50 Great Walks in Florida

Lucy Beebe Tobias

Foreword by M. Timothy O'Keefe

50 Great Walks in Florida

UNIVERSITY PRESS OF FLORIDA

Florida A&M University, Tallahassee
Florida Atlantic University, Boca Raton
Florida Gulf Coast University, Ft. Myers
Florida International University, Miami
Florida State University, Tallahassee
New College of Florida, Sarasota
University of Central Florida, Orlando
University of Florida, Gainesville
University of North Florida, Jacksonville
University of South Florida, Tampa
University of West Florida, Pensacola

University Press of Florida
Gainesville
Tallahassee
Tampa
Boca Raton
Pensacola
Orlando
Miami
Jacksonville
Ft. Myers
Sarasota

WILD FLORIDA

edited by M. Timothy O'Keefe

Books in this series are written for the many people who visit and/or move to Florida to participate in our remarkable outdoors, an environment rich in birds, animals, and activities, many exclusive to this state. Books in the series offer readers a variety of formats: natural history guides, historical outdoor guides, guides to some of Florida's most popular pastimes and activities, and memoirs of outdoors folk and their unique lifestyles.

30 Eco-trips in Florida: The Best Nature Excursions and How to Reduce Your Impact on the Environment, by Holly Ambrose (2005)

A Hiker's Guide to the Sunshine State, by Sandra Friend (2005)

Fishing Florida's Flats: A Guide to Bonefish, Tarpon, Permit, and Much More, by Jan S. Maizler (2007)

50 Great Walks in Florida, by Lucy Beebe Tobias (2008)

13 12 11 10 09 08   6 5 4 3 2 1

A record of cataloging-in-publication data is available
from the Library of Congress.
ISBN 978-0-8130-3174-3

The University Press of Florida is the scholarly
publishing agency for the State University System of
Florida, comprising Florida A&M University, Florida
Atlantic University, Florida Gulf Coast University,
Florida International University, Florida State Uni-
versity, New College of Florida, University of Central
Florida, University of Florida, University of North
Florida, University of South Florida, and University of
West Florida.

University Press of Florida
15 Northwest 15th Street
Gainesville, FL 32611-2079
http://www.upf.com

To Christopher, Martin, and Philip Tobias, my three sons.
The future is in good hands.

I only went out for a walk, and finally concluded to stay out till sundown, for going out, I found, was really going in.

John Muir

Contents

Part IV · Southwest Florida

Foreword

With Florida already ranked as one of the most populous states and hundreds of thousands more moving here every year, it seems impossible that truly wild places can remain anywhere in such a densely inhabited region. Yet in spite of the tremendous influx of people wanting to enjoy the Sunshine State's warm climate and active outdoors lifestyle, significant sections of the original, natural Florida do still endure.

In fact the amount of Florida set aside for preservation surprises many people, especially first-time visitors and newly arrived residents. As this is written, Florida terrain is protected by 3 national forests, 11 national parks, 157 state parks and 28 national wildlife refuges. In addition, individual Florida counties have designated their own protected public lands, providing for pristine rivers and sheltered coastline.

Yes, there is quite a lot of Florida that hasn't been paved over or badly disturbed by development. And it never will be.

The University Press of Florida celebrates the essential natural qualities of Florida, its environment, its creatures and its people through the broad-ranging series *Wild Florida*.

Lucy Beebe Tobias's *50 Great Walks in Florida* uses an innovative approach to help both visitors and residents experience the outdoors with a series of cleverly themed walks. No matter how well you think you know Florida, Lucy will open your eyes to new facets of which few of us are aware.

For instance, when you join Lucy on the Haunted History Walk in the small town of Monticello in the Panhandle, you will be exploring "the most haunted small town in the United States" according to ABC-TV. A title aptly deserved, since one in every three buildings is said to be presently haunted or has experienced a haunting.

Lucy's stroll through the small town of Quincy will take you past elegant homes, explaining how many were funded by the owners' investments in Coca-Cola when the drink was in its infancy. Residents owned so many shares that Quincy became known as "The Coca-Cola Town" and the company president came to address a community meeting when it decided to expand overseas; town members owned that many shares.

For those wanting to see a more natural side of Florida, Lucy will guide you to the state's highest waterfall in Falling Waters State Park, to the bottom of the Lake Eaton sinkhole in the Ocala National Forest, accompany you on a nighttime turtle nesting walk at the Archie Carr National Wildlife Refuge and escort you through the orchid gardens at the Marie Selby Botanical Center in Sarasota.

All walks are made conveniently accessible by means of a Trip Essentials box presenting contact information, when to visit and any problems you might encounter. Since most of these outings will probably be family experiences, each Trip Essentials notes whether pets are permitted and contains suggestions for meals afterwards.

Lucy literally takes you by the hand as she brings alive every walk's highlights, providing fascinating anecdotes gained from in-depth interviews and research at each location, such as the saga of the American crocodile that appeared in Ding Darling National Wildlife Refuge on Sanibel in the 1980s.

Each nesting season the female crocodile produced eggs that never hatched due to the lack of a mate. So the reptile was moved 80 miles away where she hopefully would have more success. Within six months she was back at Ding Darling, where she has stayed ever since, famous as perhaps the northernmost crocodile in Florida.

Lucy's walks are peppered with similar insightful nuggets, a reminder of her days as an award-winning columnist, photographer and graphic designer for 23 years with the New York Times Regional Newspaper Group in Florida.

Graphically, this is the most appealing walking book I've ever seen. Instead of the usual page after page of nothing but words, you will see many instances of Lucy's camera skills as her photographs illustrate points of interest. Each walk also opens with its own individualized map highlighting its location and sometimes detailed driving instructions. You will also find space to note the date on which you make the walk with space for your own observations.

If a walk only whets your appetite for a particular area, Lucy has recommendations for other nearby strolls, making it convenient to turn these excursions into weekend events. One for almost every weekend of the year.

Lucy Beebe Tobias's *50 Great Walks in Florida* will not only motivate you to explore the state's most interesting byways, it will have you seeing everything in a fresh new way.

M. Timothy O'Keefe
Series editor

Acknowledgments

My gratitude and admiration go to Patti Griffiths, former editorial page editor of the *Ocala Star-Banner*, who graciously proofread all fifty chapters.

Alan Macher provided initial enthusiasm and the phrase "walk in peace." Judy Johnson and Bob Howe shared food for thought and wine. Elena Jones gave me a refresher course in mapmaking.

Two of my sons, Christopher and Martin Tobias, walked some walks. I can recommend these Great Walks as good family experiences. Sandy and Bill Huff sheltered Christopher and me. Bill made biscuits for breakfast. We did not want to leave.

Thank you, Kathleen Carr, of the Florida Park Service, for Florida park district maps. A deep bow goes to Harvey Campbell, of the Original Florida Tourism Task Force, for a North Florida press tour.

Many thanks to Paul Kayemba with Visit Florida in Tallahassee; Carolyn Haney, Director of Tourism Sales, Nassau County at Amelia Island/Fernandina Beach/Yulee Chamber of Commerce; and Harborside Hampton Inn, Fernandina Beach. Thanks also to Debra Benjamin, Director of Sales, Tallahassee Area Convention and Visitors Bureau; Cabot Lodge, Tallahassee; the Hilton Garden Inn, Tallahassee; Mary B. Craven, Tourism Development Manager, Citrus County Visitors and Convention Bureau; Plantation Inn, Crystal River; Nancy Hamilton, Communications Director, Lee County Visitor & Convention Bureau, Bonita Springs; and AmericInn, Bonita Springs.

Carol Crawford took care of my furry family when I traveled. Two paws up! For all who prayed, cheered, and paved the way, you are a blessing. Walk in peace.

Introduction

Going on a Great Walk

A beautiful day in Florida, like fine wine, is not to be wasted. Leave behind the schedule book and the list of "must-dos." Go outside and imbibe.

How? Take a Great Walk, a short but significant jaunt through Florida's natural or historical places. The walks offer low impact and high reward for both body and soul. You'll even be done in time to do lunch.

50 Great Walks in Florida

Great Walks are affordable. Eighteen are free, and another fifteen cost less than $5 entrance fee. Distances range from less than a mile to almost 4 miles.

Finding Your Footing

With this book, you can locate a Great Walk anywhere in Florida. The table of contents divides Florida into the same five geographic sections used by the Florida Park Service.

My advice is to start by taking a Great Walk near where you live and then expand outward. Don't forget to increase your possibilities with the Bonus Points section of each chapter. With the extra experiences offered there, *50 Great Walks in Florida* offers 145 Florida destinations.

Every chapter ends with Trip Essentials, a summary of information that answers vital questions including: Are there restrooms on this walk? Can we bring our dog?

Going with a Guide

The availability of real-people guides is one of the best-kept secrets in Florida. Park rangers, greenway staff personnel, forest rangers, passionate birders, history buffs, master gardeners, and naturalists all know their special piece of Florida well. And they often share their knowledge for free.

For those who want to go on walks but are not keen on going alone, the guided-walk option has great appeal.

Some guides require a minimum number of people; others will take one or two. Appointments for a guide, where required, are a necessary courtesy for everyone's schedule—yours and theirs. If there is a fee for a guide, that is noted in the Trip Essentials for each chapter.

This book also serves as your own guide with some designer routes. Three of the walk routes—Monticello, St. Augustine, and Key West—were created for *50 Great Walks in Florida*.

Change Is Constant

Change is the only constant in our lives. Information was accurate at the time of publication. Before you go, call the location to verify current conditions. That way, your itchy feet won't turn into disappointed dogs.

Cross-reference hours for any side visits you might like to make. Tallahassee, for example, has seven parks downtown, laid out in a line called the Park Avenue Historic District. The Knott House Museum, a historic house along the way, has guided tours during limited hours on Wednesday, Thursday, and Saturday. If you want to see the Knott House inside, plan to go on those days.

High-Tech Treasure Hunt

If you are into the high-tech treasure hunt called geocaching, or if would like to begin, the GPS coordinates for every Great Walk, or its closest neighbor, are listed in Trip Essentials.

One example of a hunt: A thirteen-county area in North Central Florida has a geocache treasure hunt called "Hidden Treasures of North Florida" with places off the beaten path and thirteen red X's on a map marking areas where cache boxes are hidden. Map details are on www.geocaching.com and www.originalflorida.org.

Three of the geocaches are located in Great Walks: Alfred B. Maclay Gardens State Park, Monticello, and Madison.

Change with the Seasons

Ah, spring. Flowers in bloom. Let's see, that would be April, May, and June. No. That was up north. This is Florida. Springtime in Florida is whenever flowers bloom, and that depends a lot on how cold winter turns out to be.

For azaleas, the prime time is usually March. Take a garden walk at Rainbow Springs State Park in Dunnellon or visit Alfred B. Maclay Gardens State Park in Tallahassee.

Fall is a good time to visit forest destinations like Lake Eaton in the Ocala National Forest. By October the weather is cooler, the mosquito population is diminished, and the deer flies have gone elsewhere.

Winter is the season for migrating shorebirds and songbirds. Visit St. Mark's National Wildlife Refuge near Tallahassee, and J. N. "Ding" Darling National Wildlife Refuge on Sanibel. Walk the levee trail at Ocklawaha Prairie in Weirsdale.

What is there to say about hot, humid summer? Like an unwelcome houseguest, Florida summers come too soon and stay too long. On the bright side, June through September are the months offering the most color at Kanapaha Botanical Gardens in Gainesville. Check out the huge Victoria water lilies.

Sign up for a guided turtle walk at Archie Carr National Wildlife Refuge between Melbourne Beach and Wabasso. Female loggerhead turtles come up on beaches in June and July to lay their eggs. You may be fortunate enough to see the event happen.

Dressing for a Great Walk

Invest in a good pair of closed-toe shoes. A long-sleeved shirt to go over various T-shirts will act as a sunscreen for your arms, a bug deterrent, and, if needed, a temporary hat.

Carry rain gear in the car. Bug spray is a must. Serious sun-protection cream is critical. Consider getting a lightweight fishing vest. There are pockets for field guides, for spare lenses, notebooks, and more. I don't leave home without one.

Bugged by Bugs

Dress to discourage bugs. Wear a long-sleeved shirt and long trousers. Tuck your trousers inside your socks. Always check your clothes and your body for ticks after you've finished a walk.

DEET. Remember this word. The Centers for Disease Control recommend buying insect repellents that contain DEET (N, N-diethyl-meta-toluamide). More DEET in a repellent means longer protection. But concentrations of greater than 50 percent can cause side effects, including skin irritation. Cover your clothes and exposed skin only; avoid your eyes and mouth.

Do your Great Walks during the day after the sun has come up. Don't walk in the twilight before dawn or after dusk, the times when some mosquitoes are more active. Stay on the marked path. Don't stray into tall grass or heavily wooded areas.

On an extended reporting assignment at Everglades National Park in late May, I made the mistake of stepping outside the hotel room after dark to get something from the car. Thirty different kinds of mosquitoes live in the park. We were instantly on a first-name basis.

It was like a scene from an Alfred Hitchcock movie, and I had a starring role. Screaming, I ran into the hotel room, slammed the door, jumped into the shower with all my clothes on, and stood there with the water running.

The moral? Take mosquitoes seriously. Read the warnings about West Nile virus. Don't walk at dusk and dawn. Forewarned is forearmed.

Dancing with Wildlife, or Not

Here's a story about a guy I know. Three times a week, he sits on a stationary bike at the gym, pedaling to heavy music and turning a resistance knob to simulate hills.

He has logged hundreds of miles on that bike, but he has never set foot on a trail in a state park or anywhere else that might even mildly be considered wild Florida.

He wants to try, but Florida is so different from back home in a northern metropolitan city. Once he asked me if it were true that snakes in Florida fall out of trees when you walk underneath.

"No, only if you call them," I responded. He turned pale.

Mea culpa. I'm so sorry I said that. In self-defense, it was early in the morning. Truthfully, snakes scare many people, including me.

Walkers on the Shell Mound Trail boardwalk at J. N. "Ding" Darling National Wildlife Refuge, Sanibel.

This is a healthy fear. Here's a news flash: snakes, by and large, are afraid of us too. Two big exceptions: cottonmouth moccasins and rattlesnakes.

Florida has forty-five different kinds of snakes, with six of them listed as poisonous: the southern copperhead, the eastern coral snake, the dusky pygmy rattlesnake, the cottonmouth moccasin, the timber rattlesnake, and the eastern diamondback rattlesnake.

While walking my dogs on trails at a local state park, I've been known to sing off-key and announce: "All right, snakes, if you are going to leave, now is a good time. Here we come."

It has worked so far. Must be my off-key singing.

A Bad Overbite

Alligators are eating machines with lots of teeth and a bad overbite. Do not feed them. Do not wade into a pond to get a closer picture. Don't swim where there are alligators.

Once humans feed alligators, their fear of us is gone. An alligator's next meal could be your dog or you. They can move very quickly on land. If you must get close to one, buy a T-shirt with an alligator on it.

Going to the Birds

My very first birding walk was a disaster. Someone would say, "LBB at 2 o'clock up in the pine tree," and dozens of binoculars swiveled in that direction.

I didn't have binoculars and thought they were all nuts. What is an LBB anyway? LBB is shorthand for "little brown bird."

Birding is addictive. Do a little and you want more—more sightings and more check marks on your bird list. The Florida Fish and Wildlife Conservation Commission, along with the Florida Department of Transportation and the Wildlife Foundation of Florida, understand this addiction and have designed the Great Florida Birding Trail for birders.

Covering 2,000 miles, the trail has a total of 446 birding sites divided into four sections: East Section, West Florida, Panhandle Florida, and South Florida, and each has a free, downloadable guide. Check for birding opportunities in Trip Essentials.

Birds cannot survive without natural areas. Birders spend money. This makes conservation profitable. Reinforce this point by handing out birder calling cards that say: "I'm spending money in your community because I'm here to see your wonderful birds. Keep up the good work conserving your wildlife and wildlands and I'll keep coming back!" Download the cards and section guides at www.floridabirdingtrail.com.

The Best Buy

Fourteen Great Walks are in state parks. Both the Florida Park Service and federal lands give you a price break with annual passes good for unlimited day admissions.

An annual Florida Park Pass in 2007 cost $43.40 plus tax for individuals and $85.80 plus tax for a family, up to 8 people. Florida has 156 parks that cover 600,000 acres. Entry fees vary, but the average price of park entrance is $4.

A Florida Park Pass is honored at all state parks except Homosassa Springs Wildlife State Park and Skyway Fishing Pier State Park. At those two places, the pass is good for a 33 percent discount.

All park passes are for day admission only. Not included are charges for camping or anything extra. You can buy an annual Florida Park Pass online at www.floridastateparks.org; by calling (352) 628-1002; or at any state park.

A nice extra is the Parks Passport. Small and easy to carry, the Parks Passport is a combination journal, collectible memento, and nifty informational handbook. It contains descriptions of every state park. When you visit a state park, the ranger will stamp your Parks Passport. Your goal is to collect stamps from every park in the state. Parks Passports cost $7.95 plus tax and are available at state parks.

Frequent visitors to national parks and other federal lands benefit from buying an America the Beautiful—National Parks and Federal Recreational Lands Annual Pass. The cost is $80 and covers the pass holder plus 3 adults per vehicle. Children under 16 are admitted free to federal lands.

An America the Beautiful senior pass, for anyone 62 and over, is good for a lifetime and costs $10, admitting the pass holder and up to 3 adults in a vehicle. Buy either one at any federal lands, such as Everglades National Park or St. Marks National Wildlife Refuge. You must present proof of age.

In 2007, the America the Beautiful passes, a new program authorized by Congress, replaced the Golden Age, Golden Access, and Golden Eagle passports. All those passports, if you already have one, are still good and will be honored.

Once you get an America the Beautiful annual pass or senior pass, keep track of it. If lost or stolen, no replacement is issued. You'll have to start all over again and buy a new one.

A special passport called the America the Beautiful—National Parks and Federal Recreational Lands Access Pass is available for U.S. citizens of any age with permanent disabilities.

My Pace or Yours?

No two walkers walk alike. The slowpoke wants to read every sign and stop to admire each butterfly. That would be me. The strider is eager to make some headway fast and add up the miles.

In this book, some walks of 2 miles suggest a time of 2 hours to complete. Certainly not race pace. But this isn't a race. Great Walks are strolls to be enjoyed, sights to be seen, photographs to be taken, and they include bench time to sit and admire the view.

Your Mother Talking

As with any outdoor activity in Florida, dress sensibly for weather conditions. The sun may be shining when you leave the house. It could rain an hour later. Always carry water with you and have more available in the car. Buying a gallon of water and keeping it in the car works for refills.

Any outdoor activity carries some risk. Be aware of your surroundings. Stop from time to time to look all around you to get your bearings. When you are walking alone, be sure to tell someone where you are going and what time you expect to return home. If you have one, carry your cell phone with you. By the way, you can punch in *FHP on your cell phone to be connected to the Florida Highway Patrol.

True Confessions

I walked every step of each Great Walk and most of those suggested in Bonus Points. Sometimes I got lost and found something else quite wonderful. That is how I stumbled upon the Cloisters of the Ancient Spanish Monastery in North Miami Beach, which became a Bonus Point to go with the Art Deco Walk in South Miami.

Along the way, there have been moments that were blessings, times when I knew it doesn't get any better than this. And you will have them too.

I truly believe that getting outdoors is an act of redemption. If we stay indoors, we have no sense of being a shareholder of Florida's en-

The Cloisters at the Ancient Spanish Monastery, North Miami Beach.

vironment and people. Decision makers, including public officials and business owners, who make plans for Florida's future should be required to take at least one Great Walk.

I've lived in Florida for thirty-three years and spent twenty-three of them as a newspaper reporter and columnist writing about Florida's environment and people. During the past four years I've done a Walking Club with Lucy through Prestige 55 at Munroe Regional Medical Center in Ocala and also Great Walks with Lucy through the *Ocala Star-Banner*. By taking these walks, hundreds of people have become involved in walking and experiencing Florida's remarkable outdoors. Every walk is an unfolding adventure. We find true wealth in our natural communities and cultural heritage.

Florida is this amazing place full of history, natural beauty, artful gardens, and elegant ecosystems. Take a Great Walk, and where you came from won't be as important as being here now.

Who Needs This Book?

Grandparents looking to expose their grandchildren to the real Florida will find their way with this book. Parents opting for less glitz and more quality time as a family can discover plenty of things to do. Natives and newcomers, visitors from other countries and winter residents will uncover many adventures in these pages.

This book is for anyone who asks the question, How can I get outdoors and learn more about Florida's history, culture, and natural places? You hold the answer in your hands. What are you waiting for? Round up the family, find the car keys, get the dog's leash, pick up this book, and go.

Part I

Northwest Florida

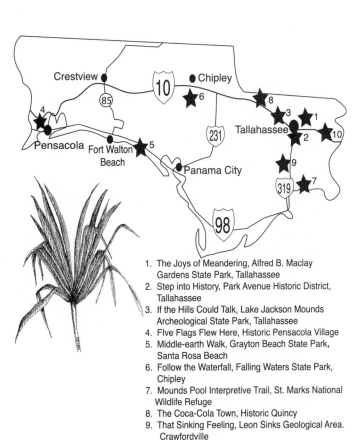

1. The Joys of Meandering, Alfred B. Maclay Gardens State Park, Tallahassee
2. Step into History, Park Avenue Historic District, Tallahassee
3. If the Hills Could Talk, Lake Jackson Mounds Archeological State Park, Tallahassee
4. Five Flags Flew Here, Historic Pensacola Village
5. Middle-earth Walk, Grayton Beach State Park, Santa Rosa Beach
6. Follow the Waterfall, Falling Waters State Park, Chipley
7. Mounds Pool Interpretive Trail, St. Marks National Wildlife Refuge
8. The Coca-Cola Town, Historic Quincy
9. That Sinking Feeling, Leon Sinks Geological Area. Crawfordville
10. Haunted History Walk, Monticello

1

The Joys of Meandering

Alfred B. Maclay Gardens State Park, Tallahassee

An old brick driveway called House Walk starts at the garden gate and goes up to the Maclay House. Lake Hall is on one side of the drive and a canopy of ancient oak trees on the other.

The morning I walked the brick road, rain from the night before made resurrection ferns live again, rising in green carpets on the tops of live-oak limbs. Resurrection ferns usually look withered, quite dead. When it rains, the ferns soak up moisture and turn green. That's how they got their name. Morning sunlight filtered through the oak-tree leaves and splashed light and shadows on the bricks.

Live-oak trees arch across the House Walk at Maclay Gardens, Tallahassee.

Off to the side of the House Walk are a number of winding paths. If there ever was a place for meandering, Maclay Gardens is it. There is no chance of getting lost. The garden paths have wonderful names like Oriental Magnolias, Azalea Hillside, Secret Garden, and Camellia Walk.

Many years ago, Alfred B. Maclay planned the gardens so prime blooming would be from January to May, the times of year his family lived here. In keeping with the best blooming times, the Maclay House Museum is open for tours from January 1 to April 30; it is closed the rest of the year.

Maclay planted hundreds of camellias and azaleas. Every year the park has a special celebration in December called Camellia Christmas.

The more I meandered, the more Maclay's creativity unfolded. A natural area of trees and bushes seems to have been in place forever. That is exactly what garden visitors are meant to think.

Original trees are augmented with plantings around them, all stair-stepped in size. Camellias grow tall in front of even taller pine trees. Native plants thrive side by side with exotics.

Near the Maclay House is a walled garden, a round enclosure with a small pond in the middle. An archway in the garden frames a long reflection pool in a grassy area next to the garden.

Next to the walled garden, a sign points to the wedding gardener's cottage. With all this beauty, it is not surprising that couples want to come here to celebrate their commitment.

Alfred Barmore Maclay bought the property in 1923, naming it Killearn Plantation and Gardens after his family's home in Scotland. Long before he arrived, American Indians lived in the area. After the Civil War, African-American farmers and plantation employees began buying land for small farms.

Maclay worked on the gardens until his death in 1944. His widow, Louise Maclay, expanded the gardens. In 1953, she donated Killearn Gardens—later renamed Maclay Gardens—to the state.

At the visitor center next to the gardens is a sign detailing what plants are in bloom every month of the year. As in all gardens and wild places, seasons change things. It is worth coming back throughout the year to see and experience those changes.

The gardens cover 28 acres and contain 160 plant species. But who's counting? The flowering plants unfold like colors on a palette, along with the richness of tall oaks and pines.

In 2002, the gardens and the park were listed on the National Register of Historic Places as the Killearn Plantation Archaeological and Historic District.

Inside the gardens, landscaped and maintained on these rolling hills, there is a strong feeling of serenity. When you visit, ponder the question I asked myself here: Does the serenity come from the architecture of the gardens or emanate from the land itself? Or is it a little of both?

Meandering through these gardens was a new and energizing experience for me, a walker who prefers going straight from point A to B. If we all worried less about reaching the destination and cared more about the journey, about strolling along the way, who knows what discoveries we'd make?

It is a shock to see how fast traffic moves and to hear the noise of cars after a few hours spent discovering the serene beauty of Maclay Gardens.

Bonus Points

Alfred B. Maclay Gardens State Park has all three of the *H* words—history, heritage, and habitats. The park also has three distinct sections: the Lake Hall Recreation Area, the gardens, and the Lake Overstreet property. Each one is reached by taking a turnoff from the one main road winding through the park.

The Lake Hall Recreation Area, located on the shore of Lake Hall, is first. A small area of the lake is cordoned off for swimming, and a large playground is situated nearby. Covered picnic pavilions, lots of tall shade trees, and a fishing dock all fit into this area. Canoes, kayaks, and other boats can be launched from a boat ramp. Only electric trolling motors are allowed on Lake Hall. Two short nature trails go through the woods overlooking Lake Hall.

Lake Overstreet is literally at the end of the main park road. Added to the park in 1994, Lake Overstreet's 877 acres include the 144-acre freshwater Lake Overstreet. This property is part of the Maclay-Phipps Cultural Heritage Greenway.

Walkers, bicyclists, and equestrians have 5 miles of multiuse trails. These include a 3-mile trail circling Lake Overstreet, a 1.5-mile Ravine Trail going through uplands, and a 2.8-mile Bike Trail with an east, north, and west loop, also traversing uplands.

Trails are marked, and free trail maps are available. A sign at the Lake Overstreet trail entrance advises walking the trail with a partner. These trails open at 8 a.m. Visitors are advised to return to the trail-head one hour before sunset. Leashed dogs are allowed.

On Meridian Road, a trailhead called Forest Meadows provides a separate entrance to the Lake Overstreet trails.

If you visit all the sections of the park, you will experience nine different natural communities along with the developed areas. These include sinkholes, slope forest, upland hardwood forest, upland mixed forest, basin swamp, bottomland forest, floodplain forest, upland lakes, and seepage streams.

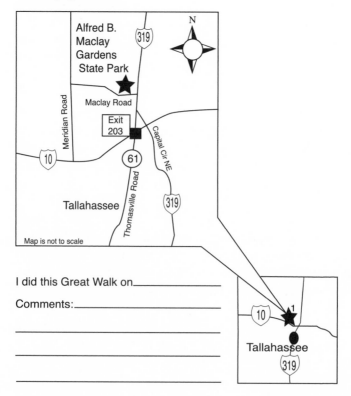

I did this Great Walk on_____

Comments:_____

_____

_____

_____

For a look at history alongside natural habitats, make a visit to the Tallahassee Museum of History and Natural Science. This is more than a museum. Bring the whole family to find Florida history, wildlife, and nature discovery all packed into 52 acres.

Walk along an elevated boardwalk and see Florida panthers taking a siesta, stroll past a farm area where a cow is curious about you, and go inside a historic schoolhouse.

The Tallahassee Museum of History and Natural Science is located at 3945 Museum Drive, Tallahassee, FL 32310, phone (850) 575-8684. Hours are 9 a.m. to 5 p.m. Monday through Saturday; and 12:30 p.m. to 5 p.m. on Sunday. Admission is $8 adults; $7.50 seniors (65 and up); $5.50 college students with identification; $5.50 children 4-15; and children under 4 are admitted free. Web site: www.tallahasseemuseum. org.

Trip Essentials

Name: The Joys of Meandering: Alfred B. Maclay Gardens State Park, Tallahassee

Type of walk: Botanical

Length of walk: Not measured

Time to finish: 2 hours

Difficulty: Easy. Wheelchair accessible.

Appeals to: Gardeners, pond enthusiasts, photographers, and birders (listed on page 22, Panhandle Florida guide to the Great Florida Birding Trail)

Guides: Self-guided. Tours for groups only; call park for arrangements.

Address: 3540 Thomasville Road, Tallahassee, FL 32309

Phone: (850) 487-4556

Web site: www.floridastateparks.org

Cost: $4 per vehicle for up to 8 people

Getting there: Take I-10 to exit 203 (U.S. 319, also called Thomasville Road). Go north about 1 mile and turn left onto Maclay Road. Park entrance is on the right.

GPS coordinates: (Maclay Gardens geocache) N 30° 30.855 W 084° 14.902

Hours: Gardens open 9 a.m. to 5 p.m. Park open 8 a.m. to 7 p.m.

Restrooms: At gardens' entrance next to the visitor center; also at Lake Hall Recreation Area

Water/food: 5 water fountains in gardens; no food or drinks allowed

Dogs: Well-behaved and on a 6-foot hand-held leash. None allowed in the gardens, on the Lake Hall beachfront, or in the water.

Lunch ideas: French cuisine, at Chez Pierre, in a restored 1920s home, 1215 Thomasville Road, Tallahassee, FL 32303, phone (850) 222-0936; eclectic, at Kool Beanz Café, 912 Thomasville Road, Tallahassee, FL 32303, phone (850) 224-2466

2

Step into History

Park Avenue Historic District, Tallahassee

No matter where you turn in downtown Tallahassee, the past meets the present. Sidewalks, steps, houses, even the very ground of this part of town are all saturated with history.

A chain of seven parks, each one block long, makes up the Park Avenue Historic District. The parks are lined up in a row on Park Avenue like a string of green pearls. Both sides of the parks are flanked with historic houses, churches, and early government buildings.

Before parks were built on this spot, early settlers kept the area cleared. It was 200 feet wide with nothing on it so they could see Indians coming. Later, as the city grew, the open area became a series of parks and buildings developed on each side. Government buildings, churches, and homes used the green spaces in the middle as a common front yard.

One of the homes has a Civil War history. In 1843, George Proctor, a free black man, built what is known today as the Knott House Museum at the corner of Park and Calhoun. Commissioned by Thomas Hatner, the home was a gift for his bride. The Union Army in 1865 temporarily commandeered the house as headquarters for General Edward Mc-Cook.

Old photographs inside the house show steps leading up to a front door on the left side. An A-shaped overhang was above the door. On May 20, 1865, McCook stood on these steps and read the Emancipation Proclamation, declaring freedom for all slaves in the Florida Panhandle.

The steps have changed since McCook's time. William and Luella Knott bought the house in 1928. To make it look grand, the steps were extended all the way across the front of the house. Thick white columns

Lunchtime walkers in the Park Avenue Historic District, downtown Tallahassee.

were added for a plantation-house look. The front door occupies the middle, with tall windows on either side so people could see furnishings inside.

The Emancipation Celebration takes place every May at the Knott House Museum. Reenactors wear period costumes. Live gospel music rings out. On the steps of the Knott House, the Emancipation Proclamation is read once again.

Many buildings on both sides of the string of parks are listed on the National Register of Historic Places. For example, First Presbyterian Church, at the corner of Park Avenue and Adams Street, is the only church still standing from Florida's territorial days. The address is: 110 North Adams Street, Tallahassee, FL 32301, phone (850) 222-4504. The Web site is: www.oldfirstchurch.org.

Each park in the Park Avenue Historic District has its own name and character. In Ponce de Leon Park, located on Park Avenue between Monroe and Adams Streets, the Downtown Marketplace takes place every Saturday, 8 a.m. to 2 p.m., from March through November. For more information, call (850) 980-8727 or visit their Web site: www. downtownmarket.com.

If your walking shoes are up to it, keep on going. The Capitol Complex, with the old and new Capitols, is three blocks south of the Park Avenue Historic District.

Admission to both Capitols is free. The Old Capitol Museum, phone (850) 487-1902, has docents who will give an introduction to the building. A free map is available for self-guided tours.

The new State Capitol stands an impressive twenty-two stories tall. A Visit Florida welcome center on the plaza level, phone (850) 488-6167, has a wealth of free brochures for both the Panhandle and all of Florida.

Three areas of interest inside the State Capitol are the governor's office on the plaza level, where you can sign a visitors' log; the observation galleries for the House and Senate on the fifth floor; and the panoramic view from the glassed-in observation tower on the twenty-second floor.

The Florida Vietnam Veterans' Memorial is across from the Old Capitol Museum. Two large slabs of polished granite reach skyward. The names of 1,942 Floridians killed in action and 83 missing in action are engraved on the memorial.

For more information on the memorial, contact the Florida Department of Veterans' Affairs, phone (850) 487-1533, or visit the Web site: www.floridavets.org.

At this point you have walked about 2 miles and traveled through several centuries of Tallahassee history.

Bonus Points

Downtown Tallahassee is addicted to one-way streets, and Park Avenue is no exception. This makes walking the way to go. If you drive, be advised that parking is metered. Bring a handful of quarters and check time limits on the meters. The closer you are to the Capitol, the shorter the time limit.

Lake Ella, less than a mile from downtown Tallahassee, is popular with walkers and joggers.

Plan your walk for a day when the Knott House Museum gives tours. Guided tours are on the hour from 1 p.m. to 3 p.m. on Wednesdays and Thursdays; on Saturdays the tours are on the hour from 10 a.m. to 3 p.m.

The house address is: 301 East Park Avenue, Tallahassee, FL 32301, phone (850) 922-2459. Admission is free, but a donation of $3 is requested. The Web site is: www.museumoffloridahistory.com.

It is named the "house that rhymes" because Luella Knott, a temperance activist, wrote poems and affixed them to pieces of furniture. You can read her rhymes.

The Calhoun Street Historic District was the "Gold Dust Street" in the 1800s. Give yourself a good hour for a walk through this district, which starts adjacent to the Park Avenue Historic District. In its day, Calhoun Street was Tallahassee's upscale neighborhood. Historic homes like the Towle House, built in 1847, and the Elizabeth Cobb House, built in 1880, reflect the area's former wealth.

George Proctor, who built many early Tallahassee homes, built a home in the Calhoun District in 1840 for Henry Rutgers, a city councilman and territorial treasurer. Located at 507 North Calhoun Street, Tallahassee, FL 32301, Rutgers's former home is now the Tallahassee Garden Center and is open to the public, phone (850) 224-3371.

After a day of walking historic districts and seeing Florida government in action, a visit to Lake Ella is a welcome respite. Lake Ella is part of Frank O. Drake Jr. Park, managed by Tallahassee's Recreation and Parks Department, phone (850) 891-3866.

Located on Monroe Street between Sharpe and 7th, Lake Ella is less than a mile from downtown Tallahassee. For locals, this spot is both an oasis and a treasure. A wide paved path, six-tenths of a mile long, surrounds the circular man-made lake. The walkway acts a magnet for walkers, joggers, strollers, and dog walkers.

A different kind of walk awaits you at Mission San Luis in Tallahassee. More than one hundred Spanish mission settlements sprang up in Florida between the 1560s and the 1690s. Mission San Luis started in 1607, when Apalachee Indians asked for Spanish friars and the soldiers that came with them.

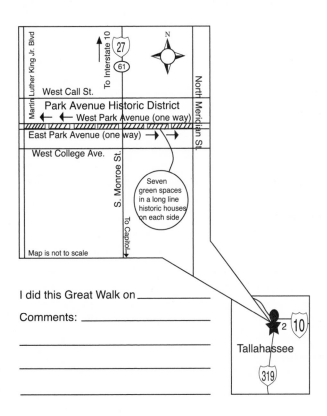

NORTHWEST FLORIDA

In 1704, the British invaded Florida. Mission San Luis was burned to the ground by the Spanish to keep the buildings from being used by the British. The Spaniards fled and so did the Apalachee.

Three centuries later, Mission San Luis is coming alive again. The council house, an immense, round building rising to an awesome height, was the center of Apalachee life. Reconstruction of a Spanish military complex is ongoing. Visitors can walk the grounds and watch archaeological excavations in progress.

One-third of a mile long, the Nature Trail goes through a mixed hardwood and pine hammock with several seep springs that provided water to the mission community. Ask for free check-off lists of birds and butterflies you might see at Mission San Luis.

The ongoing re-creation of Mission San Luis won a 2006 Preserve America presidential award. Located at 2021 West Mission Road, Tallahassee, FL 32304, phone (850) 413-9702. Admission to Mission San Luis is free. Hours are 10 a.m. to 4 p.m. Tuesday through Sunday; closed Mondays. The Web site is: www.missionsanluis.org.

Trip Essentials

Name: Step into History: Park Avenue Historic District, Tallahassee
Type of walk: Historic
Length of walk: 1.5 miles (longer if adding other historic places or districts nearby)
Time to finish: 2 hours
Difficulty: Moderate. Portions are not handicapped accessible.
Appeals to: Photographers, history buffs, and city planners
Guides: Self-guided. Free walking guide from Tallahassee Area Convention and Visitors Bureau.
Address: Self-guided tour maps are available for the Park Avenue Historic District, the Capitol area, and the Calhoun Street Historic District at the Tallahassee Area Convention and Visitors Bureau & Tallahassee Visitor Information Center, 106 East Jefferson Street, Tallahassee, FL 32301
Phone: (800) 628-2866 (toll-free)
Web site: www.seeTallahassee.com
Cost: None

Getting there: The Park Avenue Historic District runs east and west between Call Street and College Avenue, north of the Capitol Complex.

GPS coordinates: (State Library of Florida) N 30° 44028 W 084° 28333

Hours: The Visitor Information Center hours are Monday–Friday 8 a.m. to 5 p.m.; Saturday 9 a.m. to 1 p.m.; closed Sundays

Restrooms: At Visitor Information Center and Capitol buildings

Water/food: Fountains in the parks; many restaurants nearby

Dogs: Leashed on the street; not allowed in buildings

Lunch ideas: American menu with political names for entrees, at Andrew's Capital Grill & Bar, 228 South Adams Street, Tallahassee, FL 32301, phone (850) 222-3444; St. John's Café, an outreach of St. John's Episcopal Church, 211 North Monroe Street, Tallahassee, FL 32301, phone (850) 222-2636

NORTHWEST FLORIDA

3

If the Hills Could Talk

Lake Jackson Mounds Archaeological State Park, Tallahassee

The rolling hills aren't talking. And neither are the Indian mounds. But that shouldn't slow you down. Put on your moccasins, sandals, or hiking shoes. Take a walk in the footsteps of the Lake Jackson Indians and early settlers who once lived here.

If you move slowly, look and listen carefully, who knows? Perhaps the past will whisper its stories to you, unfolding them like sighs carried on the wind.

From Interstate 10, take exit 199 going north on U.S. 27. Turn right onto Crowder Road. This road winds through a heavily wooded residential area.

Entrance fee is $2 per vehicle on the honor system. Your money goes into a pay box. In the parking lot, you are faced with two choices. Take the nature trail into the woods, a 1-mile trail that starts at the end of the parking lot, or turn left toward a large grassy area with picnic tables under tall oak trees and two large historic earth mounds nearby.

The mounds are tall, and the long flight of steps up to the top is daunting from a distance. I chose the loop trail first and saved the mounds for later.

The Butler Mill Trail is about 1 mile long. Rangers say it takes 15 minutes to walk, but you might want to take longer and linger by the good stuff, like the streams, the ravine walls, or the trees and bushes in bloom.

You will be walking through upland pinelands and ravine forest. Trees include hickory, southern magnolia, and redbud. There are times on this trail when you actually walk along ridges. It is not like hiking in the Appalachian Mountains, certainly nothing that high. This terrain is a smaller echo of its bigger, taller cousins to the north.

It is a surprise to find streams meandering downhill. The streams are shallow, only 2 to 4 feet wide, and the water moves slowly. If you're not looking, you'll miss the streams at first because the sound of water is barely heard.

At one point along the trail, a small but determined stream flows right underneath the roots of a tree, exposing all the tree roots.

I wondered how the Lake Jackson Indians found their way through these woods. Did they mark trails, perhaps make a slash on a tree indicating which way to turn? Or did they follow indentations in the earth made by wildlife?

Stairs leading down from the top of a ceremonial mound, Lake Jackson Mounds Archaeological State Park, Tallahassee.

Much of the earth here is clay. Be advised that clay, when wet, can be slippery. Do watch where you walk.

The streams come together, pick up the pace, and get a little wider. Along the trail, two bridges cross the stream. At one crossing over the stream, you see exposed ravine walls with water seeping out of them.

Along the trail is an earthen dike from the old gristmill site left over from the days when Col. Robert Butler owned this land as part of a plantation. That was during Florida's territorial period, 1825–60.

Finishing the loop trail, I headed next for the flat, grassy area. Although any agricultural remains are long gone, both the Indians and the early settlers grew crops on this rich river bottomland.

A thick canopy of trees hides the lake view. But a map shows the changing shoreline, and the lake was much closer back in Indian days, called the Fort Walton period.

Tall oak trees shade picnic tables. A covered education area has benches and a number of exhibits about the past. From AD 1200 to AD 1500, this was a huge ceremonial and residential area for the Lake Jackson Indians.

Six earth temple mounds were built in this area. One is on private property. Five are located inside the park, the most Indian earthen mounds in any Florida park. Three mounds are in the forest and not currently open to the public.

Two mounds are accessible to the public in this grassy area. Just looking at the mounds raises questions: Why are they here? Without the aid of wheelbarrows or front-end loaders, how did the Indians build the mounds so high?

The largest mound is 278 by 312 feet. It is a climb to the top, some 36 feet and 64 steps, but it is worth the effort. Standing on the top of the mound, you are no longer looking up at trees; instead you are level with their top branches.

Did a chief live here? Definitely, this spot has the best view and the best breezes. Were sacrifices made? It is easy to start speculating. Was this high spot a rotating reward? If you were the best in battle or grew the most crops, maybe you and your family got to stay up here for a month or so. That would be a privilege. This is a special place. Even the sheer effort to build it makes it unique.

Archaeologists have uncovered foundation posts suggesting that there were once buildings at the top. The Indians were part of a socio-religious group called the Southeastern Ceremonial Complex. There is evidence of trade with other ceremonial centers in Georgia, Alabama, and Oklahoma.

For reasons unknown, the Lake Jackson Indians simply left the area about 1500. They abandoned the tall mounds that took so much work to construct and retreated from the lush ravine forests that provided food. It is a puzzle.

This park is self-guided, but guides for the trails and the mounds are available with two weeks' notice. Rangers manage six parks in four counties, so they need advance notice. No minimum number is needed for a guided tour. Families, small or large groups, and school

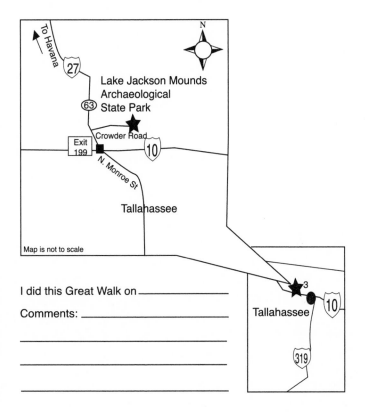

I did this Great Walk on _____

Comments: _____

_____

_____

_____

groups are welcome. There is no charge for a guided tour. To make tour arrangements, call (850) 922-6007.

Self-guided or guided, after walking the woods and climbing the mounds, you will leave with more questions than answers. And that makes this a Great Walk.

Bonus Points

Havana is 12 miles north of Interstate 10 on U.S. 27. It is a small historic town with a downtown area of old brick buildings still intact, along with several blocks of historic homes nearby.

Havana is known by several names, including "North Florida's Arts and Antiques Capital" and the "Southeast's Art and Antique Capital." The downtown area, about four blocks long and three blocks wide, boasts some forty businesses, including art galleries, antique stores, a vintage bookstore, and cafés.

Most shops are open Wednesday through Saturday; a few are open Monday and Tuesday. Street parking is free.

Trip Essentials

Name: If the Hills Could Talk: Lake Jackson Mounds Archaeological State Park, Tallahassee

Type of walk: Historic/nature

Length of walk: 1 mile for Butler Mill Trail; not measured for visiting Indian mounds

Time to finish: 15 to 30 minutes for a leisurely walk of the trail. Allow 30 to 45 minutes for the mounds.

Difficulty: Moderate. No wheelchair access to top of mounds. Parts of the trail are quite narrow.

Appeals to: History buffs, nature lovers, and photographers

Guides: Self-guided. Park staff available for guided tour at no charge with two weeks' notice.

Address: 3600 Indian Mounds Road, Tallahassee, FL 32303

Phone: (850) 922-6007

Web site: www.floridastateparks.org

Cost: $2 per vehicle; self-pay station

Getting there: Off U.S. 27, 2 miles north of I-10 in Tallahassee. Take Crowder Road and turn right onto Indian Mounds Road.

GPS coordinates: N 30° 49972 W 084° 31361

Hours: 8 a.m. to sunset

Restrooms: At parking lot

Water/food: Water at restrooms; no food sold in park. Picnic tables on the grounds.

Dogs: Allowed on 6-foot hand-held lead

Lunch ideas: American, at the Tomato Café & Tea Room inside the Planter's Exchange, 204 NW 2nd Street, Havana, FL 32333, phone (850) 539-2285; Cuban, at Mocking Bird Café, 211 NW First Street, Havana, FL 32333, phone (850) 539-2212

NORTHWEST FLORIDA

4

Five Flags Flew Here

Historic Pensacola Village, Pensacola

The French came, raised their flag, built forts, got chased out. The British came, raised their flag, built forts, left town, and came back later. The Spanish came, built forts—you get the idea.

All these comings and goings ended on July 17, 1821. Major General Andrew Jackson stood in Spanish Square and accepted West Florida from Spain. At that time, under Spanish rule, the state was divided into East Florida and West Florida (everything west of the Suwannee River).

Because history has been preserved and even celebrated in downtown Pensacola, this is a great place for a historic walk.

Three historic districts are here, starting at Pensacola Bay and moving inland for 2 miles. All three districts are easily walked and connect to one another—the Seville Historic District, the Palafox Historic District, and the North Hill Preservation District.

Start with Historic Pensacola Village, located in the Seville Historic District. A free visitor parking lot is on Tarragona Street. Historic Pensacola Village begins across the street from the parking lot. No fence separates the village from the rest of the area, so it is possible to walk right into it before you realize where you are.

The village covers an area about two blocks wide and three blocks long and is managed by West Florida Historic Preservation Inc., part of the University of West Florida. Some of the old homes in the village are occupied by businesses, others are residences, and some structures are used for historical exhibits.

Head for the Tivoli High House at 205 East Zaragoza Street, less than a block from the parking lot. The Tivoli High House looks old but was actually reconstructed in 1976 using photographs and archaeological evidence.

At the Tivoli High House, you will find free brochures to take a self-guided walking tour of the village and nearby points of interest, including the square where Jackson took possession of West Florida.

On your own or with a guide, you are likely to encounter people outside the Lavalle House dressed in early settlers' costumes. They demonstrate pioneer skills, including starting a fire using flint and steel.

The streets of Historic Pensacola Village take you on a walk back in time. Colonial architecture mingles with French Creole and Spanish influences.

On Adams Street is Old Christ Church. Built in 1832 as an Episcopal church, it has also been a public library and a museum. A landmark in downtown Pensacola, it is used for events and meetings.

Old Christ Church faces Seville Square, a one-block park with huge live-oak trees and fresh landscaping. Around the park are old homes that have been converted to modern uses, including restaurants and offices.

From Seville Square, a walk west on Zaragoza Street for two blocks puts you at another square. Originally Spanish Square, it is now the Plaza Ferdinand VII, made famous as the place where Spain ceded West Florida to the United States.

Here you will also find, fenced in a small area, the foundations of Spanish forts built from 1754 to 1821. It is a part of the Colonial Archaeological Trail, a project of the University of West Florida and the City of Pensacola along with the Florida Department of State Cultural Resources.

Across the street from the foundations sits the T. T. Wentworth, Jr. Florida State Museum. The building takes up a city block. It obviously had another life before becoming a museum. Indeed it did. This building is the old city hall, built in 1908.

Wentworth collected Florida artifacts and Americana. He never met an artifact he didn't like. His collection numbers more than 100,000 pieces. Only a small portion of it is displayed inside the museum.

The museum is located at 330 South Jefferson Street, Pensacola, FL 32591, phone (850) 595-5990. Hours are 10 a.m. to 4 p.m. Monday

The T. T. Wentworth, Jr. Florida State Museum is housed in Pensacola's 1908 city hall building.

through Saturday; closed on University of West Florida holidays. No entrance fee. Donations accepted. You can also buy guided-tour tickets for Historic Pensacola Village at the museum. The Web site is: www. historicpensacola.org.

Bonus Points

The Pensacola Historical Museum sits on the south side of Plaza Ferdinand VII at 115 East Zaragosa Street, Pensacola, FL 32591, phone (850) 433-1559. Entrance fee is $4; children under 12 admitted free. Hours are 10 a.m. to 4:30 p.m. Monday through Saturday. Their Web site is: www.pensacolahistory.com.

Big Lagoon State Park is about 10 miles southwest of Pensacola on County Road 292A. The address is: 12301 Gulf Beach Highway, Pensacola, FL 32507, phone (850) 492-1595. Damaged by Hurricane Ivan in 2004, the park is open for day use and some camping. Check to see what facilities are available. Park hours are 8 a.m. to sunset. Admission is $4 per car.

The Florida District of the Gulf Islands National Seashore has its headquarters at 1801 Gulf Breeze Parkway, Gulf Breeze, FL 32563, phone (850) 932-9654. In 2005, Hurricanes Katrina, Dennis, and Rita, along with Tropical Storms Arlene and Cindy, did extensive damage to the Mississippi and Florida Districts.

Call the Florida visitor centers to check what's open and schedules of current tours. The phone numbers are: Naval Live Oaks Visitor Center, (850) 934-2600; Fort Pickens Visitor Center, (850) 934-2635; and Fort Barrancas Visitor Center, (850) 455-5167.

The mainland forts and the National Museum of Naval Aviation are reached by going through the main entrance of the Pensacola Naval Air Station. Fort Pickens and Naval Live Oaks are east of Pensacola. Information and maps of Gulf Islands National Seashore are at: www.nps.gov/guis.

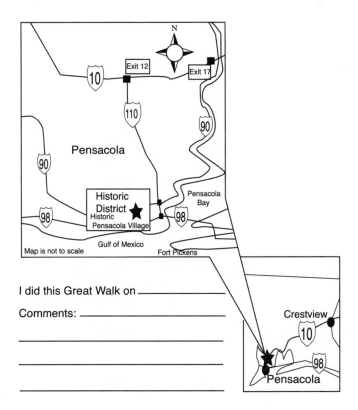

I did this Great Walk on _____

Comments: _____

_____

_____

_____

Trip Essentials

Name: Five Flags Flew Here: Historic Pensacola Village, Pensacola

Type of walk: Historic

Length of walk: 1 mile

Time to finish: 1 hour to walk; up to 3 hours if visiting museums and historic buildings

Difficulty: Easy. Wheelchair accessible.

Appeals to: History buffs, families, and photographers

Guides: Self-guided, or guided tours given three times a day at 11 a.m., 1 p.m., and 2:30 p.m. Monday through Saturday

Address: Guided-tour tickets and free brochures at Tivoli High House, 205 East Zaragoza Street, Pensacola, FL. Mailing address: Historic Pensacola Village, P.O. Box 12866, Pensacola, FL 32591.

Phone: Tivoli High House (850) 595-5993; T. T. Wentworth, Jr. Museum (850) 595-5990

Web site: www.historicpensacola.org

Cost: Guided tour: $6 adults; $5 senior citizens over 65; $2.50 children 4–16,; no cost for self- guided

Getting there: From Highway 98 east of Pensacola, cross the Pensacola Bay Bridge and turn left onto Bayfront Parkway. Turn north on Tarragona Street and go one block to Zaragoza Street. The visitor parking lot is on the left.

GPS coordinates: (Pensacola Bay Bridge) N 30° 39.361 W 087° 18.444

Hours: Daylight. For tour tickets, Tivoli High House hours are 10 a.m. to 4 p.m. Monday through Saturday

Restrooms: At Tivoli High House and T. T. Wentworth, Jr. Museum

Water/food: Bring water; numerous restaurants nearby

Dogs: Leashed on the street; none in restaurants

Lunch ideas: American, at Dharma Blue, 300 South Alcaniz Street, Pensacola, FL 32501, phone (850) 433-1275; American and seafood, at Palace Oyster Bar, Seville Quarter, 130 East Government Street, Pensacola, FL 32501, phone (850) 434-6211

5

Middle-earth Walk

Grayton Beach State Park, Santa Rosa Beach

Pressing on in their quest to return the magic ring, two hobbits come to a ridge of sand dunes. Wind-bent trees form a low archway near the crest of one dune. They move forward on bare feet, wrapping their cloaks around them to ward off the wind.

The hobbits are in Middle-earth, a place well known from J.R.R. Tolkien's novels *The Hobbit* (1937) and *The Lord of the Rings* (1954 and 1955). Middle-earth must be a long way from Florida. Or is it?

Grayton Beach State Park in the Panhandle embraces a coastal forest with a sand dune ridge. High sand dunes are covered with what looks like bonsai on a grand scale, compliments of Mother Nature. Wind pruning and salt air have gnarled the scrub oaks and magnolias and shaped them low and rounded, the better to hug the dune contours.

One dune has a low archway made by trees bent by the wind. This tree archway is the path for the 1-mile trail officially called the Grayton Beach Nature Trail. It is also called the Middle-earth Walk. Who knows? It could be true. The wide sandy path shows footprints from many travelers, including some with big bare feet.

The trail dips down the dunes toward Western Lake. You go through a scrub-oak thicket with sand live oak and myrtle oak sculpted by winds and weather.

On the far side of the lake, a hillside sprouts a long line of pine trees, tall, straight silhouettes with branches just at the tops. In the early morning, with fog rolling in from the Gulf of Mexico, the treetops are blurred, the trunks just visible. Artists will want to stop right here, open a folding chair, and begin sketching. Photographers catching the scene in the morning can come back in the afternoon and find the light totally changed.

Going into the dunes with sculpted trees at Grayton Beach State Park, Santa Rosa Beach.

In another section, you come across a basin of bushes, or so it appears. Many are actually southern magnolias and slash pines, and they are mature, as full as they are going to get in this coastal world pruned and tempered by wind and salt. The tops of the trees are bare, leaves whipped off by wind. Leaves start farther down, closer to the ground. This basin is great for wildlife. No human could penetrate the denseness. Perhaps a hobbit could.

A self-guided brochure that details numbered markers is available for the walk, but nature may determine your course. Rains had been heavy when I visited, and the path going left toward the trees was covered with water.

If that is the case for you, turn away from the lake and right toward the dunes that line the beach. A boardwalk that once served as a dune crossover has been roped off, and a sign says it is unusable. Hurricane Ivan was the culprit.

Exiting the coastal forest and stepping foot on the beach is quite a surprise. The beach is wide and flat. The Gulf of Mexico, which from a distance looks blue-grey, turns a lovely shade of emerald green up close, hence the name Emerald Coast.

Once on the beach, turn right and walk down to the dune crossover with a weather flag. This takes you back to the lot where you parked to take the nature trail. You have come full circle through time and ecosystems. You have been to Middle-earth and come back again to the twenty-first century. Congratulations.

Bonus Points

Grayton Beach State Park is located in Santa Rosa Beach on Route 30-A. Across from the park entrance is the start of the Grayton Beach Hike and Bike Trail. It is 4.3 miles long one way, with a connection trail to Point Washington State Forest.

The Hike and Bike Trail starts at Route 30-A, also known as "Scenic Route 30-A." This short road, slightly over 18 miles, drops down from heavily traveled U.S. 98 and runs along the Gulf of Mexico. A bike and foot trail parallels the road.

Beaches along the way are accessible to the public. All of them are designated Blue Wave beaches, which means that they are clean and the surrounding areas enforce strict building regulations to ensure they stay this way. Collectively, they are called the Beaches of South Walton.

Route 30-A has several communities, both developed and under construction, whose design reflects the principles of New Urbanism. Seaside, WaterColor, and Rosemary Beach are examples of these walkable New Urbanist communities.

Seaside's streets lead to a common plaza that fronts Route 30-A. But four- and five-story condos are being built right next to the road on one side of the plaza. The tall buildings overshadow—even crowd—the neat homes behind them, homes built with wide porches and picket fences.

WaterColor, a town next to Seaside, has a large, open park area that runs down the center of the town. It is accented with intensive landscaping and ponds. Sidewalks line both sides of the street.

Just east of Seaside, take County Road 395 north, cross over U.S. 98, and continue for 1 mile to the entrance for Eden Gardens State Park. The address is: P.O. Box 26, Point Washington, FL 32454, phone (850) 231-4214.

Hours are 8 a.m. to sunset. Entrance fee is $3 per vehicle; $1 for pedestrians or bicyclists. The fees are paid at a self-serve fee station. Make sure you have the correct amount to put in the envelope.

The grounds have a rich canopy of old live-oak trees and mature pines. A manicured lawn, complete with sculptures and a reflecting pool, slopes down to Tucker Bayou.

A two-story white mansion, with 5,600 square feet of space, was once home to the William Henry Wesley family. Built in 1897, it was occupied by family members until 1953. Be advised that the park is open every day, but guided house tours are only offered on the hour from 10 a.m. to 3 p.m. Thursday through Monday. The fee is $3 per adult and $1.50 per child.

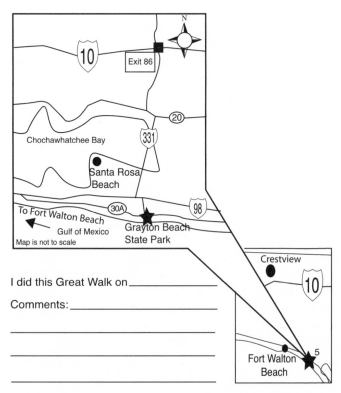

I did this Great Walk on _____

Comments: _____

_____

_____

_____

Lois Maxon bought the home in 1963. Maxon made the home a showcase for heirlooms and antiques, including a large collection of Louis XVI furniture.

Picnic tables are near Tucker Bayou. A garden trail goes through a butterfly garden, a rose garden, and camellia and azalea gardens and along Tucker Bayou. Free trail guides are available at the Fig Leaf Shop in the Wesley House.

Trip Essentials

Name: Middle-earth Walk: Grayton Beach State Park, Santa Rosa Beach
Type of walk: Nature
Length of walk: 1 mile
Time to finish: 1 hour
Difficulty: Moderate. Not wheelchair accessible.
Appeals to: Nature buffs, Tolkien fans, families, photographers, beach lovers, and birders (listed on page 9, Panhandle Florida guide to the Great Florida Birding Trail)
Guides: Self-guided
Address: Grayton Beach State Park, 357 Main Park Road, Santa Rosa Beach, FL 32459
Phone: (850) 231-4210
Web site: www.floridastateparks.org
Cost: $4 per vehicle
Getting there: Located on Route 30A south of U.S. 98, about halfway between Panama City Beach and Destin. Take County Road 283 south of U.S. 98; turn left at stop sign onto 30A and go about half a mile. The park entrance is on the right.
GPS coordinates: (Santa Rosa Beach) N 30° 39.583 W 086° 22.889
Hours: 8 a.m. to sunset
Restrooms: At beach parking lot
Water/food: Water at restrooms; no food
Dogs: Allowed in camping area, nature trail, and picnic areas on a 6-foot leash; not allowed on beach or in cabins
Lunch ideas: Mediterranean and southern, at Bud & Alley's Waterfront Restaurant, seaside on the beachside, phone (850) 231-5900; American, at Café Spiazzia, seaside on the beachside, phone (850) 231-1297

NORTHWEST FLORIDA

6

Follow the Waterfall

Falling Waters State Park, Chipley

Mention Florida and waterfalls in the same breath. See what happens. Eyebrows will go up. No waterfalls here. But we do have them. Honest.

You'll find the state's tallest waterfall along the Sinkholes Trail boardwalk at Falling Waters State Park, located 3 miles south of Chipley in North Florida.

After going through the entrance station, the road to the Sinkholes Trail winds through an upland pine forest thick with longleaf pines. A wiregrass prairie grows under the trees.

North Florida has a lot in common with South Georgia and parts of the Carolinas. The woods here have a distinct northern feel to them, with towering trees, deep green colors, and a hilly landscape. Seasons change distinctly. You know, just looking around, that you need a sweater in the fall.

The road ends at a huge parking lot flanked by restrooms, picnic tables, and playground equipment. A concrete walkway goes downhill and leads to the Sinkholes Trail, about a one-fourth-mile loop boardwalk that includes the wonderful waterfall and some pretty amazing sinkholes. At the trailhead, pick up a free numbered guide to the trees along the Sinkholes Trail.

Entering the woods, you hear the waterfall before you see it. The waterfall is off the boardwalk trail to the right. Get there by going down steps to a viewing platform. Now you are standing about halfway down a sinkhole, looking up at the waterfall cresting over the top of a cliff.

Water from Branch Creek cascades 73 feet and falls into a cavern. Where the water goes after it enters the sinkhole is a mystery. The sides

NORTHWEST FLORIDA

Waterfall
at Falling
Waters
State Park,
Chipley.

of the sinkhole are limestone rocks, massive boulders jumbled on top of each other. All the rocks are upholstered with moss and lichens. Wildflowers grow seasonally on the slopes. Ferns are abundant in this cool, shady place.

Limestone appeared over 20 million years ago, when salt water covered most of the state. It is made from animal shells deposited on the ocean floor. Water contains a weak natural acid. As it flows over the cliff and falls down into the sinkhole, the water ever so slowly but surely is dissolving the limestone rocks.

Native Americans lived on Falling Waters Hill, which rises to an elevation of 324 feet. During the Civil War, the waterfall powered a gristmill at this site. The mill ground corn into grits and cornmeal. In 1891, a legal distillery used the water to make whiskey.

Along the loop boardwalk are deep, wide sinkholes separated from each other by rocky limestone ridges. At one sink, you look down, down, down and barely see a hole at the bottom. Standing on the boardwalk peering into a sinkhole, you are literally looking at a slice of what the earth is like under your feet.

Sinkholes have a life of their own. Limey soil and moist conditions are ideal for ferns of all kinds. Ferns grow thick and sprout in bright green colors. At the bottom of a sinkhole, a thick carpet of leaves hides what is underneath. Magnolia trees grow tall enough to reach over the crest of the sinks.

Limestone sits underneath the pine forest. The sinkhole system that you can see from the boardwalk occurred because the top of the limestone dissolved. The most notable sink is Falling Waters, a pit 100 feet deep.

The waterfall is a natural Florida wonder. And it comes with its own mystery. The stream plunges down and disappears into a cavern, but where does it emerge?

Bonus Points

By climbing the stairs leading from the boardwalk, you access the Wiregrass Trail about a quarter mile along the top of the sinkhole area and out to a lake. Another quarter-mile trail, the Terrace Trail, continues uphill through the forest to the park campground.

The campground is on one of the highest points in Florida, 324 feet above sea level. That's high altitude for Florida. The whole area, including the hill, sits on a limestone base. On Saturdays, park rangers offer fireside chats.

At Florida Caverns State Park in Marianna, guided cave tours are offered every day except Christmas and Thanksgiving. The geological history of the caverns goes back 38 million years. Tours take about 45 minutes and are labeled moderately strenuous.

Native Americans used the caves for gathering clay, as shelter, and even as a place for burials. These are dry caves with limestone stalactites and stalagmites.

Florida Caverns State Park is located 3 miles north of Marianna. The address is: 3345 Caverns Road, Marianna, FL 32446, phone (850) 482-9598. Hours are 8 a.m. to sunset. Park admission is $4 a vehicle with up to 8 people. Web site: www.floridastateparks.org.

Cave tours are $8 plus tax for those 13 and up; $5 plus tax for children 3–12.

Nature trails, a historic visitor center built by the Civilian Conservation Corps during the Depression era, camping, picnicking, and swimming are all available to visitors.

The park borders both banks of the Chipola River. Spring and summer wildflowers are a popular draw.

Florida Caverns State Park is listed on page 10 of the Panhandle Florida guide to the Great Florida Birding Trail. Because of well-preserved uplands, species of birds like red-breasted nuthatches and winter wrens may be seen.

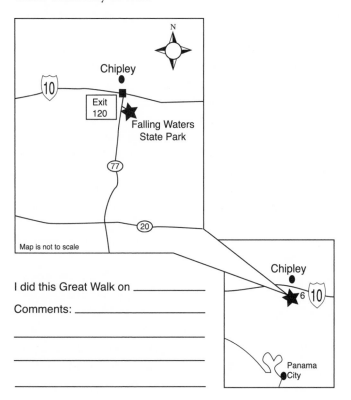

I did this Great Walk on _____

Comments: _____

_____

_____

_____

The Chipola River is listed on page 11 of the Panhandle Florida section guide to the Great Florida Birding Trail. Here the intrepid birder is advised to launch a canoe and spend the day on the river birding.

Trip Essentials

Name: Follow the Waterfall: Falling Waters State Park, Chipley
Type of walk: Nature
Length of walk: Sinkholes Trail is one-fourth of a mile long. Two other park trails are the same length.
Time to finish: 1 hour
Difficulty: Moderate. Not wheelchair accessible.
Appeals to: Nature buffs, photographers, and birders (listed on page 10 of the Panhandle Florida guide to the Great Florida Birding Trail)
Guides: Self-guided
Address: 1130 State Park Road, Chipley FL 32428
Phone: (850) 638-6130
Web site: www.floridastateparks.org
Cost: $4 per vehicle; extra fees for camping
Getting there: From I-10, take Chipley exit south on State Road 77 and follow signs to the park.
GPS coordinates: N 30° 72.778 W 085° 52.861
Hours: 8 a.m. to sunset
Restrooms: At trailhead
Water/food: Water at restrooms; no food
Dogs: Allowed on trails on a 6-foot hand-held lead. Large dogs not allowed on narrow boardwalk down to the waterfall.
Lunch ideas: Bring a picnic lunch.

7

Ducks, Shell Middens, and High-Water Marks

Mounds Pool Interpretive Trail, St. Marks National Wildlife Refuge, St. Marks

From the refuge's visitor center to the end of the road at the St. Marks Lighthouse is 6.8 miles. Fresh- and saltwater ponds are scattered along Lighthouse Road. Started in 1931, the refuge, administered by the U.S. Fish & Wildlife Service, had a mission to protect wintering waterfowl. The Civilian Conservation Corps added levees and culverts to make pools for the birds.

The Mounds Trail, also known as the Tower Pond Trail, is 5 miles down Lighthouse Road. Tower Pond is a saltwater lagoon made for ducks, wading birds, and migrating songbirds. The turnoff and parking lot are shared use for the Mounds Trail, restrooms, picnic tables overlooking Picnic Pond, and Headquarters Pool.

Free interpretive trail brochures are in a box at the trailhead. The trail begins on the right side of the parking lot near the road turnoff. You will be doing a 1-mile loop going through pine flatwoods and an oak ridge, moving past a brackish pond, a saltwater marsh, and an oak/cabbage palm hammock.

Ready? Good. Let's go. You begin by walking through thick pines alongside Tower Pond. In the pond, ducks and shorebirds come and go. The best viewing times are early in the morning and late afternoon.

The day we walked the trail, swallows were diving for flying bugs, swooping down toward the water but never touching the surface, then veering straight up into the sky, like miniature Blue Angels doing daredevil flying stunts.

NORTHWEST FLORIDA

Someday, little tree, all this will be yours. St. Marks National Wildlife Refuge.

The trail abruptly turns inland and travels up an incline. An old fire tower, in use from the 1930s to the 1950s, still stands on this high ground. Most of these lands were bought from timber companies and watching for wildfires was important. Now the refuge contracts with the U.S. Forest Service for fire suppression.

You are standing on an Indian midden, an archaeologist's term for an ancient trash pile. Indians, like migrating birds, came and went from the area from about 10,000 BC to the late eighteenth century.

Over the midden and down into the woods is marker No. 2 on the interpretive trail, and it is an eye-opener. The tree's marker is the approximate height, about 5 feet, of the wall of water that arrived on September 13, 1843. The Hurricane of 1843, as it is called, wiped out the nearby towns of St. Marks River, Magnolia, Rock Haven, and Port Leon.

Much of the trail you'll be walking is compacted sand, often with a carpet of leaves and pine needles. Pine cones are everywhere. The underbrush is thick with palmettos. Clusters of oak trees have numerous branches, twisting in many directions, and not growing very tall. Beyond the refuge is the Gulf of Mexico with its ever-changing weather patterns. Anything that grows too tall would probably not survive a severe storm.

The trail changes to grass, easy for walking. Next to another pond is a photo blind, a structure you can climb into and photograph wildlife in the pond.

Soon the trail becomes a sandy road. On our walk, a wax myrtle in bloom was heavy with bees buzzing and one monarch butterfly. Over a boardwalk with rope handles there is a raised observation deck with views of the same pond that has the photo blind on the other side.

Go straight past the observation deck and over the rise of a hill, and down at the bottom there is a trail sign with an arrow. The trail runs along the top of an impoundment.

Up high, walking on the flat top of the impoundment, the view is excellent. On one side is a salt marsh; on the other side are freshwater ponds. Two worlds, separated by a road.

An alligator suns itself on the bank of the freshwater pond. Blue crabs scuttle in the shallows of the pond. On the salt marsh side, the tide is out. Animal tracks weave patterns on the exposed flats. Ribbons of yellow-green marsh grasses go on and on as far as the eye can see, reminiscent of the Everglades and its river of grass.

The trail turns to the right into an oak/cabbage palm hammock. On your left is Tower Pond. Before long, regretfully, you are back at the parking lot. The walk showcases a wealth of natural and cultural life. It will leave you wanting more.

Bonus Points

St. Marks National Wildlife Refuge, some 68,000 acres along the Gulf coast of Northwest Florida, is divided into three units: St. Marks, the Wakulla, and the Panacea.

St. Marks, with its man-made impoundments, fishing, cycling, hiking, and wildlife observation, gets the most public use. An entrance fee of $4 per vehicle is charged. Those with all types of the America the Beautiful—National Parks and Federal Recreational Lands Pass get in free.

At the St. Marks Visitor Center you can purchase the "Lighthouse Road Drive Guide" for 50¢. The guide includes suggestions on where to park when walking the levees.

Birders, in particular, enjoy walking on levees. The elevation allows for good sight lines. You can see quite a distance. Walking is easy.

Photographers appreciate the lack of obstacles. Levees are flat, covered with grass, and unhindered by trees, tree roots, bushes, and snags.

St. Marks National Wildlife Refuge is designated a Gateway on the Great Florida Birding Trail. This means they are a hub for birding information in the area and have loaner optics available. Across the parking lot from the Mounds Nature Trail is Headquarters Pond. The Headquarters Pond Trail observation deck is a popular stop during the winter, when ducks abound.

Hikers who want to walk the distance can go 49.5 miles on the Florida National Scenic Trail as it crosses the St. Marks Unit going from east to west. Camping permits for through hikers are available at the visitor center.

The mailing address for the refuge is: St. Marks National Wildlife Refuge, P.O. Box 68, St. Marks, FL 32255, phone (850) 925-6121. Visit the Web site at: www.fws.gov/saintmarks.

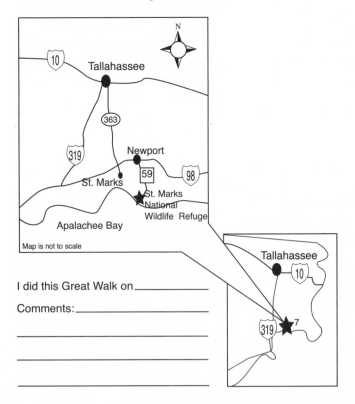

I did this Great Walk on _____

Comments: _____

_____

_____

_____

A number of free brochures are available at the visitor center. The "St. Marks Bird List," for example, is set up in checklist fashion so you can fill in the blanks. Bird species are ranked from abundant to rare. Each one is labeled with the season when it is most likely to be seen.

Families with children will want to pick up the free brochure titled "Young People's Check List." It has wildlife drawings that can be checked off as items are seen. Another page has a wildlife bingo game everyone in the car can play while driving Lighthouse Road.

A short but sweet walk starts right next to the visitor center. Plum Orchard Trail is one-third of a mile. Walking is easy. There are some boardwalks. Part of the trail goes past a pond. Like the freshwater ponds along Lighthouse Road, this one was full of water lilies in bloom. The day we visited, a stiff breeze lifted the green lily leaves, exposing their red-brown undersides. From a distance, it looked like Portuguese man-of-war were floating in the pond.

Bicyclists will find Lighthouse Road to their liking. Plenty of places to stop and nobody drives fast. In fact, cars sometimes stop on the road. You'll see a long lens protruding out of a passenger's or driver's window. Look around and sure enough there will be a photo moment close by, perhaps a great blue heron on a branch overhanging the water. By staying in the car, the photographer has a better chance of getting the picture.

Trip Essentials

Name: Ducks, Shell Middens, and High-Water Marks: Mounds Pool Interpretive Trail, St. Marks National Wildlife Refuge, St. Marks
Type of walk: Nature/historic
Length of walk: 1 mile
Time to finish: 1 hour
Difficulty: Easy. Mostly wheelchair accessible.
Appeals to: Families, history buffs, nature lovers, photographers, and birders (St. Marks Lighthouse Unit is a designated Gateway for the Great Florida Birding Trail; see page 24 of the Panhandle Florida guide.)
Guides: Usually tied in with an event. Call ahead for schedule.
Address: St. Marks National Wildlife Refuge, P.O. Box 68, St. Marks, FL 32355

Phone: (850) 925-6121

Web site: www.fws.gov/saintmarks

Cost: $5 per passenger vehicle or motorcycle. America the Beautiful pass holders pay no fee. Put pass on car dashboard when parked.

Getting there: 3 miles south of U.S. Highway 98 at Newport

GPS coordinates: N 34' 05" W 84' 20"

Hours: The St. Marks Unit gate opens at 6 a.m. and closes at 9 p.m. Visitor center hours are 8 a.m. to 4 p.m. Monday through Friday; 10 a.m. to 5 p.m. Saturday and Sunday; closed on federal holidays.

Restrooms: At trailhead and visitor center

Water/food: Water at restrooms; fountain at visitor center; no food

Dogs: Allowed; must be leashed at all times

Lunch ideas: Picnic table at visitor center; several picnic tables at Tower Pond and other locations

8

The Coca-Cola Town

A Walk around Historic Quincy

Standing outside watching the sky turn grey and clouds gather, the shop owner engaged a stranger in a conversation about the weather. Will it rain? Won't it? Walking to the next block, a local resident struck up a conversation with the same stranger.

And me? I'm the stranger, not even from around these parts. Just visiting. Come to see historic Quincy without a clue where to go or what to do. Yet I felt welcomed within minutes of parking my car and walking two blocks.

No wonder that, in 2005, *Florida Monthly* magazine readers voted Quincy "Florida's Friendliest Small Town."

Quincy has a long history, and it picked up speed in 1821, the year Spain turned Florida over to the United States. Settlers began moving into Gadsden County. Since 1827, the courthouse square has been the epicenter for government and commerce. A year later, 1828, the town was officially recognized. Tobacco crops were already growing and profitable before Quincy had an official name and built the first of several county courthouses.

Not many places can say their entire downtown is historic. Quincy can. Every bit of downtown Quincy plus some of the surrounding area is included in a thirty-six-block National Register Historic District.

The current courthouse, built in 1913, when the town was really bustling, stands two stories tall and is painted pale yellow and white, with plantation-style columns in front and a cupola on the top. It is a style that architects call "classical eclecticism," meaning the building echoes a lot of different themes. No one needs to wear a watch in Quincy because the cupola has large clock faces on all four sides—and the clocks work!

Right across the street from the courthouse, at 13 North Madison Street, sits the Gadsden Arts Center in what used to be the Bell & Bates hardware store, established in 1910. Now a modern gallery with rotating exhibits, the center could also call itself a living museum.

The building's beautifully refinished heart pine floors, along with a Victorian gingerbread office, are original, and they still have the rolling wall ladders from the hardware store days.

The Gadsden Arts Center is a good place to get two free brochures, "On the Trail in Historic Quincy: A Walking Tour Guide to the Historic District," and "Quincy/Havana/Midway/Chattahoochee." Both brochures have a map of the historic areas. The historic trail guide includes lovely pen-and-ink drawings of some buildings and descriptions of fifty-five places marked on their historic district map.

Going north on Madison for one block, you pass the Centenary United Methodist Church at 122 North Madison Street. Keep on going past the church to the next block and the church offices. Ask to see the church and the staff will be happy to open it for you. Inside the church are some outstanding stained-glass windows.

The Methodists arrived in Quincy right after it became a town and organized as a congregation in 1829. The present structure was built in 1918, the same year James Campbell was born. Campbell has spent his whole life as a member of this church. A history buff, he researched the windows and is the keeper of living history. Campbell said one window depicting Christ knocking on a door may be a Tiffany window, but it is not signed by the artist.

Back on the sidewalk, walk past the church offices to the end of the block and look to your left. The Centenary United Methodist Parsonage occupies the Smallwood-White House, built in 1843. During the Civil War, the Ladies Aid Society—formed to help wounded Confederate soldiers—used this house to tend sick and dying soldiers following the battles at Olustee and Natural Bridge.

Turn right onto East King Street for a stroll through a historic district residential area. You notice immediately that not just the houses built in the late 1800s are memorable; a number of homes built in the early part of the twentieth century are standouts.

One such house is the Gardner-McCall House, built between 1928 and 1931, at 235 East King Street. Nowhere else in Quincy will you see Spanish-style architecture, but it was typical in the 1920s.

The current Gadsden County Courthouse in Quincy was built in 1913.

What isn't typical is the story of how Quincy became known as the Coca-Cola town, a story that helps to explain the wealth of beautiful historic homes. In the early 1900s, Pat Munroe was president of Quincy State Bank. There was this newfangled soft drink called Coca-Cola. When someone came in for a bank loan, Munroe urged the borrower to take out a little extra, buy Coca-Cola stock, and hold onto it. He did the same with family and friends. They listened and made money. At one time Quincy had more millionaires per capita than any other location in Florida.

Coca-Cola stock plus the specialty trade in the surrounding area of growing shade tobacco (the tobacco used in the outer wrapping of a cigar) funded churches, elegant homes, and businesses.

Once you have your historic map, the route you take to see the thirty-six blocks of historic Quincy could go a number of different ways. Whichever way you go, the town of Quincy, past and present, will welcome you.

Bonus Points

The Gadsden Arts Center, 13 North Madison Street, Quincy, FL 32351, phone (850) 875-4866, is open 10 a.m. to 5 p.m. Tuesday through Saturday; and 1 p.m. to 5 p.m. on Sunday. Closed on Thanksgiving, Christmas, and New Year's Day. Admission to the center is $1 for adults; children get in free. Web site: www.gadsdenarts.com.

Another place to get historic brochures and more area information is the Gadsden County Chamber of Commerce, 208 North Adams Street, Quincy, FL 32351, phone (850) 627-9231. Web site: www.gadsdenfla.com.

Quincy sits midway on the North Florida Art Trail, which runs through Gadsden County. The trail includes Havana, Quincy, Greensboro, and Chattahoochee. In 1997, the Florida Legislature designated State Road 12 as Gadsden County's North Florida Art Trail. If you picked up a copy of the walking-tour guide to Quincy's historic district, a map of the North Florida Art Trail is on the back cover.

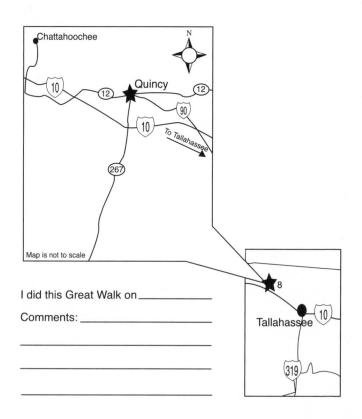

I did this Great Walk on _____

Comments: _____

_____

_____

_____

Trip Essentials

Name: The Coca-Cola Town: A Walk around Historic Quincy

Type of walk: Historic

Length of walk: About 3.6 miles

Time to finish: 1 to 2 hours, depending on route chosen

Difficulty: Easy. Wheelchair accessible.

Appeals to: History and architecture buffs and photographers

Guides: Self-guided. Walking brochures at Gadsden County Chamber of Commerce and Gadsden Arts Center.

Address: Gadsden County Chamber of Commerce, 208 North Adams Street, Quincy, FL 32351

Phone: (850) 627-9231

Web site: www.gadsdenfla.com

Cost: None

Getting there: Quincy is 16 miles northwest of Tallahassee. From I-10 take exit 192, U.S. 90, to Midway/Quincy.

GPS coordinates: (Quincy) N 30° 58694 W 084° 58333

Hours: Daylight

Restrooms: At Gadsden County Chamber of Commerce, Gadsden Arts Center

Water/food: Bring water; several local restaurants

Dogs: Leashed on the street; not allowed inside buildings

Lunch ideas: Cuban, at Lisa & Joe's Café, 114 East Washington Street, Quincy, FL 32351, phone (850) 875-1922; deli, at Kelly's Deli, 1320 West Jefferson, Quincy, FL 32351, phone (850) 627-7857

That Sinking Feeling

Leon Sinks Geological Area, Apalachicola National Forest, Crawfordville

North Carolina and Tennessee have mountains. Florida has mountains too. Honest. Only our mountains are inverted. We call them sinkholes.

To see a whole range of sinkholes and learn about the wonderful world of karst, visit Leon Sinks Geological Area, located 7 miles south of Tallahassee on U.S. 319. Leon Sinks is in Leon County, but just barely. The Wakulla County line is spitting distance away. The town of Crawfordville is 9 miles south of Leon Sinks, and Tallahassee is up the road about 6 miles.

A day-use fee of $3 is paid at a self-serve pay station. Since it is self-serve, have the correct amount with you. The holders of any of the America the Beautiful passes get in free. Display the pass on the dashboard of your car.

A free brochure has a map inside naming all the sinks along the way and contains information about the karst world. Did you know that most of Florida sits on a thick bed of limestone? Think about that. Limestone is porous and can dissolve. Rain picks up carbon dioxide from the air and from decaying vegetation. It changes into a weak acid.

Karst develops when rain and groundwater work away at and dissolve the limestone bedrock underneath. The ground drops, opening up into sinkholes of all sizes and depths, swales, caverns, natural bridges, circular depressions, and water table ponds. Leon Sinks has several prominent wet sinkholes, which are inverted mountains filled with water.

Looking at the map, you'll see several trail choices. The Sinkhole Trail is 3.1 miles and marked with blue blazes on trees. A Crossover Trail covers one-half mile and is marked with white blazes. Finally, Gumswamp Trail traverses 2.3 miles marked with green blazes.

The most popular route isn't listed. It is a do-it-yourselfer and combines all the blazes. Take the Sinkhole Trail past the sinks, and then use the Crossover Trail to shorten the hike. The Crossover Trail connects to the last two-tenths of the Gumswamp Trail leading back to the parking lot. This route makes the trip about 2.3 miles long.

You are barely on the trail when the fragrance hits you. Pinewoods, deep, aromatic—a sharp fragrance that you'll wish you could bottle

NORTHWEST FLORIDA

The aroma of pine trees permeates the blue-blazed trail at Leon Sinks Geological Area.

and take home. When southern magnolias are in bloom, their perfume adds a heavy floral scent.

The blue blazes take you along a dirt trail covered with a carpet of pine needles. Tree roots cross the trail. In some places, going uphill, the tree roots serve as steps.

To see the most wildlife, you already know the drill. Morning and early evening are the best times. Wildlife is smart enough to lie low during the heat of the day. We should be, too.

If the book field guides get to be a bit heavy, consider bringing the folded, laminated quick guides to plants, animals, and birds. They weigh a lot less and are often keyed to specific areas, making it likely that what you see is on the quick guide.

In April and May, the dogwood trees bloom, then the southern magnolias. Tupelo, ash, wiregrass, hickory, along with red and white oaks are all found along the trail.

The brochure shows a cross section of an underground cave system called the Hammock Sink Cave System. Divers have explored 41,000 feet of this cave system. Swimming is not permitted because it causes damage to wildlife. The entrance to the sink basin is underneath the deck platform overlooking Hammock Sink.

The water in the sink is a glassy blue green, but the color of water changes from sink to sink, ranging anywhere from tannic acid–brown to aquamarine blue.

After that impressive sight, the trail goes uphill and along comes Tiny Sink. It is indeed tiny. Next up on the trail is Big Dismal. Curious name. Nothing is dismal about this sink. The water is a beautiful turquoise green. Yellow and brown leaves float on the surface. Sink sides are steep. Shallow groundwater seeps from the sides into the 130-foot-deep sink.

Big Dismal is a wet sinkhole, making it an open door to the Floridan Aquifer below, a huge underground water system going underground from South Carolina to Florida and west to Alabama.

This is our drinking water. Keeping it pure means changing lifestyles, seriously curtailing fertilizer or pesticides on our lawns. Whatever you do at home seeps down into the Floridan Aquifer. Some twenty years from now, we'll be drinking our decisions.

Past Big Dismal you will encounter four more sinks and then cross over Natural Bridge and Fisher Creek Sink. Walking a bit farther, you come to signs for the Crossover Trail. On the Crossover Trail is a boardwalk through a swamp.

Usually you see cypress trees in swamps but not in this part of the world. Gum tupelo trees fill the swamp. Their shapes are almost surreal—large, bulbous bases rising up into long, stately grey trunks that end abruptly in bushy, bright green tops.

Bonus Points

Bald Point State Park was purchased in 1999 and opened in 2000. You will find 4,800 acres of coastal wilderness punctuated by freshwater ponds and tidal marshes. Their address is: 146 Box Cut, Alligator Point, FL 32346, phone (850) 349-9146.

NORTHWEST FLORIDA

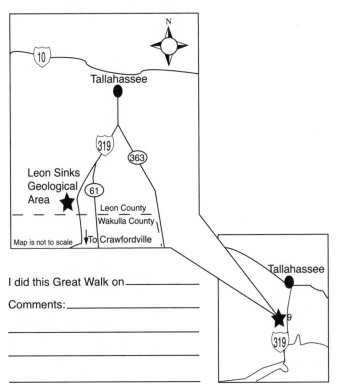

I did this Great Walk on _____

Comments: _____

_____

_____

_____

Hours are 8 a.m. to sundown 365 days a year. Entrance fee is $3 per car; $1 per pedestrian or bicyclist. Visit their Web site at: www. floridastateparks.org.

Gulf Specimen Marine Laboratory in Panacea has touch tanks. That alone makes it a worthy destination for families, grandparents with grandchildren, and adults. The focus is on marine life found along the North Florida Wilderness Coast—seahorses, starfish, octopuses, and sea anemones.

Jack Rudloe, naturalist and author, founded the business in 1963 to supply marine animals to academic scientists. Author John Steinbeck, an amateur marine biologist himself, was a friend of Rudloe's and encouraged him to start Gulf Specimen.

Located at 222 Clark Drive, Panacea, FL 32346, phone (850) 984-5297, the lab is open from 9 a.m. to 5 p.m. Monday through Friday; 10 a.m. to 4 p.m. on Saturday; and noon to 4 p.m. on Sunday. Admission is $5 for adults; $3 for children. The Web site is: www.gulfspecimen. org.

Trip Essentials

Name: That Sinking Feeling: Leon Sinks Geological Area, Apalachicola National Forest, Crawfordville

Type of walk: Nature

Length of walk: Sinkhole Trail shortened with Crossover Trail, 2.3 miles

Time to finish: 2 hours for a leisurely stroll

Difficulty: Easy to mildly moderate. Parts of trail not wheelchair accessible.

Appeals to: Nature lovers, natural history enthusiasts, and birders (listed on page 22, Panhandle Florida guide to the Great Florida Birding Trail)

Guides: Self-guided

Address: Leon Sinks, 6605 Crawfordville Highway (U.S. 319), Tallahassee, FL 32310

Phone: Wakulla Ranger District, Crawfordville (850) 926-3561

Web site: www.fs.fed.us/r8/florida

Cost: $3 per vehicle; self-pay station. Free for all America the Beautiful pass holders

Getting there: From Crawfordville, go north on U.S. 319. Leon Sinks is on the left just as you enter Leon County.

GPS coordinates: (Leon Sinks Geological Area) N 30° 30.944 W 084° 34.861

Hours: 8 a.m. to 8 p.m. April 1 to October 31; 8 a.m. to 6 p.m. November 1 to March 31

Restrooms: At trailhead

Water/food: Water fountain at trailhead; no food

Dogs: Leashed at all times

Lunch ideas: Local seafood and American, at Posey's Steam Room & Oyster Bar, 1506 Coastal Highway (US 98), Panacea, FL 32346, phone (850) 984-5243; seafood and buffet, at Coastal Restaurant, Coastal Highway 98, Panacea, FL 32346, phone (850) 984-2933

10

Got Ghosts?

Haunted History Walk, Monticello

A small town in North Florida boasts of residents who won't pay taxes and whose names can't be found in the phone book. However, they do make house calls.

The town is Monticello in Jefferson County off Interstate 10, some 23 miles east of Tallahassee. ABC-TV labeled Monticello "the most haunted small town in the United States."

Big Bend Ghost Trackers—a Tallahassee-based group of paranormal investigators who take statements of sightings and research whether witnesses are credible before stories are accepted—estimates that one out of three homes in Monticello is presently haunted or has experienced a haunting in the past. A place has to have some history under its belt before ghosts arrive. Monticello qualifies.

Jefferson County, named for Thomas Jefferson, was separated from Leon County and established in 1827. Monticello, named for Jefferson's home in Virginia, became the county seat while the state was still a territory of the United States.

The City of Monticello is a National Mainstreet Community, graced with tree-shaded streets and a wealth of Victorian and antebellum houses. It is worth a visit for the architecture alone. Twenty-seven city blocks are designated as a National Register Historic District.

The Monticello–Jefferson County Chamber of Commerce, on West Washington Street, has a free walking and driving tour brochure listing twenty-six homes and three landmarks with suggested routes for a self-guided tour.

Even the chamber building is part of the tour. Built in 1906 as a Catholic church, the entrance hall is the chamber's office. Also available at the chamber is a free pamphlet, "Jefferson County Guide," with a more detailed historical tour map and descriptions. Suggested walking or driving tours in this guide are the West Tour, East Tour, and Downtown & North Tour. If you walked them all, it would add up to over 3 miles.

The West Tour is short, just over 1 mile in downtown historic Monticello. Even if you don't see or feel the presence of a ghost, you can experience history and have, as the Ghost Trackers like to say, a haunting good time.

Brochure and guide in hand, walk two blocks east from the chamber toward the courthouse, which is easy to spot as it is located on a roundabout in the middle of West Washington Street, also known as U.S. 90.

On your right, at the end of West Washington Street, is the Monticello Opera House. A two-story brick structure built in 1890 by John H. Perkins, the opera house is listed on the National Register of Historic Places. Perkins used the whole block to construct one long building, dividing the first floor to house businesses and putting in a six-hundred-seat auditorium upstairs at the end of the building.

At the turn of the twentieth century, it was one of the largest auditoriums in Florida. When the railroad was rerouted to exclude Monticello, rich visitors from South Georgia and North Florida stopped coming. Until the entire block was purchased in 1973, the auditorium sat unused. Now it has a new life, billing itself as the Rural Center for the Arts.

The Monticello Opera House enjoys a year-round season of plays, concerts, receptions, dinners, community events, and occasional late-night ghostly visitors. Jan Rickey, executive director of the Monticello Opera House, tells of being there at night on the first floor and hearing the piano playing on the second floor. No one was up there.

Rickey believes it is Perkins himself, who loved to dance and continues to stay around for the party.

If you try the entrance door of the opera house and find it locked, go back to 185 West Washington Street, the opera house office. A staff member should be there from 10 a.m. to 4 p.m. on weekdays and often weekends. They will open the opera house.

The Big Bend Ghost Trackers have a story about the courthouse across the street from the Monticello Opera House.

Ghost Trackers in period costumes head for the Palmer House, said to be the site of hauntings, in Monticello.

Toward the end of the Civil War, a crowd gathered at the courthouse for news. It was a hot August night. Tempers flared. One man pulled a gun. Another man pulled his gun. The two shot each other and died on the spot.

During full moons on hot summer nights, witnesses report driving by and seeing two men shooting at each other on the courthouse steps. Ghost researchers call this a residual haunting, where an event is played back without any interaction between the ghosts and the viewer.

Continue right on U.S. 19 two blocks to the Palmer House, a white, two-story structure at 325 South Jefferson Street. It is currently an antique store, only open on weekends. The Ghost Trackers label this building the South's most haunted house in the South's most haunted town.

Martin Palmer built the home in 1840 for his son, Dr. John Palmer. The senior Palmer was so distraught after the South lost the Civil War that he killed himself in this house.

At the Palmer House there is a geocache. The GPS coordinates are in Trip Essentials.

Lovely old homes with wide porches line the street called Palmer Mill Road behind South Jefferson Street. The John Denham House, built in 1872, stands out by having a cupola above the second story. This was so Denham could oversee his plantation and watch the cotton workers without having to leave his house.

The 1872 John Denham House today is an award-winning B&B, famous for weddings, family stays (children and pets are welcome), and its ghosts. Not only is Denham said to still be present but also a lady named Aunt Sarah, who once occupied a front room and had an affair with a prominent politician.

Where Palmer Mill Road ends, you are back at West Washington Street. If you turn left, there are eight more places to see on the West Tour. By turning right, you are headed back toward the chamber.

Right across the street from the chamber is Jefferson County High School. Built in 1852, it was the first brick schoolhouse in Florida. School bells no longer ring here—that stopped in 1992—though the Ghost Trackers say "tap-tap" sounds have been heard, perhaps schoolteachers from long ago tapping rulers on desks, trying to bring students to attention.

Bonus Points

Along the West Tour route, four of the historic homes you will walk by are currently operated as B&Bs: The Cottage Bed & Breakfast Inn; Palmer Place Bed & Breakfast Inn; Avera- Clarke House; and the John Denham House. If the owners are home, do knock and ask to see a room or two.

Betty Davis is the director and founder of Big Bend Ghost Trackers. Their Haunted History Walking Tours in Monticello on the third Saturday of each month start at 8 p.m. at the chamber. Ghost Trackers wear period costumes from the Civil War era and are versed in local history.

The tour costs $10 and lasts 90 minutes. Should you want more, they offer a Haunted Cemetery Tour/mini–ghost hunt starting at 10:30 p.m. This tour is also $10 per person.

Call ahead of time to verify tour dates, times, and prices. Mailing address: Big Bend Ghost Trackers, P.O. Box 38141, Tallahassee, FL 32315, phone (850) 508-8109 or (850) 562-2516. Web site: www. bigbendghosttrackers.homestead.com.

The Monticello–Jefferson County Chamber of Commerce is at 420 West Washington Street, Monticello, FL 32344, phone (850) 997-5552. They are open from 9 a.m. to 3:30 p.m. Monday through Friday; closed during the lunch hour.

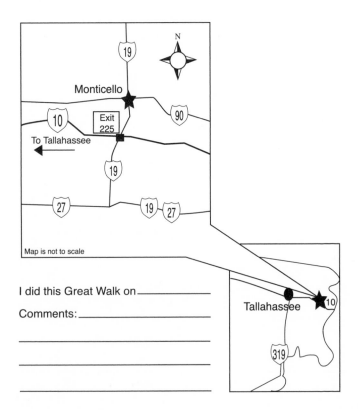

Trip Essentials

Name: Got Ghosts? Haunted History Walk, Monticello

Type of walk: History

Length of walk: Slightly more than 1 mile for the West Tour section

Time to finish: 45 minutes to 1 hour

Difficulty: Easy. Handicapped accessible.

Appeals to: History buffs, ghost hunters, lovers of architecture, geocachers, and photographers

Guides: Self-guided. Free brochure at Monticello–Jefferson County Chamber of Commerce. Ghost tours given third Saturday of the month. Cost $10 per person. Contact Big Bend Ghost Trackers, Betty Davis, director, phone (850) 508-8109.

Address: Monticello–Jefferson County Chamber of Commerce, 420 West Washington Street, Monticello, FL 32344

Phone: (850) 997-5552

Web site: www.monticellojeffersonfl.com

Cost: None for self-guided; $10 for ghost tours

Getting there: 25 miles east of Tallahassee at the intersection of U.S. 90 and U.S. 19

GPS coordinates: (Palmer House geocache) N 30° 32.631 W 083° 52.220

Hours: Daylight; or night if you take the ghost tour

Restrooms: At Monticello–Jefferson County Chamber of Commerce

Water/food: No water fountains on street (bring your own); restaurants nearby

Dogs: Leashed on the street; not allowed in buildings

Lunch ideas: American, at Jake's Sub & Grill, 180 West Washington Street, Monticello, FL 32344, phone (850) 997-0388; Mexican, at Rancho Grande, 320 North Cherry Street, Monticello, FL 32344, phone (850) 997-0087

NORTHWEST FLORIDA

Part II

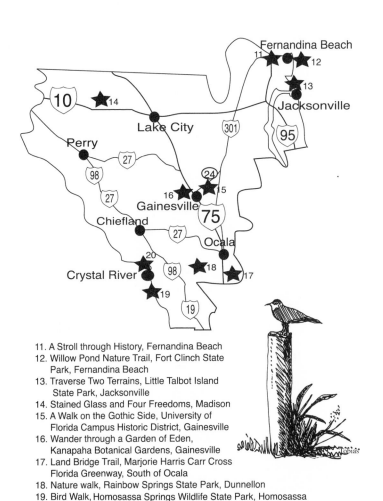

11. A Stroll through History, Fernandina Beach
12. Willow Pond Nature Trail, Fort Clinch State Park, Fernandina Beach
13. Traverse Two Terrains, Little Talbot Island State Park, Jacksonville
14. Stained Glass and Four Freedoms, Madison
15. A Walk on the Gothic Side, University of Florida Campus Historic District, Gainesville
16. Wander through a Garden of Eden, Kanapaha Botanical Gardens, Gainesville
17. Land Bridge Trail, Marjorie Harris Carr Cross Florida Greenway, South of Ocala
18. Nature walk, Rainbow Springs State Park, Dunnellon
19. Bird Walk, Homosassa Springs Wildlife State Park, Homosassa
20. EcoWalk, Crystal River Preserve State Park, Crystal River

A Stroll through History

The Historic Downtown Fernandina Beach Centre Street Stroll, Fernandina Beach

Fernandina Beach has a bawdy past and a genteel present. Both are alluring.

A good way to answer their siren call is to sign up for a stroll with a long name—the Historic Downtown Fernandina Beach Centre Street Stroll.

Strolls take place on Friday and Saturday. Tickets are required. Purchase them at the Amelia Island Museum of History, located in the old Nassau County Jail at the corner of 3rd and Cedar Streets.

When it is time for the stroll, a museum volunteer will arrive at the starting point, a plaza area in front of the old railroad depot, 102 Centre Street.

The docks, freshly built a few years ago with floating walkways, are the first stop. To get there requires crossing the railroad tracks next to the old railroad depot. They may look ordinary, but these railroad tracks hum with history.

In the 1850s, a U.S. senator by the name of David Yulee had both vision and a plan, but first he needed the townspeople to move off their high bluff.

Fernandina's original settlement—Old Town, as it is now known—was located high on a bluff overlooking the Amelia River. Yulee had a problem with that. He wanted to build a cargo railroad between Fernandina and Cedar Key. But there was a catch. He didn't want to build the railroad through some wetlands and up the bluff. Yulee suggested the town move south about a half mile to dry land that he owned and generously offered for $1 per acre.

Old Town was abandoned. Yulee built the 155-mile-long Florida Railroad from both ends, meeting in the middle. His railroad began operating in 1861, one month before the Civil War started. Bad timing, but who knew?

Our guide for the stroll told us how Florida seceded from the Union to join the Confederacy. In 1862, Union troops arrived in Fernandina. Townspeople fled as the Union army took over Fort Clinch and Fernandina.

The last flatcar out of town was loaded with furniture. Two men on the flatcar stood up and taunted the Union soldiers. A soldier fired one shot, killing them both. Our guide said that as far as anyone knows, those were the only shots fired here during the Civil War.

With these stories in mind, we cross the railroad tracks and look down at the rails with newfound respect.

From the docks, the stroll turns around to walk up Centre Street. Both sides of the street are lined with historical buildings occupied by modern-day businesses. The stroll does not go into any buildings except St. Peter's Episcopal Church if it is open.

Warning to parents with children: Fernandina's Fantastic Fudge, located at the corner of 2nd and Centre, is going to get their attention. Since the stroll doesn't go inside any of the shops, promise your children to come back later, a promise you'll want to keep not only for them but, let's be honest, for yourself as well.

Fernandina's Golden Age lasted from 1870 to 1910. Union officers liked what they saw in Fernandina during their tour of duty. They returned after the Civil War to build businesses and a slew of Victorian homes.

Tourists came on steamboats. Sailing ships brought cargo from around the world. The railroad flourished. It was said that you could walk from Fernandina across the river to Georgia without getting wet just by stepping from one ship's deck to the next.

All those ships meant all those sailors were looking for a good time. At one point, Fernandina had twenty-two bars and eight bordellos.

The late Angel Davis, born in the Lesesne House at 7th and Centre, was a child in the early 1900s. She remembered that kimono-clad prostitutes scandalized her mother.

The modern shrimping industry had its birth here during the

A horse-drawn carriage mixes with combustion engines in historic downtown Fernandina Beach.

Golden Age. Some five to six shrimpers still remain. A cargo port now sits where tall sailing ships once docked.

Memories of the past are well preserved in entire neighborhoods of late Victorian architecture. Fifty blocks of downtown Fernandina, including Centre Street, have the honor of being on the National Register of Historic Places.

One example is the Palace Saloon on the corner of 2nd and Centre. On the stroll, our guide told us a tale—never verified but widely believed—that Andrew Carnegie and his friends would come over from Cumberland Island, belly up to the long wooden bar in the Palace, and light their cigars with $20 bills.

At the end of Centre Street sits St. Peter's Episcopal Church, built in 1884. In a visual and moving way, the best part of the stroll is saved for last. If St. Peter's is open and not being used for a service, the stroll will enter the church. There are stained-glass windows of breathtaking beauty.

Bonus Points

Volunteers with the Amelia Island Museum of History must like to walk. In addition to the Centre Street Stroll, the museum offers walk-

NORTHEAST FLORIDA

ing tours of Victorian homes north of Centre Street and a separate tour of Victorian homes south of Centre Street. On the south tour, it is possible to enter three homes.

If that's not enough, there are ghost tours that begin in St. Peter's graveyard. Many of the Victorian houses have haunting tales. Some of the ghosts are benign, some are not. Another popular highlight is the illuminated tours. Call the museum at (904) 261-7378 for all these tour schedules.

After a Centre Street stroll, go to the old railroad depot. No longer a place to wait for trains, the depot now houses the Amelia Island–Fernandina Beach–Yulee Chamber of Commerce.

The staff is friendly and helpful. Racks of free brochures cover a multitude of possible trips and relocation information. Do-it-yourselfers should ask for the brochure called "A Walking or Driving Tour of Centre Street Fernandina."

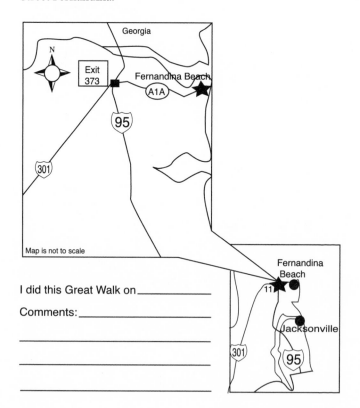

Georgia

N

Exit 373

Fernandina Beach

A1A

95

301

Map is not to scale

I did this Great Walk on _____

Comments: _____

_____

_____

_____

Fernandina Beach

11

301

Jacksonville

95

Growth on Amelia Island even touches historic downtown, but the new buildings stay in character with their surroundings. Hampton Inn & Suites on South 2nd Street, for example, is designed to look like building fronts on Centre Street, using the same color schemes as the historic buildings. This attention to historic detail allowed them to easily sail past historic boards and get permits to build.

Trip Essentials

Name: A Stroll through History: The Historic Downtown Fernandina Beach Centre Street Stroll

Type of walk: Historic

Length of walk: 1.2 miles round trip

Time to finish: 1 1/2 hours

Difficulty: Easy, entirely on pavement. Wheelchair accessible.

Appeals to: History buffs and families

Guides: Amelia Island Museum of History provides guides for the stroll.

Address: Stroll begins at old railroad depot, 102 Centre Street. Buy tickets inside the Amelia Island Museum of History, 233 South 3rd Street, Fernandina Beach, FL 32034

Phone: (904) 261-7378

Web site: www.ameliamuseum.org

Cost: $10 adults; $5 students.

Getting there: From Interstate 95, take exit 373 east onto A1A and go to Amelia Island. After crossing the bridge, A1A becomes 8th Street. In Fernandina Beach, turn left onto Centre Street. The old railroad depot is on the left just before railroad tracks.

GPS coordinates: N 30° 66.944 W 081° 46.278

Hours: Strolls conducted on Friday and Saturday at 3:30 p.m.

Restrooms: Inside museum and next door to the old railroad depot

Water/food: No store to buy water; numerous restaurants

Dogs: Leashed on the street; not allowed inside buildings

Lunch ideas: Ethnic cuisine, at Café Karibo, 27 North 3rd Street, Fernandina Beach 32034, phone (904) 277-5269; American cuisine, at La Bodega, 19 South 3rd Street, Fernandina Beach 32034, phone (904) 321-1922

NORTHEAST FLORIDA

12

Nature's Classroom

Willow Pond Nature Trail, Fort Clinch State Park, Fernandina Beach

Being in an outdoor classroom, where Mother Nature provides the curriculum, is ideal for Carl Watson, a volunteer at Fort Clinch State Park in Fernandina Beach. He gets to do three things he really enjoys: guide walks, teach people, and learn new things through research.

On the Saturday morning we arrive for a nature walk, it does not take long for the small trailhead parking lot to fill up with cars. Cub Scout Troup 25 from Jacksonville showed up along with assorted adults. Carl waits for latecomers. A few families with children of various ages arrive, and a selection of senior citizens rounds out the group.

The nature trail has two loops. Willow Loop takes 25 minutes, so the sign says, while Magnolia loop is 45 minutes. If you stop and chat about things, and we do, double that to an hour and a half.

We step onto the trail and almost immediately are engulfed in a coastal maritime hammock. Wax myrtles and magnolias and a squadron of scraggly oaks have their branches bent in contorted shapes, the result of growing up in a storm-laced, windy environment. Before developers ripped out maritime hammocks, this is how coastal Florida looked.

A coastal hammock is not an overnight sensation. Ancient dunes along the shore gave way over time to low, dense forests. Trees and bushes start with seeds dropped accidentally by birds and animals. Animal trails wear grooves in the forest floor. Carpets of leaves cushion the footfalls of both humans and animals.

Carl stops by a saw palmetto, one of the oldest plants in the hammock. It is one of his favorites. He confesses that he could spend all day talking about this plant. A member of the palm family, a saw palmetto

NORTHEAST FLORIDA

Volunteer guide Carl Watson explains the role of saw palmettos to members of Boy Scout Pack 25 from Jacksonville, on the Willow Pond Trail at Fort Clinch State Park.

is the plant that keeps on giving. Indians boiled the leaves to make a purgative drink. The fanlike leaves became shelter material for both Indians and early settlers, while the plant's roots produced tannic acid, useful for tanning leather.

In modern times, saw palmetto berries are processed into capsules for easy ingestion. Saw palmetto is suggested as a supplement for prostatic hyperplasia. It is claimed to improve urinary flow and help decrease prostate size.

Wild animals know a good thing. All animals eat the saw palmetto berries. An autopsy of a roadkill bear near Ocala revealed thirty pounds of saw palmetto berries in her stomach.

For those who are afraid of encountering wildlife, a guided walk is a good option. A group of humans walking and talking loudly is enough to spook any self-respecting wildlife.

Carl finds deer tracks and stands over them, cautioning people to step aside so they can sight along the trail and see them. The deer trail crosses the Willow Pond Trail. We squint and see cloven-shaped indentations in the dirt.

Turns out that raccoons scorn trails made by deer. They make their own trails through the woods, even setting aside bathroom areas—raccoon rest areas.

Sooner or later, all the trails lead to water. A number of freshwater ponds dot the area, including Willow Pond. All were man-made, it is speculated, for an indigo-processing plant long ago. Willow Pond is covered in duckweed, a small green plant that floats on the surface. This is like sushi for ducks. They like it a lot.

Before crossing over a boardwalk at Willow Pond, Carl cautions us to stay in the middle of the path because poison ivy grows everywhere. Good advice. Any time, anywhere, stay on the trail and don't pick any plant. You only have to get poison ivy once to forever remember the mantra: Leaves of three, leave it be.

Live oaks dip graceful curved limbs toward the pond. All along the trail, we've seen live oaks, but these are not the original trees that explorers saw centuries ago. Those were cut down to fill orders from naval architects.

Years ago, these graceful trees were in demand for ship building, especially for support timbers and knees. The natural crooks in the tree, when shaped a bit, became ship's knees. *Old Ironsides* was made out of live oak. Carl has researched the subject and found it would take from four hundred to seven hundred live oak trees to build a ship.

As we walk along, there are potholes in the path. Some look fresh. Armadillos made them, digging in the ground for insects. Armadillos, sad to say, seem to be supremely dumb. How else do you explain the way they walk right up to a tree and bump into it, or why there are so many dead armadillos on the road?

The answer is poor eyesight. Their hearing is keen, and so is their sense of smell. We don't actually see any armadillos this day. Perhaps they heard us with those keen ears.

Hanging down from the live oaks is a grey plant called Spanish moss. If you owned a car before 1975 and slashed open a seat, what you'd find inside was Spanish moss.

Spanish moss was big business for a long time. Pillows, mattresses, and furniture were stuffed with it, along with those car seats. Indians made clothes out of it. Jacksonville almost ceased to exist because of Spanish moss. A fire that started in a moss plant on May 3, 1901, burned the whole city down.

We're surprised to find that we've finished the loop and the parking lot is in sight. After being in the coastal hammock, the sudden sight of vehicles, a sure sign of civilization, seems out of place.

Carl is one of a number of volunteer guides who give this nature walk every Saturday at 10:30 a.m., weather permitting. There is no extra charge for the walk. Reservations are not required. Just show up.

Ask for a free Willow Pond nature trail guide at the ranger station. It is worth having both for reference value and for those who want to do the walk on their own. The brochure has a map and the location of thirteen numbered markers along the trail. Some of the markers explain life processes like succession, a word biologists use to describe change.

Plants come and go. New trees adapt to the area. Change, the only constant in our lives, enriches Willow Pond even as we pass by on the nature trail.

Bonus Points

Fort Clinch State Park has campgrounds on the Amelia River and the Atlantic Ocean. There is fishing from several locations, including the pier, and shark-tooth hunting on the beaches.

The main paved drive through the park meanders some 3 miles through a coastal hammock whose trees form a shady canopy over the road. Locals use this beautiful roadway as a jogging destination. Bicyclists discover it to their delight. It is a cheap thrill. Pedestrians and bicyclists pay $1 to enter the park. Motorcyclists pay $3 admission.

Fort Clinch State Park is a designated Gateway for the East Section of the Great Florida Birding Trail. Check the hammock and the marsh for warblers, waders, wrens, and sparrows. At the fishing pier, there might be seabirds, purple sandpipers, and gannets.

Every Saturday at 9 a.m., weather permitting, a park ranger will give a beach walk around the northeasternmost point of Florida. Meet at the Fort Clinch parking lot.

Living-history buffs re-create life at Fort Clinch during the Civil War. Check with the park for the dates, usually the first weekend of the month, when Union garrisons occupy the fort. There are also special

NORTHEAST FLORIDA

NORTHEAST FLORIDA

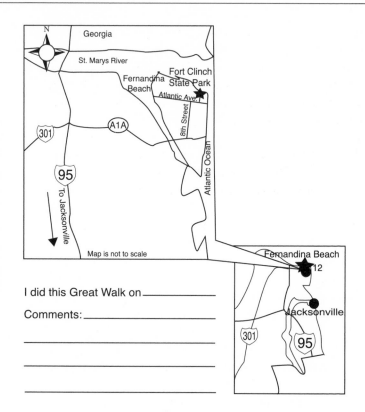

I did this Great Walk on _____

Comments: _____

_____

_____

_____

activities including Confederate garrisons and a Spanish-American War event. Day admission to the fort is $2 per person for those 6 and up. A small museum displays daily fort life.

To really know what life was like for a soldier, take a candlelight tour of the fort. There was no electricity in the early 1800s. When the sun went down, the candles came out. Guided tours take place after sundown on Friday and Saturday nights beginning in May and running through Labor Day. Reservations required.

Trip Essentials

Name: Nature's Classroom: Willow Pond Nature Trail, Fort Clinch State Park, Fernandina Beach
Type of walk: Nature trail inside a state park
Length of walk: Not measured, less than a mile

Time to finish: Willow Loop takes 25 minutes; Magnolia Loop takes 45 minutes

Difficulty: Easy. Wheelchair accessible, but some short inclines and wet areas after rain.

Appeals to: Nature buffs, families, and birders (Fort Clinch is a designated Gateway for the Great Florida Birding Trail; see page 2 of the East Section guide.)

Guides: Self-guided, or nature walk guided on Saturdays at 10:30 a.m., weather permitting

Address: Fort Clinch State Park, 2601 Atlantic Avenue, Fernandina Beach, FL 32034

Phone: (904) 277-7274

Web site: www.floridastateparks.org

Cost: None for the walk; park admission $5 per vehicle for up to 8 people

Getting there: I-95 to Fernandina Beach/Callahan exit; stay to the right, traveling east; this is A1A. In Fernandina, A1A becomes 8th Street. Go to the intersection of 8th Street and Atlantic Avenue. Turn right and go about 2 miles; park entrance is on the left.

GPS coordinates: (Fort Clinch State Park) N 30° 69.611 W 081° 44.139

Hours: Fort Clinch State Park is open from 8 a.m. to sundown, 365 days a year.

Restrooms: None at trailhead. Restrooms in park campgrounds and at the park's fishing pier.

Water/food: Water at restrooms; no food sold inside park.

Dogs: Well-behaved on a 6-foot hand-held lead. No pets on beaches, on boardwalks, in buildings, or on the fishing pier.

Lunch ideas: American and seafood, at Marina Seafood Restaurant, 101 Centre Street, Fernandina Beach 32034, phone (904) 261-5310; Florida upscale, at Brett's Waterway Café, 1 South Front Street, Fernandina Beach 32034, phone (904) 261-2660

NORTHEAST FLORIDA

13

Traverse Two Terrains

Little Talbot Island State Park, Jacksonville

A walk through two worlds begins just before the entrance station to Little Talbot Island State Park.

Laid out like a large rectangle, the hiking trail goes north through a coastal hammock for 2.6 miles, followed by a 1.2-mile walk going south along the Atlantic Ocean.

Park rangers suggest going through the entrance gate and parking in the first parking area, the North Beach Pavilion Area, then walking back to the trailhead. Makes sense. By taking their advice, you are coming back to your vehicle at the end of the walk.

Start this walk with your shoes on. Carry drinking water. Wear insect repellent and sunscreen. Bring a camera. Along the way there will be textures, shapes, sweet details, and sweeping vistas. You'll want to capture these moments.

Hikers should check in at the ranger station before going on the trail. Pick up a free trail brochure. You can't get lost, so why carry a brochure? Because on the back are explanations of the terrains you'll see.

All of the Talbot Islands are a seasonal nesting area for songbirds including the painted bunting, a vibrant bird of many colors that looks like a flying artist's palette. Little Talbot Island State Park is on page 3 of the East Section guide to the Great Florida Birding Trail. Look for buntings and songbirds in the hammock portion of the trail. On the beach you may catch sight of skimmers, oystercatchers, and seven different species of sandpipers, and that's just for openers.

Once on the hiking trail, the world of a coastal hammock surrounds you. A dirt path rolls up and down sand dunes. The aroma of red cedars mixes with salt air. The surprise to me was the richness and

NORTHEAST FLORIDA

Tides and weather have overcome this tree on the beach at Little Talbot Island State Park, Jacksonville.

complexity of the coastal hammock and dune world. Every time the trail drops downhill, so does the temperature. Flowers show up unannounced—tiny white star-shaped blossoms on a ground-hugging plant or a purple iris-shaped flower on a long stem.

From the very first step, the sound of the ocean plays like a siren call. When you're surrounded by the coastal hammock, ocean waves rumble low in the background. As you progress, the sound gets louder and moves into the foreground.

Reaching the northern end of the rectangle, the trail turns east and runs through sand dunes. Coming out of the dunes onto the beach, you see where red cedar trees once grew. Tides and time have eaten away their surroundings. The trees are dead but still upright, not quite driftwood but headed in that direction.

On the beach, kick off your shoes and walk the edge of the surf. Look for sharks' teeth. Stop to admire the horizon. In our daily lives, our horizon may be limited by the view of the house across the street. Here the horizon goes on forever, or so it seems.

Watch the skimmers, with their lower jaw longer than their upper jaw, skimming along just above the surface, scooping up anything edible. Walking the beach is a time for daydreams and reflections, a time to inhale the sea breeze and exhale stress. All too soon the boardwalk comes into view. Beyond the boardwalk are the parking lot and your vehicle, your four-wheeled connection to the outside world.

You may, as I did, drag your feet in the sand, reluctant to leave. Let the busy world take care of itself a bit longer. You need to be here now.

Bonus Points

Little Talbot Island is part of the Talbot Islands State Parks, with access to 40 miles of shoreline and 10,000 acres for recreation and conservation. The parks were acquired from 1951 to 2004 and include Little Talbot Island, Big Talbot Island, Amelia Island, Fort George Island, Yellow Bluff Fort, Pumpkin Hill Creek Preserve, and the George Grady Bridge Fishing Pier. All are accessed from Heckscher Drive (State Road 105), which joins with A1A at the Mayport Ferry Landing.

The entrance station at Little Talbot has information on all the parks.

Multiple state and federal agencies partner to manage these areas and more sites in the area. The National Park Service manages the Kingsley Plantation, part of the Fort George Island Cultural State Park, which includes Kingsley and the Ribault Club, on Heckscher Drive shortly before you get to Little Talbot.

You access the Ribault Club from Heckscher Drive/A1A one-half mile north of the St. Johns River ferry landing. Turn at the sign saying Kingsley Plantation and Ribault Club. It will also say Timucuan Ecological & Historical Preserve. Getting to the club involves driving a narrow, two-lane road that runs alongside the Fort George River. Opened in 1928 as a winter resort, the Ribault Club declined during the Depression, and the club sold its property. The building is listed on the National Register of Historic Places.

Open 9 a.m. to 5 p.m., closed Mondays and Tuesdays, the Ribault Club has interpretive and interactive exhibits about the 12,000-year history of the area. One room has a bookstore run by the National Park Service.

There is no charge to visit. The grand rooms (and they are grand) in the club are restored and available for rent. Web site: www.ribaultclub. org. The club was restored through a partnership between the City of Jacksonville, the National Park Service, and the Florida Park Service.

The main plantation house at Kingsley Plantation, accessed on the same road as the Ribault Club, is the oldest plantation house remaining in Florida. Built in 1798, the main plantation house was closed in 2003 for restoration to correct damage by termites and the stress of 55,000 visitors a year.

Kingsley Plantation is open 9 a.m. to 5 p.m. seven days a week except on Thanksgiving, Christmas, and New Year's Day. Admission is free. Call (904) 251-3537 for information about Kingsley and to find out if the main house is open for tours.

The plantation is listed on page 3 of the East Section guide to the Great Florida Birding Trail, as is the Fort George Island Cultural State Park. For information about Fort George Island Cultural State Park, call (904) 251-2320.

The same partnership of state, local, and federal agencies that saved the Ribault Club later led to the formation of the Timucuan Ecologi-

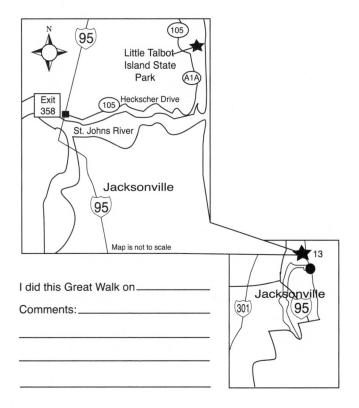

I did this Great Walk on _____

Comments: _____

_____

_____

_____

cal & Historical Preserve in 1988, also called Timucuan Trail State and National Parks. These titles can be confusing, but the bottom line is simple: a number of agencies who don't always see eye to eye cooperated to save and protect valuable cultural and natural resources in the Jacksonville area.

You can learn about all the places on the Timucuan Trail by visiting the Web site www.nps.gov/timu and then going to "Partnerships" on the menu.

Trip Essentials

Name: Traverse Two Terrains: Little Talbot Island State Park, Jacksonville
Type of walk: Nature
Length of walk: 3.8 miles
Time to finish: 1 to 2 hours (includes walking on the beach)
Difficulty: Moderately easy. Soft sand areas not wheelchair accessible.
Appeals to: Nature lovers, photographers, and birders (listed on page 3 of the East Section guide to the Great Florida Birding Trail.)
Guides: Self-guided
Address: 12157 Heckscher Drive, Jacksonville, FL 32226
Phone: (904) 251-2320
Web site: www.floridastateparks.org
Cost: $4 per vehicle for up to 8 passengers
Getting there: In Jacksonville, take I-95 to Heckscher Drive (milepost exit 358A) and go east for 17 miles.
GPS coordinates: N 30° 45222 W 081° 41889
Hours: 8 a.m. to sundown
Restrooms: At both the North Beach Pavilion Area and the South Beach Pavilion Area
Water/food: Water at restrooms adjacent to parking lots; no food sold inside park
Dogs: Not permitted on beaches; may take trail walk. Must be well-behaved and on a 6-foot hand-held leash.
Lunch ideas: The north parking lot has covered picnic pavilions with a grand ocean view, perfect for a picnic lunch

14

Stained Glass and Four Freedoms

Madison

Small town hospitality is alive and well in Madison, Florida, population three thousand.

If you call the Madison County Chamber of Commerce to say you are coming, they will gladly put together an information packet for you. Should you arrive after the chamber closes at 5 p.m., you will find your packet waiting for you on the office porch.

Inside the packet, among other things, will be a brochure about a walking/driving tour of historic Madison. More than fifty historic homes, buildings, places, and churches are listed. This free brochure is available at the chamber and many local businesses.

Four Freedoms Park, the center of historic Madison, is a great place to start. Street parking is free. The park occupies a full block at 100 North Range Street. On the northwest corner of the park, at Base and Range Streets, stands the Four Freedoms Monument. This is listed as number 1 on your map, and it is definitely a camera moment.

The angels represent freedom of worship, freedom of speech and expression, freedom from want, and freedom from fear everywhere. These are the four freedoms enunciated by President Franklin D. Roosevelt in his 1941 State of the Union address to describe American values. The monument is dedicated to the memory of Colin P. Kelly Jr., the first declared hero of World War II and a Madison native. There is a geocache at Four Freedoms Monument.

Across the street from the park is the Manor House, a brick hotel built in 1883 that takes up almost an entire block. A renovation under way will turn some of the hotel area into apartments.

In the next block, at 205 North Range Street, is the Presbyterian Church, built in 1851. The congregation, established in 1840, met in a

Four Freedoms Monument in historic Madison.

storefront until the church was built. The funeral service for Colin P. Kelly Jr. was held here.

The church is now a privately owned wedding chapel, and the former pastor's residence next door is currently the Four Freedoms Wedding Chapel Bed and Breakfast. Stephen and Rae Pike own both buildings. Their Web site is: www.madisonfourfreedoms.com.

In a six-block area on Range Street you will find twelve of the historic buildings or areas listed on the brochure. Neighboring streets are similar. Four Freedoms Park with its monument is a must-see. After that, pick and choose a walk based on your interests. The entire route, seeing everything, is about 4 miles.

Civil War buffs will want to visit the Wardlaw-Smith Goza Conference Center, North Washington Street, built about 1860. North Florida Community College bought the property in 1988. The house was used as a field hospital for soldiers from both the North and the South after the Battle of Olustee near Lake City. For tour information, call (850) 973-9432.

You can uncover more Civil War history at Oak Ridge Cemetery, dating back to 1800. Located at the north end of Meeting Street, thirty-one Confederate soldiers killed at Olustee are buried here. The World War II hero Colin P. Kelly Jr. is also buried at Oak Ridge Cemetery.

If church architecture and church interiors are to your liking, you are in luck. Church roots run deep in Madison. Six churches are listed in the historic walking brochure.

To tour the inside of the Presbyterian church—the oldest church in Madison and now the Four Freedoms Wedding Chapel—call Rae Pike at (850) 673-9462. She can usually arrange a time to meet you at the church and show you the interior. There is no charge.

The stained-glass windows will take your breath away. Design details are deep and intricate. A combination of time and North Florida weather has not been so kind to the leading that holds the stained glass together. And time has taken its toll on the outer wooden frames. The windows need total restoration or they will fall apart. Pike hopes that future visitors to Madison will be able to see the restoration in progress. Plans are under way to set up a workshop next door for a master stained-glass craftsman.

At 200 West Rutledge Street is the First United Methodist Church, built in 1921. This is the fourth building for a congregation that was established in 1830. Inside there are over seventy stained-glass windows. Usually a church staff member is at the rectory from 9 a.m. to 3 p.m. on weekdays and available to answer questions. There are no formal tours. You are welcome to visit the sanctuary. The phone number is (850) 973-6295.

The 1895 First Baptist Church at South Orange Street and West Pinckney Street has an architectural secret you don't see until you get inside. The outside is rectangular while the inside is an octagon. Call (850) 973-2527.

Built in 1907, the Catholic church of St. Vincent DePaul, 402 West Sumter Street, is noted for its faceted windows. The church is open. Call (850) 973-2428.

The honor of being the oldest church building in continuous use in Madison goes to St. Mary's Episcopal Church, 108 North Harry Street, built in 1881. The white frame church is carpenter Gothic style architecture. If the pastor is in, he will be happy to show you the church. Call (850) 973-8338.

NORTHEAST FLORIDA

What was the Old Jail Museum has a new name—the Treasures of Madison County Museum—and a new location in the W. T. Davis Building, 214 South Range Street. Hours are 10 a.m. to 2 p.m. Monday through Friday; and 10 a.m. to noon on Saturday.

The museum has a good collection of Madison County history from cotton to turpentine and hometown heroes, with a sampling of Colin Kelly Jr. memorabilia. Perhaps the highlight is their treasure trove of more than three thousand old photographs of people and places in Madison County. To know more about the museum, call the chamber at (850) 973-2788.

Next to the Madison County Courthouse at 101 South Range Street stands a structure that easily qualifies as a museum piece. It is the standpipe/water tower built in 1894 as part of the first public water supply. A ring was anchored in place and filled with water, and a raft placed on the water. The next ring was assembled from the raft, the water raised, and up it went. When the tower was finished, the raft was taken apart and lowered to the ground by ropes. Pretty amazing.

Downtown Madison from 100 North Range to 400 South Range Street has many buildings going back to the 1800s, buildings now filled with antique shops, bookstores, restaurants, and more. This area is definitely a lunch destination after your historic walk.

As you take your walking tour and visit sites, do ask questions. Locals love to talk about their historic past and the surrounding natural resources plus their plans for preserving their treasures for the future. They get excited thinking about the possibilities, and so will you.

Bonus Points

The chamber and many shops in downtown historic Madison carry the free walking brochure. Visit the chamber at 105 North Range Street, open 9 a.m. to 5 p.m. Monday through Friday. Their Web site is: www.madisonfl.org. Also check out the Madison County Tourism Development Council Web site at: www.madisonfla.com.

On the outskirts of Madison, Betty and Jim O'Toole have a certified organic farm. The land has been in the same family for five generations. Stroll around a garden that attracts birds and butterflies. Visit the greenhouses loaded with herbs, perennials, and vegetable plants for sale. Browse the two gift shops.

The address is: O'Toole's Herb Farm, 305 Northeast Artemesia Tri, Madison, FL 32341, phone (850) 973-3629. Web site: www.otoolesherb farm.com.

There is only one park in Greenville. You'll find it easily on U.S. 90. Haffye Hays Park has a pond, walking paths, picnic tables, playground equipment, and something unique—a bronze statue of the multitalented musician Ray Charles.

Born in Albany, Georgia, Charles (1930–2004) was raised in Greenville until the age of fifteen. Greenville mayor Elesta Pritchett was his next-door neighbor. The town was busy when she and Ray were growing up, with some five thousand people, most working in pulp mills.

Greenville is down to eight hundred people these days, but they have remembered the hometown boy blessed with great musical talent. Pritchett says the statue looks just like the Ray she knew, and it is good to have him here, forever playing in Greenville.

NORTHEAST FLORIDA

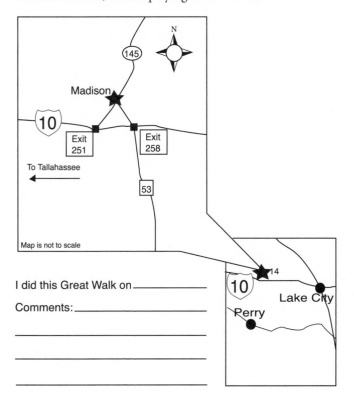

Trip Essentials

Name: Stained Glass and Four Freedoms: Madison

Type of walk: Historical

Length of trail: 1.2 miles to 3 miles, depending on route

Time to finish: 1 to 2 hours, includes going inside buildings

Difficulty: Easy. Wheelchair accessible.

Appeals to: History buffs, stained-glass admirers, geocachers, and photographers

Guides: Self-guided

Address: Free walking/driving guide to historic Madison at Madison
County Chamber of Commerce, 105 North Range, Madison, FL 32340

Phone: (850) 973-2788

Web site: www.madisonfl.org

Cost: None

Getting there: On I-10, take exit 28 and Highway 53 going north to Madison

GPS coordinates: (Four Freedoms Monument geocache) N 30° 28.201 W
083° 24.747

Hours: Chamber open 9 a.m. to 5 p.m. Monday through Friday. They will
mail information or, if you arrive after hours, leave it for you on their
porch.

Restrooms: At chamber

Water/food: Water fountain at Four Freedoms Park; restaurants in downtown area

Dogs: Leashed on sidewalks; none in buildings

Lunch ideas: American, at One Eleven Grill, 307 Southwest Pinckney
Street, Madison, FL 32340, phone (850) 973-4115; American, at Lady-
bug Café inside Morris Pharmacy, 110 South Range Street, Madison,
FL 32340, phone (850) 973-2222

15

A Walk on the Gothic Side

University of Florida Campus Historic District, Gainesville

A student ambled along a walkway on the Plaza of the Americas, reading from a book held open by both arms. He looked up, startled, to see twenty adults bearing down on him. Were we replacement teachers? Lost parents?

Nope. We were history hunters, putting feet on the ground, stepping out at a fast clip, moving across the Plaza of the Americas as if we were late for a date with history.

Our tour leader was Steven A. Rajtar, attorney-at-law. In fact, Steve got his law degree here at University of Florida. As a student, he didn't even notice the historical buildings and acknowledges that few students, even today, have a clue that these buildings are historic.

In 1989, twenty-two academic buildings and dormitories were listed on the National Register of Historic Places (drum roll, please), and the University of Florida Campus Historic District was created.

On this summer Sunday afternoon, Rajtar is returning to his alma mater to lead a free tour.

A quick quiz: When was University of Florida started? If you said 1905, with the passage of the Buckman Act that consolidated a number of small colleges into three universities—one for blacks, one for white women, and one for white men, you'd be right.

Gainesville got the university with the all-white male student body. In 1906, two buildings opened to serve the entire student body—102 male students. Women were not admitted until 1947.

You'd also be right if you said 1853, the date on the university's seal. UF has ancestors that merged and consolidated their holdings. They include the Florida Agricultural College, the South Florida Military

College, and the East Florida Seminary, which was founded in Ocala in 1852 and merged with Gainesville Academy in 1866.

In 1853, the seminary started receiving money from the state (that would be our tax money). UF decided that becoming a state-supported higher institution marked its beginning in 1853.

Forget the test. Enjoy the architecture. From the beginning, the Collegiate Gothic style was enthusiastically embraced, first by architect William A. Edwards from 1905 to 1925, then by Rudolph Weaver from 1925 to 1944. Weaver, the first dean of the College of Architecture, succeeded Edwards as the campus architect.

These brick buildings are beautiful. Two and three stories tall, they have entranceways outlined in cast stone. Stop and admire the details—Gothic tracery around the windows, gargoyles, medallions, and soaring rooflines. They fulfill their mission—to reinforce the environment of scholarship in a place set aside from the demands of everyday life.

The Collegiate Gothic style adapts the nineteenth-century Gothic revival style. Both spring from medieval roots in England, where masters and students studied together in centers of learning meant to be solid and permanent—an ongoing institution. These buildings are built to last, and their very endurance gives a sense of place.

The University of Florida gives guided campus tours for prospective students Monday through Friday at 10 a.m. and 2 p.m. History buffs can come along too. On Saturday the tour starts at 10 a.m. There is no charge. Preregistration is advised but not required.

Meet at the Welcome Center inside of the University Bookstore located on Museum Road. Tours begin with an information session in an auditorium, followed by a 90-minute walk around campus. There are no walking tours on state holidays or during special events such as Homecoming.

While these tours are designed to show the campus to prospective freshman and their families, the tour guides do talk about the school's history, and the walk goes past most of the historic buildings. Many of these buildings are clustered around the Plaza of the Americas. Some buildings have plaques describing their history.

The University Auditorium is the high point, literally, of Collegiate Gothic style architecture on campus. Designed by William A. Edwards,

The front of Weil Hall, built in 1949 at the University of Florida, has cast-stone trim around the doors.

it includes a 190-foot tower. Take time to look up at the vaulted ceiling in the auditorium. Allegorical figures are numerous, put there as symbols for learning, professions, and athletics.

Weil Hall, built in 1949, houses the College of Engineering's Department of Civil and Coastal Engineering. Located at the intersection of Stadium Road and Gale Lemerand Drive, a small landscaped area next to Weil Hall has a mini-tower. The tower is new and built to blend in and look old. What is inside is historic. Look inside to see a 1913 Howard clock mechanism.

Finding a parking place on campus can be difficult. Two information/parking kiosks have attendants who can point out garages and spaces for public parking. One kiosk is on Gale Lemerand Drive (next to Ben Hill Griffin Stadium); the other kiosk is next to Tigert Hall on SW 2nd Avenue.

Bonus Points

Paynes Prairie Preserve State Park, south of Gainesville, was designated Florida's first state preserve in 1971. The preserve is also a National Natural Landmark. Naturalist William Bartram came through in 1774 and called the area the "great Alachua Savannah."

The preserve has 21,000 acres. Hours are 8 a.m. to sundown. Admission is $4 per vehicle for up to 8 passengers. The park's address is: 100 Savannah Boulevard, Micanopy, FL 32667, phone (352) 466-3397. Web site: www.floridastateparks.org.

To get oriented, start at the visitor center, watch a historic video, and visit the exhibits. For a panoramic view, climb the 50-foot observation tower near the visitor center. Within the preserve are eight trails for hiking, horseback riding, and bicycling. A number of ranger-led activities take place in the fall, winter, and spring months.

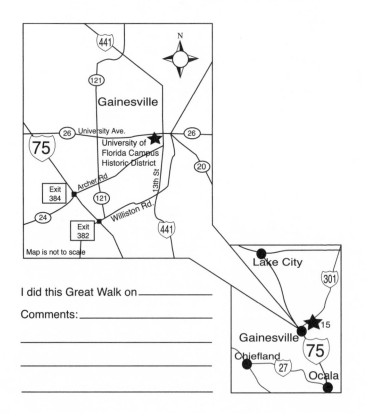

I did this Great Walk on _____

Comments: _____

_____

_____

_____

Trip Essentials

Name: A Walk on the Gothic Side: University of Florida Campus Historic District, Gainesville

Type of walk: Historic

Length of walk: 2 to 4 miles, depending on route

Time to finish: 1 to 2 hours

Difficulty: Moderately easy. Pavement. Wheelchair access. Parking is scarce.

Appeals to: Architecture enthusiasts, Florida history buffs, and photographers

Guides: Self-guided, or take a campus tour given at 10 a.m. and 2 p.m. on weekdays; 10 a.m. on Saturdays, which lasts 90 minutes and goes into many of the historic buildings. Occasional historical walking tours by Steven Rajtar; contact for schedule (srajtar@rajtar.com).

Address: University of Florida Campus Historic District starts at the intersection of West University Avenue and SW 13th Street. The campus tours start at the Welcome Center inside the University Bookstore on Museum Road.

Phone: Welcome Center (352) 392-2959

Web site: www.admissions.ufl.edu/visit

Cost: None

Getting there: From I-75, take exit 387, Newberry Road, and go east for 5 miles. Newberry Road becomes University Avenue. At the intersection of University Avenue and 13th Street, take a right. Enter parking lot at SW 2nd Avenue.

GPS coordinates: N 29° 64.833 W 082° 34.944

Hours: Daylight hours, year-round

Restrooms: Inside food courts on campus and at Welcome Center

Water/food: Water fountains at entrances of some buildings, vending machines in scattered campus buildings. Food court and restaurants inside Reitz Union.

Dogs: No

Lunch ideas: Pizza & Italian, at Leonardo's Pizza by the Slice, 1245 West University Avenue, Gainesville, FL 32601, phone (352) 375-2007; pan-Asian, at Chopstix, 3500 SW 13th Street, Gainesville, FL 32608, phone (352) 367-0003. Chopstix has a view of a lake.

16

Wander through a Garden of Eden

Kanapaha Botanical Gardens, Gainesville

If you have ever wondered what the Garden of Eden might have looked like, then make a visit to Kanapaha Botanical Gardens. Surely there are similarities—a diversity of habitats, all wondrous, with paths for walking in the cool of the evening and the warmth of early morning.

In the beginning, Kanapaha was a land of meadows fringed with woods and a lake. Then, in 1978, the North Florida Botanical Society signed a lease with Alachua County to develop a public botanical garden on 33 acres. Later, 29 more acres were added. Fourteen different gardens are clustered on the site.

A map and garden guide, given when you pay admission, will show the garden walkways. Leading out of Summer House, the visitor center, are doors going right and left. Go left and the path is about one-half mile through the Azalea-Camellia Garden, Rose Garden, Butterfly Garden, and the extraordinary Kanapaha Water Gardens.

Take the right-hand door out of Summer House, and the path winds about a mile through eleven different gardens, including the famous Bamboo Garden, with Florida's largest collection of bamboo species and a limited view of Lake Kanapaha.

If you like ponds, then exit Summer House from the left-hand door. Past the Azalea-Camellia Garden you come to a stream, all man-made, but so artfully done it looks as if it has been here for centuries.

In 1994, Kanapaha paired with Gainesville Regional Utilities, using water from the Kanapaha Wastewater Treatment Plant. As the treated effluent flows through the water gardens, it percolates, infiltrating the soil. Reclaimed water is used throughout Kanapaha for irrigation.

Stay to the left, follow the stream a short distance, and the stream

Waterfall at Kanapaha Botanical Gardens, Gainesville.

ends, or rather begins, with a waterfall. The day we visited, a bright green chameleon sunned itself on a yellow bamboo stalk. It is moments like these that make garden walks memorable.

On the walkway, horsetails spring up—tall, thick, and leggy. They reached the peak of their existence 200 million years ago, before dinosaurs appeared.

When you find yourself back at Summer House, go past it to the path on the right. It quickly splits but is a large loop so you will see everything either way you go.

On this walk, you'll find surprises not mentioned in the brochure. A little path will go off to the side, and there you find a memorial waterfall, plantings, a bench, and a plaque telling about a special person's life.

You will enter the bamboo forest on a brick path. Who knew bamboo came in so many colors? Bamboo with bright green stalks, mustard yellow stalks, and a purple brown stalk variety called black bamboo.

Farther along you pass a deep sinkhole and then enter a hardwoods area with tall trees. The Vinery has a variety of vines, many on arbors. Before long, you are back at Summer House. Pots and plants for sale just outside the door tempt you.

June through September are the months offering the most color at Kanapaha. This is when the huge Victoria water lilies, looking like floating platforms, are in bloom along with Asian snake arums. Kanapaha has become well known for two annual events: the winter bamboo sale and spring garden festival. All events at the gardens are posted on their Web site: www.kanapaha.org.

Bonus Points

The Butterfly Rainforest, a huge outdoor exhibit attached to the Florida Museum of Natural History on the University of Florida campus, brings you up close and personal with hundreds of butterflies from around the world. Plus, a Wall of Wings exhibit outside the enclosure has thousands of preserved butterfly and moth specimens. Both are part of the McGuire Center for Lepidoptera and Biodiversity.

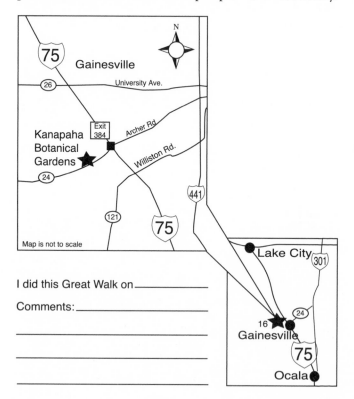

I did this Great Walk on _____

Comments: _____

_____

_____

_____

NORTHEAST FLORIDA

The Florida Museum of Natural History is part of the University of Florida Cultural Plaza at SW 34th Street and Hull Road, Gainesville, phone (352) 846-2000. Hours are 10 a.m. to 5 p.m. Monday through Saturday; 1 p.m. to 5 p.m. Sunday. Web site: www.flmnh.ufl.edu.

Parking costs $3 a day Monday through Friday, but is free on weekends and state holidays. Museum admission is free, but there are charges for special exhibits and donations are suggested. The Butterfly Rainforest has a separate charge: $8.50 adult; $7.50 Florida resident; $6.50 senior (62 and over); $6.50 college student with identification; $6.50 student 13–17; $4.50 children 3–12; those under 3 are admitted free.

Devil's Millhopper Geological State Park, 4732 Millhopper Road, Gainesville, FL 32653, phone (352) 955-2008, has a sinkhole 500 feet across and 120 feet deep. Hours are 9 a.m. to 5 p.m. Wednesday through Sunday. Admission is $2 per vehicle for up to 8 people. Dogs are welcome on a 6-foot leash. A one-half-mile trail goes around the top of the sinkhole. On Saturdays at 10 a.m., a park ranger gives a guided walk.

Trip Essentials

Name: Wander through a Garden of Eden: Kanapaha Botanical Gardens, Gainesville

Type of walk: Botanical

Length of walk: 1.5 miles for entire gardens

Time to finish: 1 1/2 to 2 hours

Difficulty: Easy. Paved and brick walkways. Mostly handicapped accessible.

Appeals to: Gardeners, photographers, pond enthusiasts, and butterfly lovers

Guides: Self-guided

Address: 4700 S.W. 58th Drive, Gainesville, FL 32608

Phone: (352) 372-4981

Web site: www.kanapaha.org

Cost: $5 adult; $3 children 6–13; children under 6 admitted free

Getting there: On SW Archer Road (State Road 24), 1 mile west of I-75 (exit 384)

GPS coordinates: (Lake Kanapaha) N 29° 61.778 W 082° 40.472

Hours: 9 a.m. to 5 p.m. Monday, Tuesday, Wednesday, and Friday; 9 a.m. to dusk, Saturday and Sunday; closed Thursday

Restrooms: Inside visitor center

Water/food: Water fountains in garden and visitor center; no food

Dogs: Well-behaved; leashed

Lunch ideas: Vietnamese family style, at Saigon Café, 808 West University Avenue, Gainesville, FL 32601, phone (352) 338-0023; Cuban and Caribbean, at Emiliano's Café, 7 SE 1st Avenue, Gainesville, FL 32601, phone (352) 375-7381

NORTHEAST FLORIDA

17

East Meets West

Land Bridge Trail, Marjorie Harris Carr Cross Florida Greenway, South of Ocala

Spanish explorers thought of it first. Wouldn't it be nice to carve a ship canal from the Atlantic to the Gulf of Mexico? Conquistadors could get to Mexico quicker where there was gold to plunder. When no gold was found in Florida, the land was seen as a mosquito-ridden obstacle on the way to Mexico.

Centuries came and went. The idea of a cross-Florida ship canal never died. During the Depression in the 1930s, the Works Progress Administration funded a sea-level ship canal project. Land was purchased along a corridor 110 miles long, running from the St. Johns River to the Gulf of Mexico.

Men using shovels carved valleys in the landscape. Work continued in fits and starts for decades. In the 1960s, the project took on new life as the Cross Florida Barge Canal, for barges instead of ships this time, with a system of locks and dams.

Concerns persisted that digging into the Floridan Aquifer would be a disaster for the environment. In 1969, a group of scientists including Marjorie Harris Carr of Gainesville founded the Florida Defenders of the Environment. Their first project: stop the canal.

That same year the National Environmental Policy Act passed, mandating that projects using federal dollars have an environmental impact study. The canal flunked their study. The canal work was stopped in 1972 and deauthorized by Congress in 1990, and canal lands in Citrus, Levy, Marion, and Putnam Counties were turned over to Florida. Today the former canal project is a long ribbon of green across the state known as the Marjorie Harris Carr Cross Florida Greenway.

The Land Bridge Trail is part of that greenway. It is nine-tenths of

Suzi and Annie, the author's two dogs, take a break on the Land Bridge Trail.

a mile long one way. Once you step through the fence posts and onto the dirt trail, an oak hammock surrounds you. Orange blazes, each one within line of sight of the next one, show the way for hikers. This is part of an area stretching east and west of Interstate 75 with trails that are part of the Florida Trail. The orange-blazed portion is officially designated as Florida National Scenic Trail.

After going through the woods, you come to the Land Bridge connecting the east and west sides of the greenway. Old coquina rock was used to landscape terraces for the native plants and trees. Tons of dirt made up the roadway. No asphalt. No cars.

Horses, hikers, bikers, and wildlife all cross this bridge built over the Interstate. It is the only safe way to get across Interstate 75 where it bisects the greenway. The span is 52 feet wide and 200 feet long.

In the middle of the bridge are large grated openings to view traffic on Interstate 75 below. For those who came to see the Land Bridge only, it is time to turn around and amble back to the parking lot and the trailhead.

Bonus Points

On the other side of the bridge is another information kiosk and several trails including a 2.4-mile section of the Florida National Scenic

Trail going to the 49th Avenue Trailhead, an equestrian trail about 8.7 miles long, and a mountain bike trail about 2.5 miles long.

You're not only taking a nature walk going to the Land Bridge and possibly beyond; this is also a history walk. The Cross Florida Barge Canal could have been built. Some of it was started in this area. A historic digging, as the excavated valleys are called, is located a short distance from the Land Bridge. With the passage of time, diggings have filled in with loblolly pines and other trees. There are no directional markers to the digging.

The "49th Avenue to Land Bridge" brochure, available free, has a map showing the different trails and the digging location. Brochures are available from the Florida Department of Environmental Protection Greenways & Trails. The toll-free Tallahassee phone number is (877) 822-5208. Web site: www.floridagreenwaysandtrails.org.

NORTHEAST FLORIDA

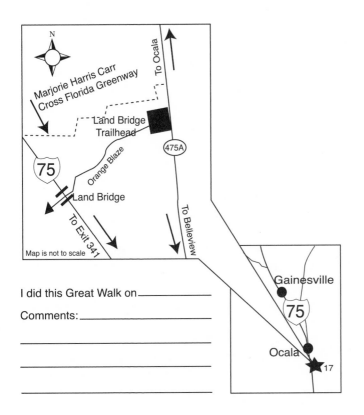

I did this Great Walk on _____

Comments: _____

_____

_____

_____

The Florida Trail Association has detailed maps, segment by segment, for hiking any part of the Florida Trail. See their Web site: www.florida-trail.org.

Mountain bikers from many areas find their way to the Santos Trailhead on 80th Street near Belleview. Over 30 miles of unpaved trails are available, color-coded for difficulty ranging from beginners to experts. Santos is part of the Marjorie Harris Carr Cross Florida Greenway. For more information, call (352) 236-7143.

Trip Essentials

Name: East Meets West: Land Bridge Trail, Marjorie Harris Carr Cross Florida Greenway, South of Ocala

Type of walk: Nature/historic

Length of walk: About 1 mile

Time to finish: 1 hour

Difficulty: Easy to slightly moderate. Not wheelchair accessible.

Appeals to: Nature and history buffs, photographers, and anyone wanting to see a land bridge

Guides: Self-guided

Address: Land Bridge Trailhead 475A, 11100 SW 16th Avenue, Ocala, FL 34476

Phone: Greenways & Trails Field Office, Ocala (352) 236-7143

Web site: www.floridagreenwaysandtrails.org

Cost: None

Getting there: From I-75 south of Ocala, take exit 341 to County Road 484. Head east on C.R. 484 toward Belleview. In about 1.4 mile, you come to the intersection with County Road 475A. Take a left, and go on C.R. 475A for about 2 miles. Trailhead is on the left.

GPS coordinates: (Land Bridge) N 29° 0521 W 82°169

Hours: Sunrise to sunset

Restrooms: At trailhead

Water/food: Water at trailhead; no food available

Dogs: Leashed

Lunch ideas: New American, at BD Bean's Coffee Company, 5148 Southeast Abshier Blvd., Belleview, FL 34420, phone (352) 245-3077; American, at Farm House Restaurant, 11077 SE 57th Court, Belleview, FL 34420, phone (352) 307-7100

18

Flowers, Waterfalls, and Headsprings

Rainbow Springs State Park, Dunnellon

Ever so long ago, U.S. 41 was a major route into Florida. The road ran right past Rainbow Springs, a privately owned attraction and a popular place from the 1930s to the 1970s.

Billed as the largest attraction in the United States, Rainbow Springs had a monorail, rodeo shows, azaleas by the bushel, a sky tram that went through a gigantic aviary, and glass-bottom boat rides on the Rainbow River.

Then Orlando gave big chunks of itself away to a man named Walt Disney, and Interstate 75 was built. Who needed U.S. 41 or U.S. 441 anymore? There was Mickey Mouse and a fast road to get there.

The owners of Rainbow Springs went bankrupt and closed the attraction in 1974. A developer bought the springs, adding the enticement that building a home at his already-named Rainbow Springs subdivision meant you had your own spring nearby to visit.

Homeowners from the Rainbow Springs development, calling themselves the Friends of Rainbow Springs, began volunteering their time to clean up the park area.

Upon learning the developer wanted to put condominiums right on the slopes leading down to the headsprings, homeowners lobbied state officials not to issue permits because of the watershed. In 1990, the state—with help from Marion County's Pennies for Parks program—purchased the former attraction.

Taking a guided garden walk—given the first and third Saturday of the month from November through April—is a good way to get a sampling of the park's history and natural beauty. The walk begins at the most civilized hour of 11 a.m. and lasts about 45 minutes. No reservations necessary.

The Rainbow River begins at the headsprings inside Rainbow Springs State Park, Dunnellon.

Any time of year, the headwaters of the Rainbow River are awesome. The Rainbow River is 5.7 miles long and ends where it joins the Withlacoochee River.

Walking through the gardens and taking the nature trail at Rainbow Springs State Park means literally stepping on or near history. Some of the old brick pathways from the private attraction days meander past man-made waterfalls.

The brick walkways descend to a level where you are looking straight out over the river. Marsh grasses line the water's edge. Wading birds work the shoreline. Looking more closely at the water, you see boils in the sand, water coming up from the Floridan Aquifer.

You'll come across waterfalls cascading over mounds of limestone rock, all laid by hand between 1935 and 1937. All the falls in the park are man-made, but they look like they've belonged here forever. Water is pumped from the river into a holding pond. The rocks were tailings, leftovers from mining phosphate in the late 1800s and early 1900s.

Along the way, there are side detours you can take. Visit the butterfly garden with native plants. Or, if you stay on the main path, you'll see the remnants of stalls where horses used in the rodeo were once kept.

As the walkway rises up an incline to the top of a hill, you find the pond that supplies water to the waterfalls. Our guide reminds us that what we put on our lawns goes down into the aquifer and that someday it will show up in the Rainbow River.

Old Florida attractions like Rainbow Springs on U.S. 41 and Silver Springs on State Road 40 faded for a while with the coming of Walt Disney World. They have been discovered again and are celebrated anew as Florida's premier natural attractions.

Bonus Points

At 8:30 a.m. on the second Saturday of every month, except June, July, and August, there is a guided bird walk. No reservations are necessary, and there is no extra charge for the walk. They do have some binoculars to loan.

A backcountry nature trail goes to the old pastures and past phosphate pits. The full length of the white trail is 2.5 miles. A shorter yellow trail splits off from the white trail, making the total length 2.2 miles.

Although almost all evidence is gone, and you won't see any buildings along the trail, a community named Juliette once thrived near the springs during the phosphate boom that began in the late 1800s.

History buffs will enjoy stepping inside the park's visitor center next to the veranda. In addition to memorabilia from the attraction days, there is a selection of little paperbacks, local history written by local people who have lived here or heard the stories.

In 1972, the entire Rainbow River was designated as a Registered Natural Landmark. Then, in 1986, the area became an Aquatic Preserve, and in 1987, the Rainbow River was named an Outstanding

I did this Great Walk on _____

Comments: _____

_____

_____

_____

Florida Waterway. Swimming and picnicking at the headwaters are both popular.

Trip Essentials

Name: Flowers, Waterfalls, and Headsprings: Rainbow Springs State Park, Dunnellon

Type of walk: Nature/historical

Length of walk: 2.5 miles for the nature trail. Less than 1 mile to walk around the gardens.

Time to finish: 45 minutes to 1 1/2 hours

Difficulty: Moderate. Not handicapped accessible. Old brick walkways are slippery.

Appeals to: Nature lovers, history buffs, families, photographers, and birders

Guides: Self-guided, or guided garden walks first and third Saturday of the month at 11 a.m. from November through April. Guided bird walk the second Saturday at 8:30 a.m., except June, July, and August.

Address: Rainbow Springs State Park, 19158 SW 81st Place Road, Dunnellon, FL 34432

Phone: (352) 465-5555

Web site: www.floridastateparks.org

Cost: $1 per person; children under 6 admitted free

Getting there: From I-75. exit at State Road 40. Take S.R. 40 west until it dead-ends at U.S. 41. Turn left. The park entrance is on the left. Rainbow Springs State Park is 3 miles north of Dunnellon on the east side of U.S. 41.

GPS coordinates: N 29° 10.417 W 082° 4375

Hours: 8 a.m. to sundown

Restrooms: At visitor center and swimming area

Water/food: Water fountains at visitor center and bathing beach; no food sold inside park

Dogs: Not allowed on bathing beach or concession areas. Allowed on trail if well-behaved and on a 6-foot hand-held leash.

Lunch ideas: American, at Front Porch Restaurant & Pie Shop, U.S. Highway 41 South, Dunnellon, FL 34431, phone (352) 489-4708; American, at Stumpknockers Restaurant, 13821 SW Highway 200, Dunnellon, FL 34432, phone (352) 854-2288

19

Bird Walk on Pepper Creek Trail

Homosassa Springs Wildlife State Park, Homosassa

Birds of a feather, whether novice or experienced, flock together the last Saturday of the month for a free guided bird walk at Homosassa Springs Wildlife State Park.

Assemble at the visitor center parking lot on U.S. 19 in Homosassa. Pepper Creek Trail is totally paved and wheelchair accessible. It runs alongside Pepper Creek for 1.2 miles. The bird walk starts at 8 a.m. and ends at 9:30 a.m. Walks take place each month except June, July, August, and December.

At the start of our bird walk, our guide takes us from the parking lot to a bridge behind the visitor center. The bridge spans Pepper Creek. We stand in the center of the bridge and look down at creek water stained deep brown by tannic acid. In winter months, wood ducks nest along this creek. Wading birds work the creek edges. Ospreys fly overhead.

On the far side of the parking lot, away from the visitor center, runs a long line of tall pine trees. Those with binoculars scan for birds of prey and migrants. Then we turn away from the parking lot and enter Pepper Creek Trail.

Immediately we're in a hardwood hammock and wetland. Our guide advises novice birders like me on binocular technique. If you see a bird, fix your eyes on its location and set your chin in concrete, pointing right there. Then lift your binoculars to your face and hopefully you'll be on target.

Birders on a walk go through a six-step process:

1. Hear the call or see a bird.
2. Stop, listen, and look.

3. Locate the bird with binoculars.

4. Once the bird is sighted and in focus, call out possible names.

5. Put down binoculars and open guidebook.

6. Have an intense identification discussion.

Even if you bring nothing with you except a desire to learn, you will find birders are incredibly generous with sharing guidebooks and binoculars.

Walking past the park's pontoon boat dock at the end of the trail, our guide led us through the west entrance parking lot and into a meadow surrounded by tall trees. A red-shouldered hawk called repeatedly and then landed on a bare limb.

Birders on the Pepper Creek Trail, Homosassa Springs Wildlife State Park.

NORTHEAST FLORIDA

At the end of the walk, some people elected to cross the street and pay the admission fee to visit the park. Others took a free pontoon boat ride back to the visitor center. A few chose to walk the trail back to the visitor center parking lot and do more birding along the way.

Homosassa Springs Wildlife State Park is on page 13 of the West Florida guide to the Great Florida Birding Trail. The guide recommends just what we did—walk the paved trail along Pepper Creek. For me, the morning outing provided a double adventure—a birding walk and a boat ride. And both are free.

Bonus Points

The Pepper Creek Trail is one of a number of birding trails in Citrus County listed in the West Florida guide to the Great Florida Birding Trail. These guides are free and available at any state park or downloadable at www.floridabirdingtrail.com.

Visiting Homosassa Springs Wildlife State Park provides an excellent way to view West Indian manatees without causing them stress by swimming in their water environment.

Homosassa Springs Wildlife State Park, a rehabilitation center for injured and orphaned manatees, is located 6 miles south of Crystal River at 4150 South Suncoast Blvd., Homosassa, phone: (352) 628-5343. Web site: www.floridastateparks.org.

The park can be accessed two ways. Drive directly to the park itself and use the west entrance parking lot, or go to the visitor center and main entrance on U.S. Highway 19. From here, a pontoon boat takes visitors down Pepper Creek to the park. The boat ride is included in the park admission fee. Trams are also available to take visitors to the west entrance via the Pepper Creek Trail.

Park entrance fees are $9 for an adult; $5 for children 3–12; and children under 3 are admitted free. The park opens at 9 a.m. and closes at 5:30 p.m. A number of animal encounter programs are given daily. Manatee feedings are at 11:30 a.m., 1:30 p.m., and 3:30 p.m. Other animal encounter programs include: wildlife encounters at 10:30 a.m. and 2:30 p.m. and an alligator and hippo program at 12:30 p.m.

In the 1940s, Elmo Reed opened "Nature's Giant Fish Bowl," and it is still there, with huge viewing windows that look out into the spring.

NORTHEAST FLORIDA

Winding through the park is a 1.1-mile nature trail with both paved and elevated boardwalk sections.

Yulee Sugar Mill Ruins Historic State Park is in Homosassa. From U.S. 19, turn west onto County Road 490 West (Yulee Drive), drive about 2.5 miles, and the ruins of the mill are easily seen. There is no admission charge. Picnic tables are available, and interpretive stations around the mill explain sugar making.

The Crystal River Preserve State Park oversees the Yulee Sugar Mill Ruins. Their address is: 3400 North Museum Pointe, Crystal River, FL 34428, phone (352) 563-0450. Web site: www.floridastateparks.org.

Trip Essentials

Name: Bird walk on Pepper Creek Trail, Homosassa Springs Wildlife State
  Park, Homosassa
Type of walk: Birding/nature
Length of walk: 1.2 miles one way
Time to finish: 1 1/2 hours
Difficulty: Easy. Pavement. Wheelchair accessible.
Appeals to: Photographers and birders (listed on page 13 of the West
  Florida guide to the Great Florida Birding Trail)
Guides: Guided bird walk on the last Saturday of the month from 8 a.m.
  to 9:30 a.m. This walk can also be self-guided.
Address: Homosassa Springs Wildlife State Park, 4150 South Suncoast
  Blvd., Homosassa, FL 34446
Phone: (352) 628-5343
Web site: www.floridastateparks.org and www.homosassasprings.org
Cost: Free for the bird walk, which takes place outside the park. Admis-
  sion is charged to enter park.
Getting there: Homosassa Springs is 75 miles north of Tampa on U.S. 19,
  and 90 miles northwest of Orlando.
GPS coordinates: N 28° 48.00 W 082° 35.15
Hours: 8 a.m. to sundown
Restrooms: At visitor center and west entrance to the park
Water/food: At restrooms. The Remember When restaurant is over the
  visitor center on U.S. 19, and the Manatee Café is located at the park's
  west entrance.
Dogs: Permitted on Pepper Creek Trail on 6-foot hand-held leash. Dogs
  not recommended on a bird walk. No dogs allowed inside the park.
  Self-service outside kennels provided at visitor center at no charge.
Lunch ideas: American, at Remember When restaurant, 4150 South Suncoast Boulevard, Homosassa, FL 34446, phone (352) 628-1717; American, at Emily's Family Restaurant, U.S. 19, 7181 West Cardinal Street,
  Homosassa Springs, FL 34446, phone (352) 628-6559

NORTHEAST FLORIDA

20

EcoWalk in Wild Florida

Crystal River Preserve State Park, Crystal River

Getting to know wild Florida is a little bit like falling in love with someone you missed the first time around.

The second time around it is not going to be a dramatic swoon. No, finding wild Florida is much more subtle. The affair unfolds gradually until one day you know.

You'll walk down a trail and it hits you. Everything—the changing seasons, the wetlands, prairies, hammocks, beaches, flora, fauna, sky, and earth—every bit of it stirs your heart. You feel bonded, connected in a deep and abiding way.

To help get in touch, and maybe fall in love, put on your walking shoes and take the 2.5-mile EcoWalk Trail, a loop trail that is part of the Crystal River Preserve State Park. Located near busy U.S. 19, the EcoWalk area was once a cattle ranch. J. D. Mendenhall, the park's education coordinator, recalled that when the former cattle ranch was added to the park, the staff put their heads together trying to figure out how to open this area to the public.

With open meadows left from the cattle days, the site was, and is, a wet/dry prairie that edges into a hammock. Birds are all over the place—bluebirds, American kestrels, red-tailed hawks, swallowtail kites, black vultures, osprey, red-shouldered hawks, and bald eagles are just a few.

But Mendenhall and the crew realized they were up against some pretty stiff competition. In Crystal River, the park has to contend with the West Indian manatee for public attention. Manatees are a hard act to follow. And the staff was also concerned about visitors who arrive already disconnected from the natural environment.

The start of the EcoWalk, Crystal River Preserve State Park.

The staff sought to close the people/environment disconnect by creating a different kind of exercise trail. There are eleven Discovery Zones that offer "sensory sensitivity" tips. In this age of cell phones, headphones, and computer games, people actually need directions on how to slow down, use their senses, get in touch with the world around them.

The EcoWalk starts in an oak clearing. Pick up a trail guide brochure at the information board and sign the log. Be sure to take water with you. You can choose to start with the left or the right part of the loop. We chose the right-hand trail because this is where the sensory zones begin, as well as signs about the environment.

Very soon you'll come across a sign informing you there are aliens among us. They invade wild Florida because people accidentally or intentionally release them outdoors. We're talking about plants and animals including feral cats, wild hogs, and the dreaded hydrilla that clogs waterways. Letting them loose upsets the balance with native plants and animals.

Next to a pond you find the first sensory sign, which says: "The key is to relax. The first thing you must do to restore your sensory sensitivity is to relax. Leave those everyday problems right here. Take them no further."

We visualize leaving heavy backpacks of problems next to the bench and feel lighter already. We're instructed to take five deep breaths, then five more with our eyes closed. Breathe deeply, feel the breeze and the sun.

Sound plays a big role in the natural world. We're bombarded with sounds in our daily lives. We can't possibly use our ears the way animals do—to stake out territories, find mates, divide food, or escape from predators.

A sensory sign asks us to concentrate all our senses on the sounds around us. How many birdcalls do you hear? Focus on just one birdcall. What is the power and pitch of the song? If you don't have a clue as to what kind of bird it is, what name would you give it based on its song? Children will have fun with this one.

We move into a live-oak forest. Massive trees with huge, spreading limbs cover the landscape. The stand of trees goes so deep we can't even tell where it ends.

The oaks have an ancient, prehistoric feel. Spanish moss drapes down from tree limbs. Only spotted sunlight gets through the thick canopy of leaves. Without light, we would not see colors. Animals use light and color on their bodies, to communicate, protect, and conceal.

Of course, there would not be complete sensory exercises without smell. For animals, most of what they know about the world comes to them through their noses. Pick up something and smell it. Be sure you know what you are picking up. Don't step off the trail to pick up anything. A few pine needles found on the trail will do nicely.

The same caution applies to the sensory exercise about touch. Pick an object that you know is safe. A nice, small rock ought to be just fine. Close your eyes. Feel its texture, its temperature. Then put it back where you found it.

After walking 2 miles, we've edged a hammock, traveled along a swamp, seen open prairie, and now we're entering a bottomland hardwood.

Gone is the easy, grassy trail, replaced by a dirt trail strewn with pine needles. The last sensory sign gives us a final direction to take home with us: "Leaving the trail is just the beginning of learning sensory awareness. If you leave with more questions than when you started, then you can call your excursion an overwhelming success."

Bonus Points

In conjunction with the EcoWalk is the 9-mile South Loop Bicycle Trail, a good choice for those who want to come back with their off-road bicycles.

Either before or after the EcoWalk, be sure to visit the Crystal River Preserve State Park Visitor Center at 3266 North Sailboat Avenue, Crystal River, phone (352) 563-0450. It is open 9 a.m. to 5 p.m. every day. There is a logbook you can sign at the EcoWalk, but if you forget, the visitor center also has a logbook.

On the third Saturday of every month, environmental videos are shown in the visitor center's Redfish Revue Theatre. Topics vary. Try the matinee show at 3 p.m. or the evening video at 7 p.m. All shows are free.

State Park Drive also has a turnoff for Crystal River Archaeological State Park, 3400 North Museum Point, Crystal River, phone (352) 795-3817. It is well marked. The entrance fee is $2, paid at a self-serve station. A voice recording tells you how to pay and how to get started. A small but beautifully appointed museum explains the history of the Native Americans who lived here until five hundred years ago. They built this ceremonial mound complex and burial ground. It is the longest continuously occupied pre-Columbian site in Florida and has the honor of being listed as a National Historic Landmark.

Brochures are free and include a map of the mound complex. Be sure to carry one with you to identify the mounds, as they are not all labeled. Periodically, the citizens' support group for the park has moonlight walks through the mound complex. Donations are requested.

On Friday mornings, the park has a heritage eco–river tour. The boat tour departs at 9:30 a.m. and lasts about an hour and a half. Cost is $10 for adults; $8 for children ages 7–12; children under 7 are admitted free. The boat seats 24 people on a first-come, first-served basis; no reservations. Departure is from inside the park, near the new picnic area next to Crystal River. The park provides loaner binoculars.

Back on U.S. 19, more walks are part of the Crystal River Preserve

State park trail system: the Churchhouse Hammock Boardwalk and the Path to the Past primitive trail. The address for these trails is 1510 N. Suncoast Blvd., U.S. 19, Crystal River. A large, shaded parking area, restrooms, and a covered picnic pavilion are all grouped together at the trailhead entrance, directly across from the Crystal River Mall.

Churchhouse Hammock Boardwalk is an elevated wooden boardwalk covering one-third of a mile. It is handicapped accessible. This short walk goes through a pinewoods ecosystem that is being taken over by a mesic hammock, according to the free Crystal River Preserve State Park Trails brochure. There were no informational signs posted along the boardwalk at the time of our visit.

In addition to the Boardwalk Path, try the three-quarter-mile Path to the Past primitive trail. It begins off the boardwalk entrance and will loop back to the boardwalk.

Of course, manatees are the big draw. To guarantee a manatee sighting without the environmental effects that come when you jump into the water with them, plan a visit to Homosassa Springs State Wildlife Park, located 6 miles south of Crystal River. The address is: 4150 South Suncoast Blvd., Homosassa, phone (352) 628-5343.

Viewing manatees this way is far less stressful for the animals than jumping into their water world at Crystal River, Kings Bay, or Homosassa River. A whole tourist industry is geared to this endangered animal. Some manatees seem to like company; others are shy. They can be deeply stressed by all the visitors, especially the ones who try to swim with them.

Kings Bay is the headwaters of Crystal River and a huge gathering place for humans, manatees, and entire flocks of waterbirds. More than thirty artesian springs are grouped in Kings Bay.

Some tour operators offer other manatee paddles that are less invasive. These include Save the Manatee Club's "Do Not Disturb" kayak tours in Crystal River. Save the Manatee Club is located in Maitland. See their Web site, www.savethemanatee.org, or call (407) 539-0990 or toll-free (800) 432-5646.

Lars Andersen of Adventure Outpost in High Springs conducts paddling tours around Kings Bay, but no swimming with the animals is allowed out of respect for them. See their Web site, www.adventure outpost.net, or call (386) 454-0611.

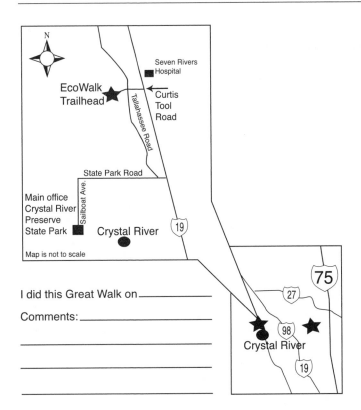

NORTHEAST FLORIDA

Captain Mike's Sunshine River Tours is an ecotourism guide service in Homosassa. From November through April, they do not go to Crystal River or Kings Bay but offer snorkeling tours in the Homosassa River, where snorkelers are few. Their Web address is: www.sunshinerivertours.com; or call (866) 645-5727.

Trip Essentials

Name: EcoWalk in Wild Florida: Crystal River Preserve State Park, Crystal River

Type of walk: Nature trail

Length of walk: 2.5 miles

Time to finish: 1 1/2 to 2 1/2 hours

Difficulty: Easy; mowed grass walkway most of the way. Wheelchair accessible, but there may be wet spots at bottom of inclines.

Appeals to: Families (minors must be accompanied by an adult), teachers, nature lovers, and birders (see page 12, West Florida guide to the Great Florida Birding Trail)

Guides: Self-guided with sensory exercises along the walk

Address: EcoWalk is at 5990 N. Tallahassee Road, Crystal River

Phone: Crystal River Preserve State Park office (352) 563-0450. The park office is 2 miles from the EcoWalk trailhead.

Web site: www.floridastateparks.org

Cost: None

Getting there: For the EcoWalk, take U.S. 19 north. Just before Seven Rivers Hospital, turn left onto Curtis Tool Road.

GPS coordinates: (Crystal River) N 28° 92694 W 082° 69722

Hours: Sunrise to sunset

Restrooms: None on trail

Water/food: None; bring your own.

Dogs: Leashed

Lunch ideas: American, at Jones Restaurant, 216 Northeast U.S. Highway 19, Crystal River, FL 34429, phone (352) 563-1611; Italian, at Scampi's, 773 NE 5th Street, Crystal River, FL 34429, phone (352) 564-2030

Part III

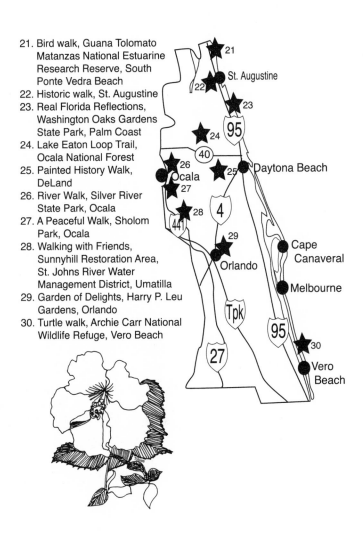

Central Florida

21. Bird walk, Guana Tolomato Matanzas National Estuarine Research Reserve, South Ponte Vedra Beach
22. Historic walk, St. Augustine
23. Real Florida Reflections, Washington Oaks Gardens State Park, Palm Coast
24. Lake Eaton Loop Trail, Ocala National Forest
25. Painted History Walk, DeLand
26. River Walk, Silver River State Park, Ocala
27. A Peaceful Walk, Sholom Park, Ocala
28. Walking with Friends, Sunnyhill Restoration Area, St. Johns River Water Management District, Umatilla
29. Garden of Delights, Harry P. Leu Gardens, Orlando
30. Turtle walk, Archie Carr National Wildlife Refuge, Vero Beach

21

Birds, Botany, and Breakfast

Guana River Site, Guana Tolomato Matanzas National
Estuarine Research Reserve, South Ponte Vedra Beach

This is a test. Have you seen a red maple or a roseate spoonbill lately?

Your answer may be a yes, and maybe you found them at Guana Tolomato Matanzas National Estuarine Research Reserve in South Ponte Vedra Beach. The reserve is 8 miles north of Vilano Beach.

The reserve covers 60,000 acres that are geographically separated into two sections: a northern section, where the Tolomato and Guana rivers run into the Atlantic Ocean, and a southern section that runs along the Matanzas River from Moses Creek to Palm Coast.

The northern section encompasses Deep Creek State Forest, Stokes Landing Conservation Area, Guana River Wildlife Management Area, Guana River Marsh Aquatic Preserve, and Guana River Site.

Color-coded trails for hiking and biking, covering 9 miles, are found in the 2,400 acres designated as the reserve's Guana River Site. You will find a mother lode of habitats, including beaches and dunes, mangrove tidal wetlands, a maritime hammock, and pond pine flatwoods. Most of the wetlands are in an estuary, a semi-enclosed body of water where salt water and freshwater intermingle.

From October through April, when the weather is cooler, the reserve's staff conducts nature walks. Starting times vary. Reservations are required.

There is a Salt Marsh Walk, an Uplands Walk, and the Birds, Botany, and Breakfast Nature Walk, a personal favorite of mine since breakfast is on the menu. The BBB walk has a fee of $10 for nonmembers and $5 for Friends of GTM Reserve members. Fee includes free admission to the reserve's Environmental Education Center.

Whether taking a guided walk or trying a trail on your own—I recommend the yellow trail—stop first at the Environmental Education Center, open 9 a.m. to 4 p.m., and pick up free trail guides along with species lists.

An admission fee is charged for the center. You will want to come back and visit that later. As you come in the front door, the extensive brochure racks are in a foyer on the right. There is no charge to come in and get brochures.

With so many natural communities, those free species lists in the brochure rack are going to come in handy, especially with children. Have a contest—who can check off the most items? Maybe the one who wins could get to pick where to have lunch and even the menu.

Hiking trails, located through the gate next to the center, are open 8 a.m. to sunset. An automated pay station, cash only or the annual reserve pass, requires $3 per vehicle for up to 8 people.

Park your vehicle at the west end of the Guana River Dam. Birders will want to start looking for anhingas, cormorants, brown pelicans, ducks, and wading birds. A short walk along a service road leads first to a covered pavilion and then to the trailhead with signs showing different colored trails and their directions.

The yellow trail begins by going along the edges of two communities. On one side sits a freshwater marsh; the other side contains a dense oak hammock.

A covered overlook with a bench has a marsh view. A sign asks: What can you see? Another queries: Have you seen this? Pictures of animal tracks and animals are helpful to get all ages looking for tracks.

People came here as far back as four thousand years ago, and they stayed long enough to leave artifacts. Items found in twenty-three archaeological and historic sites date from 2,500 BC to the late nineteenth century.

Back at the covered pavilion, a breakfast of juice, coffee, and donuts is waiting. We walked for our breakfast.

Bonus Points

A highlight of your day here will be a visit to the Environmental Education Center that opened in 2005. Admission is $2 adults; $1 children

A bench overlooking a marsh on a Guana River trail.

CENTRAL FLORIDA

10–17; those under 10 are admitted free. An exhibit hall explores the importance of estuaries and oceans, with exhibits including life-size replicas of a North Atlantic right whale and aquariums with live ocean and estuarine animals.

Along a bank of windows, a spotting scope was set up to observe an eagle's nest across the estuary. The day we were there you could see both the parents and the chicks.

The reserve's Guana River Site, including the Environmental Education Center, is located at 505 Guana River Road, South Ponte Vedra Beach, FL 32082, phone (904) 823-4500. Their Web site is: www.gtm nerr.org.

The National Oceanographic and Atmospheric Administration (NOAA) and the Florida Department of Environmental Protection, Office of Coastal and Managed Aquatic Areas, are partners in the reserve's management.

Next door to the reserve is the Guana River Wildlife Management Area, maintained by the Florida Department of Environmental Protection; the Division of Forestry; and the Florida Fish & Wildlife Conservation Commission.

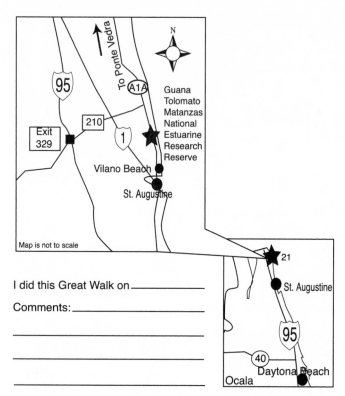

CENTRAL FLORIDA

The grey trail on the reserve goes from the reserve into the Wildlife Management Area (WMA). Be advised that hunting is allowed in the WMA, and that walk-in access is restricted during hunting season. Check the Web site www.myfwc.com for dates.

The reserve has beach-access points a few miles north of the Guana River Road. On the west side of A1A are three beach parking lots. The parking fee is $3 per day. Park here and walk across the road to dune walkovers.

Fort Matanzas National Monument is located 14 miles south of St. Augustine. This national monument is part of the southern section of the reserve. The fort was built in 1740. Hours are 9 a.m. to 5:30 p.m. The visitor center is at 8635 State Road A1A, St. Augustine, FL 32080, phone (904) 471-0116. Web site: www.nps.gov/foma.

High season for fort visitation is March through Labor Day and the December holidays. On holiday weekends there may be a wait to take the ferry.

Trip Essentials

Name: Birds, Botany and Breakfast: Guana River Site, Guana Tolomato
   Matanzas National Estuarine Research Reserve, South Ponte Vedra
   Beach
Type of walk: Birding/nature
Length of walk: 1 mile each way for the yellow trail
Time to finish: 45 minutes to 1 hour, includes stops for bird watching
Difficulty: Easy. Dirt trail. Wheelchair accessible.
Appeals to: Nature buffs, photographers, and birders (listed as Guana
   River State Park on page 6 of the East Section guide to the Great
   Florida Birding Trail)
Guides: Self-guided. Nature walks with a guide, including the Birds,
   Botany, and Breakfast Nature Walk are given fall to spring for a fee.
   See Web site for schedule.
Address: The Reserve Environmental Education Center, Guana River Site,
   505 Guana River Road, South Ponte Vedra Beach, FL 32080
Phone: (904) 823-4500
Web site: www.gtmnerr.org and www.dep.state.fl.us/coastal/sites/gtm
Cost: $3 per vehicle, cash only, to enter the reserve's Guana River Site
   at Guana River Dam Recreation Area. *Note*: The reserve is not a state
   park and does not accept annual state park passes.
Getting there: Off A1A, 7 miles north of Vilano Beach (Vilano Beach is 2
   miles east of historic St. Augustine)
GPS coordinates: N 30° 01' 21.70687° W 081° 19' 34.22991°
Hours: 8 a.m. to sunset
Restrooms: At Environmental Education Center and Guana River Dam
   Recreation Area
Water/food: Water at restrooms; no food available
Dogs: 6-foot hand-held leash on trails. No dogs on beach.
Lunch ideas: American, at Mary's Harbor View Cafe, at the Monterey Inn,
   16 Avenida Menendez, Suite A, St. Augustine, FL 32084, phone (904)
   825-0193; new American, at A1A Ale Works (sit upstairs for great view),
   1 King Street, St. Augustine, FL 32084, phone (904) 829-2977

CENTRAL FLORIDA

22

Coquina and Conquistadors

Build Your Own Historic Walk, St. Augustine

In 1565, an expedition from Spain led by Pedro Menéndez de Avilés established St. Augustine. That was sixty-five years before the Pilgrims set foot on Plymouth Rock.

The ancient city wears its age well. To be authentic, do what the early explorers did. Discover St. Augustine on foot and build your own historic walk.

First, find a parking space for your twenty-first-century vehicle. It won't be easy. Streets in the historic district are narrow, made for horse-drawn wagons and not SUVs. Some street parking is free, but there are 2-hour time limits. Other street parking is metered. King Street and Cathedral Place have on-street parking, but spaces fill up fast, especially around the Plaza de la Constitucion.

After parking, walk to the intersection of St. George Street and King Street. The plaza, the center of the colonial town, is to your right. Across the plaza on the north side is the Basilica-Cathedral of St. Augustine, built in 1797; the church is open to visitors.

On the west side of the plaza, the Government House, built in 1710 and restored in 1937, serves as a city information center. Pick up a free sightseeing map of St. Augustine and its beaches along with another free brochure, "Historic Saint Augustine."

St. Augustine has 144 blocks of notable buildings divided into four historic districts covering an area roughly 1 mile long and a half mile wide. The map inside the historic brochure has color-coded the four historic districts, making it easy to navigate.

St. Augustine's Colonial City, 1565 to 1821, runs along Matanzas Bay, as you would expect, since in the beginning everything arrived by ship.

North of Colonial City is the Abbot Tract, a neighborhood built after the Civil War and St. Augustine's first suburban development.

Henry Flagler, a builder of railroads and tourist towns, developed the Model Land Company, now a historic district situated west of Colonial City. The architecture is early twentieth century and includes the Ponce de Leon Hotel, now converted to Flagler College and Flagler Memorial Presbyterian Church. South of the Model Land Company is Lincolnville, the fourth historic district, an African-American neighborhood. Started after the Civil War, Lincolnville has many examples of Victorian-era houses.

Where to begin? At the beginning. The Plaza de la Constitucion. Side streets near the plaza are all pedestrian friendly, meaning no cars. Where to go next is a personal choice. For me, the two must-see places in historic St. Augustine are the Lightner Museum, housed in the Alcazar Hotel, built 1888, and the Castillo de San Marcos National Monument, a fort built between 1672 and 1695. A close third is Flagler College, occupying the Hotel Ponce de Leon, built by Henry Flagler in 1887.

Since we're standing on the plaza and can see water, let's head that way. From the plaza, walk east to Avenida Menendez. Directly ahead of you is the Bridge of Lions, built in 1927, with a new bridge alongside it. Turn left onto Avenida Menendez and begin your promenade down this wide boulevard facing Matanzas Bay.

Sailboats are anchored in the bay. The smell of salt air carries on sea breezes. Horse-drawn carriages are lined up along the sidewalk, waiting for passengers. The ancient roadway has a decidedly modern feel. Cars clog the roadway. Joggers and bicyclists use the wide sidewalks.

After about four blocks, the road turns to the left and becomes Castillo Drive. Directly ahead is the fort built of coquina rock, still guarding the bay though its cannons are plugged and silent.

When the weather is fine for walking, I like to make the entire stroll, take in the surroundings, then come back later for visits inside buildings. Walking back from the fort, take Charlotte Street, the next street up from Avenida Menendez. It is charming and not overdeveloped, and along the way there are galleries, shops, restaurants, and B&Bs, many housed in old, restored buildings.

Back at the plaza, turn right on King Street and go west, back to

The San Agustin Bastion at Castillo de San Marcos National Monument, St. Augustine.

the intersection of St. George Street and King Street. On the southeast corner of King Street and St. George Street is Trinity Episcopal Parish, built in 1830 and justly famous for its twenty-eight stained-glass windows installed between 1859 and 1972.

Continue going west on King Street up to Cordova Street. The Lightner Museum is on the left, and Flagler College is on your right. You have walked approximately 1.5 miles, past centuries of history, and now you know that the Oldest City, at more than four hundred years old, comes by its name honestly.

Bonus Points

In addition to the visitor information center inside Government House, which is free, you will find the Government House Museum. Admission is $2.50 per person. The address is: 48 King Street, St. Augustine,

FL 32084. Phone (904) 825-5033 for the museum and (904) 825-1000 for the visitor information center.

The National Park Service has the Castillo as one of its duty stations. The Castillo de San Marcos National Monument, 1 South Castillo Drive, St. Augustine, FL 32084, phone (904) 829-6506, is open from 8:45 a.m. to 4:45 p.m. every day except Christmas. Admission is $6 adults; children 15 and under are admitted free when accompanied by a responsible adult. Web site: www.nps.gov/casa.

The former Hotel Alcazar, built in 1887 in a flamboyant Spanish Renaissance style, is now the Lightner Museum. Address: 75 King Street, St. Augustine, FL 32084, phone (904) 824-2874. Hours are 9 a.m. to 5 p.m. daily. Admission is $8 adults; $2 children 12–18; children under 12 with an adult are admitted free. Web site: www.lightnermuseum.org.

Across from the Lightner is the Hotel Ponce de Leon, also built in 1887 and even more elaborate with its Spanish Renaissance style. Flagler College occupies the former hotel located at 78 King Street, St. Augustine, FL 32084, phone (904) 829-6481. Web site: www.flagler. edu.

Historic guided tours of the old hotel, called legacy tours, are given daily on the hour from 10 a.m. to 3 p.m. Tickets are $6 adult; $1 children under 12. The tours last about an hour.

Trinity Episcopal Parish, 216 St. George Street, St. Augustine, FL 32084, phone (904) 824-2876, is across from the plaza. Open to the public, the stained-glass windows are masterpieces worth seeing. Web site: www.trinityepiscopalparish.org.

Across the Bridge of Lions, it is easy to spot the St. Augustine Lighthouse & Museum, 81 Lighthouse Avenue, St. Augustine, FL 32080, phone (904) 829-0745. Allow at least an hour to climb the lighthouse and tour the site that includes a former light keeper's home. Hours are 9 a.m. to 6 p.m. every day except Thanksgiving, Christmas Eve, and Christmas Day. Web site: www.staugustinelighthouse.com.

Admission to the museum and tower is $7.75 adults; $6.75 seniors 60 and older; $5 children 6–11. For their safety, children must be 44 inches tall to climb the tower and be able to climb under their own power.

To view the museum and grounds, but not climb the tower, admission is $5 adults; $4 seniors 60 and older; $3 children 6–11.

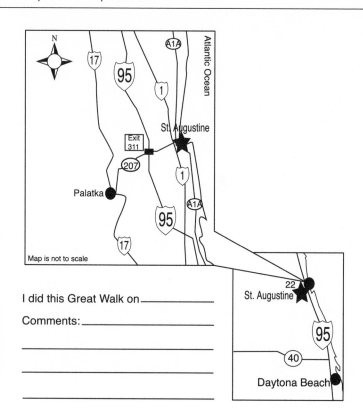

I did this Great Walk on _____

Comments: _____

_____

_____

_____

Practically next door to the lighthouse, and right on the beach, is Anastasia State Park, 1340-A A1A South, St. Augustine, FL 32080, phone (904) 461-2033. Hours are 8 a.m. to sundown. Admission is $5 per vehicle for up to 8 people; $3 for single-occupant vehicle. Web site: www.floridastateparks.org.

Anastasia has a tidal salt marsh that is popular with birders. Other birding sites are the maritime hammock trail and the beach. The park is on page 7 of the East Section guide to the Great Florida Birding Trail.

Before you get to the park's entrance station and have to pay a fee, a piece of history sits off to the right. Remember the Castillo with its thick coquina walls? Those blocks of coquina were dug here at Old Spanish Quarries. Native Americans were used as slave labor to cut out the coquina rock—from the very ground their ancestors had walked.

Trip Essentials

Name: Coquina and Conquistadors: Build Your Own Historic Walk, St. Augustine

Type of walk: Historic

Length of walk: 2.5 miles, more or less depending on the route you design for yourself

Time to finish: 2 hours

Difficulty: Easy. Pavement. Wheelchair accessible.

Appeals to: History buffs, families, and photographers

Guides: Self-guided

Address: Brochures at visitor information center inside the Government House, 48 King Street, St. Augustine, FL 32084

Phone: (904) 825-1000

Web site: www.visitoldcity.com and www.staugustine.com

Cost: None for self-guided walking tour

Getting there: Historic downtown St. Augustine is about 20 minutes from I-95. From I-95, take State Road 207 exit, go to U.S. 1, turn left, and follow signs to downtown.

GPS coordinates: (St. Augustine Historical Society Library) N 29° 89167 W 081°3125

Hours: Daylight

Restrooms: Inside visitor information center

Water/food: Water at restrooms; numerous restaurants

Dogs: Leashed on sidewalks; not allowed in buildings

Lunch ideas: New American, at the Sunset Grill, 421 A1A Beach Boulevard, St. Augustine, FL 32080, phone (904) 471-5555; Greek, at Athena Restaurant, 14 Cathedral Place, St. Augustine, 32084, phone (904) 823-9076

23

Real Florida Reflections

Washington Oaks Gardens State Park, Palm Coast

Washington Oaks Gardens State Park sits not so far off the beaten path that you can't find it at all but removed enough that you must make an effort to arrive.

Situated on the Atlantic coast 2 miles south of Marineland on State Road A1A, the park has land on both sides of the road. On the east side, scrub jay habitat gives way to a beach with coquina rock formations hugging the Atlantic Ocean shoreline. The west side of A1A is a different habitat, a coastal hammock bordering the Matanzas River. The park's centerpiece is its formal gardens known for roses, camellias, and azaleas.

History plays a part in the plantings. Native Americans came here to hunt. A shell midden—a mound of oyster shells and other discards—is now a hill in the rose garden.

In 1818, Jose Mariano Hernandez bought the land and named it Bella Vista. In 1845, his daughter Luisa married George Lawrence Washington, who shared a common ancestor with President George Washington. Hernandez gave them the land as a wedding present, but they never lived at Bella Vista.

After Luisa died, George started visiting Bella Vista, now owned by another daughter of General Hernandez. He bought the entire property in 1888, and it became known as the Washington Place. When George died in 1894, his heirs kept the land until 1923, when they sold it to developers. They planned a subdivision to be called Hernandez Estates, but Florida's land boom collapsed.

During the Great Depression, land in Florida went for garage-sale prices. Louise Powis Clark bought the land in 1936 as a retirement home for herself and fiancé, Owen D. Young, who would become her third husband.

The day after their wedding, February 20, 1937, they threw an outdoor party and renamed the estate Washington Oaks. It speaks volumes that the couple celebrated their commitment here, a place that became their winter home and a favorite retreat for them. Many of the formal garden areas, the footpaths, and reflecting pools were landscaped during their tenure.

Owen Young died in 1962. Before her death in 1965, Louise donated the property to the state with the stipulation that the gardens be maintained "in their present form" and expanded when moneys allowed. Their home became the Owen D. Young Visitors Center.

After going through the park's entrance gate and down a long driveway, park in the garden parking lot, walk across the road, and follow the path to the center. Stepping through the front door of their home makes you a guest in the Youngs' living room, re-created as it might have been in the 1940s and 1950s. An old television set is turned on, playing black-and-white sitcoms. You can even sit on the couch and watch television.

The formal gardens begin behind the visitor center. Connecting ponds are lined with grasses and banana trees. Koi and grass carp live in the ponds.

There really is no need for a map. Garden paths interconnect, meandering from one area to another. You find you come to this spot for the same reasons that Louise and Owen came—to have a respite. Washington Oaks is the perfect place for reading, journaling, and sketching, and artists will want to bring painting gear.

At the end of the day, what really matters is not whether you walked 2.5 miles or sampled every trail, but what happened to you along the way and whether you opened up enough to let a splendid place like Washington Oaks have its way with you.

Bonus Points

Washington Oaks Gardens State Park is listed on page 7 of the East Section guide to the Great Florida Birding Trail.

Across from the visitor center, the Mala Compra hiking loop, one-half mile, goes from the center to the picnic area. An estuarine tidal

CENTRAL FLORIDA

A female Palmedes swallowtail feeds on a white penta at Washington Oaks Gardens State Park, Palm Coast.

marsh is on one side of the trail and a coastal maritime hammock on the other.

In the park are trails for both hiking and biking. The Bella Vista Trails cover 1.7 miles and include the Timucuan Hiking Trail, Jungle Road Hike and Bike Trail, along with the Old A1A Hike and Bike Trail. The hiking trails were developed in partnership with the Florida Trail Association and the Florida Department of Environmental Protection.

Fishing from the seawall at the Matanzas River or surf fishing across the road on the beach are popular activities. Saltwater fishing workshops for children 10–15 are scheduled. Call (386) 446-6783 or (386) 931-4123 for schedules.

Gamble Rogers Memorial State Recreation Area at Flagler Beach, 3100 South A1A, Flagler Beach, FL, 32136, phone (386) 517-2086, has beach access on one side and picnic pavilions on the other side, facing the Intracoastal Waterway. A boat launch area is on the Intracoastal. The folksinger Gamble Rogers was Florida's troubadour. He drowned nearby while trying to save a swimmer in distress.

Park hours are 8 a.m. to sunset. Admission fee is $4 per vehicle for up to 8 people. The Web site is www.floridastateparks.org.

Trip Essentials

Name: Real Florida Reflections: Washington Oaks Gardens State Park, Palm Coast

Type of walk: Botanical/historical

Length of walk: Not measured

Time to finish: 30 to 45 minutes minimum

Difficulty: Easy. Dirt trail. Some facilities wheelchair accessible.

Appeals to: Gardeners, nature lovers, photographers, artists, and birders (listed on page 7 of the East Section guide to the Great Florida Birding Trail)

Guides: Self-guided

Address: Washington Oaks Gardens State Park, 6400 North Oceanshore Blvd., Palm Coast, FL 32137

Phone: (386) 446-6780

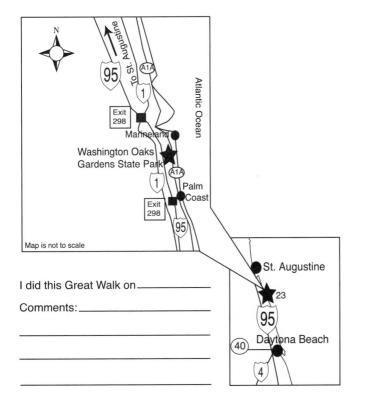

I did this Great Walk on _____

Comments: _____

_____

_____

_____

Web site: www.floridastateparks.org

Cost: Park admission fee $4 per vehicle for up to 8 people

Getting there: 2 miles south of Marineland, off A1A

GPS coordinates: N 29° 63.528 W 081° 20.417

Hours: 8 a.m. to sundown

Restrooms: At visitor center and picnic area

Water/food: Water at restrooms; no food sold inside park.

Dogs: Not allowed on beaches or in gardens. Well-behaved dogs on 6-foot hand-held leash are allowed on biking and hiking trails and in the picnic area.

Lunch ideas: Bring a picnic lunch. There is a separate picnic area.

CENTRAL FLORIDA

24

Walk with a Lake View

Lake Eaton, USDA Forest Service, Ocala National Forest

A great blue heron carved in wood forever looks at a map showing the Lake Eaton Loop Trail. He seems to be trying to make up his mind. Left or right?

The loop trail map shows trail sections eight-tenths of a mile long with a half-mile section in the middle alongside Lake Eaton. The total trail length is 2.1 miles.

Another sign tells you this used to be a mature sand pine stand. Hurricanes Francis and Jeanne put an end to that. Timber was harvested to open the trail, utilize damaged wood, and ensure public safety. Walkers are asked to "Please excuse Mother Nature's and our mess."

We can do that. Off we go, choosing the right side of the loop as a starting point. If you are not comfortable walking a trail without seeing any signs, blazes, or arrows for quite some time, say one-quarter of a mile, this forest walk is not for you. Those two signs we just talked about? They are the last you will see for quite a distance.

That said, once you start walking, the trail immediately gets your attention. Those storms that wiped out the mature sand pine stand also opened up the view to a wide, sweeping vista. Far away on the horizon are tall sand pines in a long line. Nearby, palmettos are abundant. Woodpeckers are heard but not seen.

Scrub oaks sprout gnarly limbs curling in interesting shapes. The tree trunks often sport several different kinds of lichens in a variety of colors, including a deep shade of pink. If you didn't know it was lichen, from a distance the pink color looks like paint. Fortunately, it is natural and not the result of a human defacing trees with a paint can.

All lichens, including the deer moss, the spongy green clumps on the ground, are algae. When found on trees, they do not hurt the trees.

A walker on the Lake Eaton Loop Trail, Ocala National Forest.

The relationship with the trees is called symbiosis. It is a healthy sign to see them because lichens only grow where the air quality is good.

Signs of the natural kind are everywhere on the trail. Pressed into the dirt are fresh footprints of deer and other wildlife tracks. A brochure with footprint diagrams of various kinds would be good to bring along, especially when walking with children.

Three lake overlooks are marked on the map, with one approached by two separate paths. All have platforms that jut a short way out into the lake.

The first overlook, if you are going on the trail from right to left, has a large platform with benches. Water plants float on the lake. Two ospreys fly nearby calling to one another. Cypress knees stick up in clumps along the shoreline.

A little farther along the trail is the middle overlook. This one has a boardwalk going out over the water that forms a *U* shape, so you can approach it from two paths. Photographers may want to bring long lenses, the better to capture scenes out in the lake, such as a fisherman in a small skiff anchored among water plants.

Between two overlooks we see a dead tree riddled with large holes, a high-rise apartment for woodpeckers. Throughout the entire walk, we hear woodpeckers hammering on trees but never see them.

After the three overlooks, the loop trail turns away from the lake and begins a gradual ascent. Notice that the coolness diminishes as the lake is left behind. You are on the last leg of the loop now, moving through a stand of sand pine that survived.

Why is it that the last half of a loop trail always seems shorter than the first half? It is one of life's mysteries. Before you know it, you are crossing the dirt road named Forest Road 79 and are back at the parking lot.

Bonus Points

The same trailhead and parking lot are shared by Lake Eaton and Lake Eaton Sinkhole Trails. On the west side of Forest Road 79 is Lake Eaton, the walk you just finished. On the east side are several trails to Lake Eaton Sinkhole. Choose a 1-mile loop or a 2.2-mile loop. An informational sign at the start of the trail shows the routes.

An old stand of sand hill pine was culled in 1982, and the Lake Eaton Sinkhole area reseeded. The newer pines provide habitat for the Florida scrub jays. Along the way, walking through sand pine, scrub oak, and palmetto, you'll also see rusty lyonia, called crooked wood and silk bay. When crushed, the leaf of a silk bay smells just like bay leaves.

Lake Eaton Sinkhole has a diameter of 450 feet and sinks down to 80 feet in the ground. Hardwood trees grow in the sinkhole, a stark contrast to the surrounding sand-pine forest.

Salt Springs is on the northeast side of Ocala National Forest. On the east side of State Road 19, a half mile south of the Salt Springs Campground, you will find the trailhead for the Salt Springs Trail. No fee to walk the trail.

The wooded trail, slightly over 1 mile each way, leads to an observation platform overlooking Salt Springs Run. Plan to bring binoculars and look for waders and limpkins. This trail is listed on page 8 of the East Section guide to the Great Florida Birding Trail.

Ocala National Forest covers 383,573 acres. Going to one of their three visitor centers helps one learn about the varied recreational opportunities in the forest. The centers, open 9 a.m. to 5 p.m. every day, have free brochures along with books, maps, and other items for sale, as well as helpful staff to answer questions.

CENTRAL FLORIDA

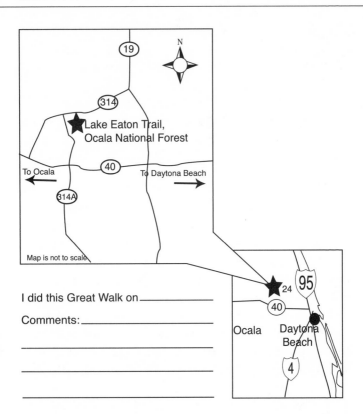

CENTRAL FLORIDA

I did this Great Walk on _____

Comments: _____
_____
_____
_____

Before taking a hike in the forest, it is good to know what areas are open to hunting and when. Hunting is permitted in Ocala National Forest from mid-September through January. Both Lake Eaton Sinkhole and Lake Eaton are areas where hunting is permitted. To learn more about hunting season, go to the Florida Fish & Wildlife Conservation Commission Web site at www.myfwc.com.

Trip Essentials

Name: Walk with a Lake View: Lake Eaton, USDA Forest Service, Ocala
    National Forest
Type of walk: Nature
Length of walk: 2.1-mile loop
Time to finish: 1 to 1 1/2 hours
Difficulty: Moderately easy. Dirt trail. Wheelchair accessible except for
    one lake overlook that has stairs.

Appeals to: Nature buffs, photographers, and birders

Guides: Self-guided

Address: Forest Road 79 is off County Road 314. Free brochures of Lake Eaton Loop and Sinkhole at Salt Springs Visitor Center, 14100 North State Highway 19, Salt Springs, FL 32134; or Ocklawaha Visitor Center, 3199 Northeast Highway 315, Silver Springs, FL 34488; or Pitman Visitor Center, 45621 State Road 19, Altoona, FL 32702.

Phone: Salt Springs Visitor Center (352) 685-3070; Ocklawaha Visitor Center (352) 236-0288; Pitman Visitor Center (352) 699-7495.

Web site: www.fs.fed.us/r8/florida

Cost: None

Getting there: From downtown Ocala, take State Road 40 east 10 miles to County Road 314. Turn left onto C.R. 314 and go 8.6 miles to Forest Road 86. Turn right (east) onto F.R. 86 and go 1.2 miles to Forest Road 79. Turn right (south) on F.R. 79 and go about one-half mile to trailhead on the left.

GPS coordinates: N 29° 25.694 W 081° 52.15

Hours: Daylight

Restrooms: None

Water/food: None

Dogs: On a 6-foot leash at all times

Lunch ideas: Barbecue, at Rogers Bar-B-Que, 10863 East Highway 40, Silver Springs, FL 34488, phone (352) 625-2020; American, at Jakes Place, 16275 East Highway 40, Silver Springs, FL 34488, phone (352) 625-3133

CENTRAL FLORIDA

25

Painted History Walk

DeLand

DeLand does not hide its past in a dusty tome on a bookshelf. Instead, you can walk right up to it. Visit the past on the DeLand Historic Mural Walk as you stroll downtown along wide sidewalks to see eleven murals.

Your first stop is the MainStreet DeLand Association at 100 North Woodland Boulevard. The door on the front of the building, built in 1887 as Miller's Hardware, leads to a hallway and Mural No. 11. It is called *Bicycling the Boulevard* and shows three men on bicycles in the 1920s—a time when bicycling between communities was a common event.

The mural walk is a project of the MainStreet DeLand Association (MSDA). It is funded by local businesses and residents who donated money to be models for some of the murals.

Once inside the office, ask for the mural pamphlet, a full-color glossy beauty that looks and feels like a catalog from a major art exhibit. The pamphlet was made possible by a grant from the Florida Humanities Council and costs $2. You will want to have it with you as you walk.

This booklet gives you the history of each mural, asks you to find hidden elements in some of them, contains a biography of the artists, and, in the middle, has a two-page locator map.

Eight murals are located on a seven-block stretch of Woodland Boulevard. Three more are on side streets, one block off of Woodland. Walking to see them all covers a little over a mile. The association hopes to add more murals in the future.

We exit the MSDA office, turn right, cross the street to see Murals Number 9 and 10, starting with Number 10, *Living at the Landmark*.

Detail from the mural *Living at the Landmark* by Courtney Canova, part of the DeLand Historic Mural Walk.

The Landmark Hotel opened in 1927. It is now the DeLand Artisan Inn and has won awards for its restoration work.

Almost every window on the first two floors of the south wall has a mural inserted that looks like it was painted right on the window. It depicts life in the hotel during the 1930s and 1940s.

We decide to have lunch and sit where we can see Mural No. 9. It is the most unusual of all the murals, using mosaics while all the others are painted. Titled *River Life*, it depicts Florida manatees that winter in warm waters flowing out of nearby springs.

The mural, surrounded by waterfalls, is located on the lower level of Wachovia Bank. Also on the lower level is a restaurant with outdoor seating that faces the mural.

Be sure to turn down Indiana Avenue to see Mural No. 8, *Strolling through Time with Bill.* He may look nineteenth century, but he's quite modern. Bill Dreggors, a fourth-generation Floridian, has an interest in local history. He helps keep it alive with slide shows, books, and presentations and portrayals of historic figures, including Henry De-Land, the baking-soda magnate from New York who wanted to build an Athens of Florida and founded DeLand in 1876.

Downtown historic DeLand is rich with old brick buildings that have been restored and revitalized. Every store is occupied, and there is a waiting list. Downtown is very pedestrian friendly. Pots full of flowers adorn every corner. Many restaurants have both indoor and outdoor seating. Little vest-pocket parks with benches are sprinkled liberally along the way. Crosswalks and sidewalks are designed for walkers.

Drivers, however, need to be wary. Meter patrols take seriously their task of marking car tires with chalk. Parking is free and abundant, but keep posted time limits in mind. You are going to want to give yourself a good 3–4 hours to complete the mural walk, plus a detour or two into shops that interest you and a stop for lunch.

Note: While the murals are available for viewing seven days a week, a number of businesses in the downtown area close on Sundays.

Bonus Points

As you travel the mural walk, look up and notice the dates on the buildings—1910 or 1887. Downtown DeLand is listed on the National Register of Historic Places. The MainStreet DeLand Association has a pamphlet, "DeLand: A Walk through Time," that will direct you to a number of historic buildings. Another pamphlet worth having is "The Road to DeLand," by the City of DeLand, the West Volusia Historical Society, and the Florida Humanities Council.

Stetson University in DeLand is right in the historical mainstream, starting out as DeLand Academy in 1883. Henry DeLand thought the town could attract more people if it had a university. DeLand Hall, built in 1884, has been used continuously for education ever since its doors opened.

Four "must-sees" are the Stetson University buildings, the Historic Volusia County Courthouse, the Athens Theater, and the DeLand House Museum.

The Henry A. DeLand House, one block off Woodland Boulevard, is home to the West Volusia Historical Society. The address is: 137 North

Michigan, DeLand, FL 32720, phone (386) 740-6813. It is open to the public at no charge. Hours are Tuesday through Saturday from noon to 4 p.m.; closed Sunday and Monday. The Web site is: www.delandhouse. com.

At the DeLand House you will also find the Robert M. Conrad Educational Research Center and the Lue Gim Gong Memorial Garden. Gong, who developed orange hybrids and a grapefruit that grew singly instead of in bunches, is the subject of Mural Number 3 on Woodland Boulevard near Wisconsin.

DeLeon Springs State Park is about 6 miles north of DeLand. The address is: 601 Ponce DeLeon Boulevard, DeLeon Springs, FL 32130, phone (386) 985-4212. Web site: www.floridastateparks.org. Hours are 8 a.m. to sundown. Admission is $5 per vehicle for up to 8 people.

DeLeon Springs State Park is listed on page 12 of the East Section guide to the Great Florida Birding Trail. Look for coots, ducks, limp-

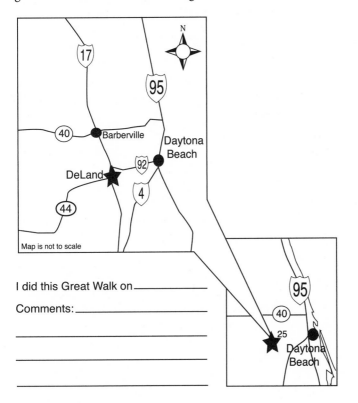

CENTRAL FLORIDA

kins, and waders at the springs or hike a 5-mile hammock trail, where you may see migrating birds.

Inside the park is the Old Spanish Sugar Mill Restaurant, famous for having griddles on the tables so guests can make their own pancakes for breakfast. Hours are 9 a.m. to 4 p.m. Monday through Friday; 8 a.m. to 4 p.m. Saturday and Sunday. Breakfast served all day, plus a full lunch menu is available. Phone (386) 985-5644.

Trip Essentials

Name: Painted History Walk: DeLand

Type of walk: Historic

Length of walk: 1 mile

Time to finish: 1 to 1 1/2 hours for the murals or 3 to 4 hours, which includes stopping to go in shops and having lunch

Difficulty: Easy. Pavement. Wheelchair accessible.

Appeals to: History buffs, art lovers, and photographers

Guides: Self-guided

Address: Mural walk pamphlets at MainStreet DeLand Association, 100 North Woodland Blvd., DeLand, FL 32720. (Mural walk brochures cost $2.)

Phone: (386) 738-0649

Web site: www.mainstreetdeland.com

Cost: Free

Getting there: Take Highways 17/92 from Daytona Beach. DeLand is approximately 15 miles southwest of Daytona Beach.

GPS coordinates: (Stetson University) N 29° 03528 W 081° 30361

Hours: Daylight

Restrooms: In restaurants and at the MainStreet DeLand Association

Water/food: Did not see water fountains; numerous restaurants

Dogs: Leashed on street

Lunch ideas: American, at MainStreet Grille, 100 East New York Avenue, DeLand, FL 32724, phone (386) 740-9535; American, at Cook's Café & Sandwich Shop, 101 North Woodland Blvd., DeLand, FL 32724, phone (386) 738-5030

CENTRAL FLORIDA

26

Two Rivers Run Through It

Silver River State Park, Ocala

My dog Suzi and I have a turkey story to tell you.

A pair of wild turkeys walked through the River Trail underbrush, gobbling to one another. We were about 10 feet away, standing still and watching them. Suddenly the turkeys spotted us and stopped in their tracks. Emitting a huff, as though we were not worthy to be there, they turned away and vanished into the underbrush. Suzi's eyes went wide. She'd never seen birds that big.

Two separate trails lead to the Silver River. Together they are called the River Trails. Each goes through a variety of terrain, and each has a big payoff at the end—a great view of the pristine and undeveloped Silver River.

To get to the River Trails, drive the paved park road all the way to the stop sign. On your left you'll see a large parking area. This is the trailhead for the Sinkhole Trail on the left and the River Trails on the right. The same parking lot is also used for a reconstructed Florida Cracker village and the Silver River Museum and Environmental Education Center.

On the right side of the parking lot, look for a wood pole entranceway with a hanging sign in the middle that says River Trails. Once on the trail, it splits almost immediately.

The Swamp Trail, 1.8 miles round trip, goes to the left and has a boardwalk over a swamp ending in an overlook on the Silver River. To the right, the River Trail, 1.2 miles round trip, goes to a canoe/kayak launching site with benches overlooking the Silver River.

Shortly after it begins, the River Trail takes a bend to the left, going past the backyard of a cabin. Cabins for rent are a new addition to

CENTRAL FLORIDA

The Silver River and its banks change with the seasons at Silver River State Park, Ocala.

Silver River State Park. These are built Florida Cracker style with tin roofs and wraparound porches and fit right into the landscape.

In places, the dirt trail is rubbed away and raw limestone rock is exposed, worn down by years of foot travel. Florida is built on limestone, but it isn't often you get to actually walk on it.

All along the trail birders will hear and perhaps see songbirds. At the water's edge, where there is a canoe and kayak launch ramp, there's a chance to see waders and limpkins. Turtles may be sunning themselves on a log. Alligators and otters may be spotted.

Across the river is a scene that is truly wild Florida. This is the Silver River State Park Wilderness Preserve, inhabited by wildlife, uninhabited by people.

If you have binoculars or very good eyes, you may spot monkeys in the trees or near the waterline. Rhesus monkeys were brought to the park in the 1930s to enhance a jungle cruise at Silver Springs. Placed on an island, it was thought the water would act like a fence and keep them confined. Who knew the monkeys could swim?

They can, and they did swim away from the island. The monkeys took a liking to bottomland river life. Several monkey troops live along

Silver River as well as parts of the Ocklawaha River. Monkeys are aggressive. Leave them alone. Do not feed them.

Both sides of the Silver River are part of the Ocklawaha river basin. The shoreline is rich with cypress trees, gums, and red maples. Every season has a special beauty along the shoreline. Walking down to the river is a different experience every time.

Bonus Points

Except for summer months, you can have "coffee with the birds" at Silver River State Park. The first Saturday of the month a bird-watching trail hike leaves at 8 a.m., and usually the guide takes one of the River Trails. Regular admission fees apply. No charge for the guided walk.

Bring your own coffee or tea. A bonus for birders who keep lists: after the walk everyone stays a while to bring their lists up to date. Call ahead, (352) 236-7148, to confirm. Silver River also has "coffee with a ranger" (do you sense a trend?) with talks on various subjects. Call or check their Web site for schedules. Also look for occasional nighttime stargazing events.

Inside the park is the Silver River Museum and Environmental Education Center. Owned by the Marion County School Board, students come on field trips for archaeology, history, and natural history Monday through Friday.

On Saturday and Sunday, the museum is open to the public. Hours are 9 a.m. to 5 p.m. Admission is $2 per person, in addition to the park entrance fee. The address for the Silver River Museum and Environmental Education Center is 7189 NE 7th Street, Ocala, FL 34470, phone (352) 236-5401.

The Silver Springs attraction was built to showcase the headwaters of the Silver River. The river flows from the headwaters downstream past Silver River State Park and beyond for a little over 5 miles, then joins the Ocklawaha River.

The second river in the park is the Ocklawaha River, which runs along the park's eastern edge. Boat and fishing access is outside the park boundaries. Ray Wayside Park, also called the Ocala Boat Basin, is on east State Road 40 just before the Ocklawaha Bridge. Inside the park is a boat launch with a short canal that leads to the point where

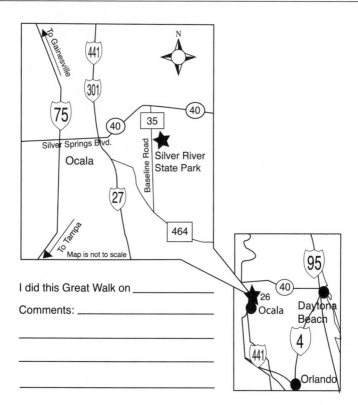

I did this Great Walk on _____

Comments: _____

_____

_____

_____

the Silver and Ocklawaha rivers meet. Admission to the boat basin is $3 per vehicle. For more information, call Marion County Parks and Recreation at (352) 236-7111.

The southern boundary of Silver River State Park faces County Road 314, also known as Sharpes Ferry Road. Across the road, at 8282 Southeast Highway 314, is the Sharpes Ferry office for the Office of Greenways and Trails, phone (352) 236-7143. Web site: www.dep.state. fl.us/gwt.

Part of the Marjorie Harris Carr Cross Florida Greenway is accessed by a trailhead right next to the Greenway office. The Sharpes Ferry Trailhead provides parking for walkers using the Marshall Swamp Trail, an unpaved hiking trail, 3 miles one way, that goes from C.R. 314 to the Southeast 64th Avenue Road Trailhead.

Once you are at the Southeast 64th Avenue Trailhead, you can use a 5-mile paved multiuse trail favored by bikers, inline skaters, and walkers.

Trip Essentials

Name: Two Rivers Run Through It: Silver River State Park, Ocala

Type of walk: Nature

Length of walk: River Trail is 1.2 miles round trip; the Swamp Trail is 1.8 miles round trip.

Time to finish: 45 minutes, includes time spent at the water's edge watching wildlife

Difficulty: Moderately easy. Dirt trail. Mostly wheelchair accessible.

Appeals to: Nature lovers, photographers, and birders (listed on page 9 in the East Section guide to the Great Florida Birding Trail)

Guides: Self-guided. Once a month, except summer months, a guided walk called "Coffee with the Birds" is given. Guided trail walks available with advance request.

Address: Silver River State Park, 1425 NE 58th Avenue, Ocala, FL 34470

Phone: (352) 236-7148

Web site: www.floridastateparks.org

Cost: $4 per vehicle for up to 8 people

Getting there: From I-75, take exit 352 onto State Road 40 east and go about 9 miles to State Road 35 (Baseline Road). Turn right. Go one mile. Park entrance is on the left.

GPS coordinates: N 29° 12.30 W 082° 01.10

Hours: 8 a.m. to sunset

Restrooms: Next to museum near trailhead

Water/food: Water at restrooms; no food sold in park.

Dogs: Well-behaved dogs permitted on trails on a 6-foot hand-held leash

Lunch ideas: Mexican, at El Taxco Mexican Restaurant & Cantina, 4901 East Silver Springs Blvd. #800, Ocala, FL 34470, phone (352) 438-0075; American, at Uptown Grill, 2436 East Silver Springs Blvd., Ocala, FL 34471, phone (352) 732-4737

CENTRAL FLORIDA

27

A Peaceful Walk

Sholom Park, Ocala

Years ago, developer Sidney Colen saw a prairie and a high ridge of land in Ocala. He decided this was a special place. No houses would be built on this site located off busy State Road 200. It is surrounded by the residential and commercial Colen family development known as "On Top of the World."

Sidney Colen's dream for the property was to leave the world a peace park. Steve Curl, a landscape designer, was hired in 2001 to design a master plan for a place where people could meditate on peace. Three years in the making, on the site Colen set aside years ago, Sholom Park opened in October 2004.

The park is open to the public from 8 a.m. to 5 p.m. daily. There is no fee.

Sholom Park is named after Sidney's grandfather. Sholom was his first name. The spelling of "sholom" is different from the more familiar "shalom," but the word means the same—peace. Like peace itself, the park is a work in progress, with more garden areas being added and planned for the future.

Sidney envisioned the world's leaders coming here to sit and talk of peace. Well, why not? As we wait for the world's leaders to figure out how to get here, you and I have Sholom Park to ourselves—a place of peace, refuge, and serenity.

More than 2 miles of paved walkways wind through different gardens, past several ponds, and through a labyrinth. All garden areas are designed to enhance serenity. Except for land that was leveled for the parking lot, walkways and gardens follow natural contours of the land including a high ridge, a sloping prairie, and deep woods.

Over 80 percent of the gardens are planted with foliage that thrives in the Central Florida climate without the aid of irrigation.

There are sixty benches in Sholom Park. The message they send is clear—walk slowly, stop often, sit a while, meditate, think about nature and your life, and feel at peace.

And look closely. Even the walkways are special. Leaves of different shapes were pressed into the concrete as it dried. Rock salt was thrown on the wet concrete for a pitted look. The walkways look old; the leaf patterns look like fossilized images.

As you reach the parking lot, the entry pavilion is ahead of you, located at the crest of a hill. Here you will find garden maps and a park flyer with distances of each garden path marked. The brochures are free.

To the left of the pavilion is the Formal Garden, a fenced area with a fountain at its entrance. This 20 percent of the park is irrigated. But formal doesn't mean it looks like an English garden. Most of the area sits on top of a limestone shelf, the garden showcasing some of the rocky ledges.

After the Formal Garden, which includes a side path to a butterfly garden, take the trail out and connect with the Azalea Trail. This goes past a small bridge, stream, and water garden to the Labyrinth.

Curl says this labyrinth is unlike any other. It meanders with open paths, no dead ends or wrong ways. There are over twenty reflection points with meditation signs.

Embedded in the walkways are old bricks laid in an hourglass shape that helps define the Labyrinth's entry and exit. A rose garden, part of the Labyrinth, features old garden roses, no hybrids.

Another route to the Labyrinth is the Azalea Trail, which starts at the parking lot. Azaleas are planted under oak trees and in open spaces along the trail. In the spring they are there, vibrant and colorful, wherever you turn.

Across from the parking lot, on the right side, is the largest manmade feature—the Pond, covering three-fourths of an acre.

The Pond, with a covered sitting area, is a popular place for bringing a brown bag lunch or a book. Moving down the pathway toward the prairie, you pass an octagonal structure, its eight posts lining up perfectly with eight compass points, so you can't get lost. This outdoor

A winding path at Sholom Park, Ocala.

structure, which seats forty people, is called a "pergebo"—a combination of "pergola" and "gazebo."

This pergebo is part of the Pergebo Trail, which wanders past ornamental grasses, perennials, and blooming shrubs. It is quite a sight to look across the prairie in the fall and see large clumps of pink Mel grass in bloom, their pink filigree tops moving, swaying, and actually dancing in a breeze.

Beyond the trail is the Enchanted Forest, a short walk through a native hammock of hardwood trees. It is always ten to fifteen degrees cooler in the Enchanted Forest.

At the entrance to the forest is a huge limestone rock smoothed on the top to make a seat. A clear acrylic sign next to the rock has Sidney Colen's words: "Come and sit and meditate on me. Together we can possibly see tomorrows that are yet to be."

Visitors wonder why there are no identification signs on plants. Curl says Colen did not want the horticulture to overpower the experience of peace. Curl hopes to produce a plant-identification brochure in the future. Also in the future is an education component, including horticulture classes.

Sidney Colen's peace park is a first for Marion County and Florida. In the first year, Curl said, sixty thousand cars came into Sholom Park, an eye-opening figure. I'm not surprised. Everyone who has been here tells me they love this park. I do too. It is my hope that you will come to walk in peace as well.

Bonus Points

The Ross Prairie Trailhead, part of the Marjorie Harris Carr Cross Florida Greenway, is located off State Road 200 about 1.5 miles north of the intersection of County Road 484 and State Road 200. If you are coming from Ocala, the trailhead is approximately 10 miles from the intersection of State Road 200 and Interstate 75. No fee required.

The hiking trail, about 2.5 miles, is part of the Florida Trail and

CENTRAL FLORIDA

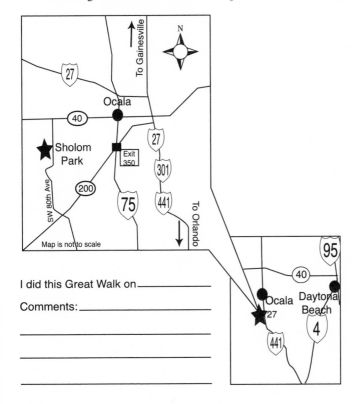

I did this Great Walk on _____

Comments: _____

_____

_____

_____

designated also as a Florida National Scenic Trail. There are connector trails and alternate routes that could alter the distance. See the Web site www.floridagreenwaysandtrails.org for Ross Prairie and other local trails for hikers, horses, and mountain bikes. The phone number for the Greenway office in Ocala is (352) 236-7143.

The Ross Prairie Trailhead is adjacent to, and shares the same entrance as, the 3,500-acre Ross Prairie State Forest at the southern end of the Ross Prairie wetlands. A longleaf pine/turkey oak/wiregrass ecosystem comprises most of this forest.

There are a number of trails in the forest. No charge for parking or visiting the forest. For more information, call the Division of Forestry, Marion County Forester, at (352) 732-1201.

Trip Essentials

Name: A Peaceful Walk: Sholom Park, Ocala
Type of walk: Horticulture and meditation
Length of walk: 2 miles
Time to finish: 1 to 2 hours
Difficulty: Easy. Pavement. Wheelchair accessible.
Appeals to: Gardeners, artists, photographers, and anyone seeking
     refuge from stress
Guides: Self-guided. Docents available for groups by request in advance.
Address: 6602 SW 80th Ave., Ocala, FL 34481
Phone: (352) 427-1628
Web site: www.hapi-info.org
Cost: None
Getting there: In Ocala, at intersection of I-75 and State Road 200, take
     S.R. 200 south for 6.7 miles. At the 80th Street stoplight, turn right, go
     a half mile. Park entrance is on the left.
GPS coordinates: (Ocala) N 29° 18694 W 082° 14028
Hours: 8 a.m. to 5 p.m.
Restrooms: At entrance pavilion
Water/food: Water at restrooms; no food sold in park
Dogs: No
Lunch ideas: Bring a brown bag lunch and sit on one of the sixty benches
     or go to the covered bench area next to the pond.

28

Walking with Friends

Sunnyhill Restoration Area, St. Johns River Water Management District, Umatilla

Two sandhill cranes walk along the top of the levee. They come toward me confidently as though we had scheduled this spot for a meeting. Tall grey birds with long legs and an even longer neck, both wear toupees of bright red and walk with an undulating gait.

Once alongside, both turn their heads and look directly at me with huge yellow eyes. No fear coming from them but rather a sense of camaraderie. Well? Are we walking or not? I turn and walk with them. It seems expected.

When the levee ends, they go right into a meadow, leaving without a farewell. I turn left onto a grassy indentation, a faint path that leads back to the trailhead parking lot.

Welcome to Sunnyhill Restoration Area on the upper Ocklawaha River. Sandhill cranes may not be your walking companions every day, but thousands of them do come for the winter. Some stay into spring and summer.

Purple gallinules nest here. So do least bitterns and ibises. Wintering ducks like the marshes. Even on a hot summer's day, at the very least you'll hear the call of a mockingbird and see a flash of cardinal red in the bushes, plus have a Great Walk.

A former muck farm where vegetables were raised, Sunnyhill has more than 4,000 acres with miles of levees and hiking trails. Turning into the Sunnyhill entrance, continue past several houses on your right (including the St. Johns River Water Management District office) until, on your left, you see a brown sign depicting white binoculars, which identifies this as part of the Great Florida Birding Trail. Nearby will be a sign saying Blue House.

CENTRAL FLORIDA

Sandhill cranes at Sunnyhill Restoration Area, St. Johns River Water Management District, Umatilla.

Go left at the signs, drive past the Blue House, and park in the large open lot. If staff is in the area, they will open the Blue House for you. Inside are exhibits explaining river restoration. Steamboats navigated the Ocklawaha River in the 1800s, but in the 1920s a 15-mile stretch of the river was abandoned.

River water was diverted to a canal called the C-231 Canal, and the nearby marshes were then drained to become muck farms. St. Johns River Water Management District bought the land in 1988. In cooperation with the U.S. Army Corps of Engineers, wetlands are being restored along a 9-mile stretch of the Ocklawaha River floodplain along with some of the old channels for the Ocklawaha River.

An informational sign to the right of the parking lot shows an area map. The levee trail runs for 7.4 miles from the Blue House trailhead to the Moss Bluff trailhead. But the nice thing about a levee trail is the simple ability to turn around at any point and retrace your steps. There is no way to get lost.

My suggestion to see several habitats and have a walk of about 2 miles is to combine some walking on the levee with a portion of the White Trail, which begins at the informational sign.

Right behind the sign, the woods begin. Walking through an oak hammock deeply shaded by spreading limbs of old live-oak trees, you see an occasional white four-inch diamond on a tree. This means you are on the White Trail.

You come to a wooden fence opening and a dirt road. The White Trail continues across the road for 3 miles to the south trailhead, or turns left onto the road and leads to an observation tower overlooking the marshes. This is a side spur and part of the White Trail. From the Blue House trailhead to the observation tower is eight-tenths of a mile.

Coming back from the tower, turn right onto a road running along a marsh until it runs into the levee trail. Levees are elevated berms built along straight lines. The tops are wide and level, and the grass is kept mowed. Walk a bit to see the canal on your left and marshes on your right. Turning around, head to the end of the levee trail and back to the parking lot at the Blue House.

Bonus Points

Sunnyhill Restoration Area is found on page 11 of the East Section guide to the Great Florida Birding Trail. Nearby, Ocklawaha Prairie Restoration Area is another piece of the puzzle for restoring 15 miles of the historic Upper Ocklawaha River Channel. From State Road 40, take County Road 314A going south; then turn right on 137th Street and go to the grassy parking lot and trailhead. An informational kiosk has free brochures with a trail map. From the trailhead to an observation platform is eight-tenths of a mile, while an upland loop trail is 3.4 miles, and a levee walk goes for 10.8 miles.

After walking along a grassy area with a hardwood hammock on one side, you cross over a canal to access the levee. Once over the canal and up on the levee, look for a boardwalk that goes out into the marshes. This is prime bird watching, especially in winter months. Plus

CENTRAL FLORIDA

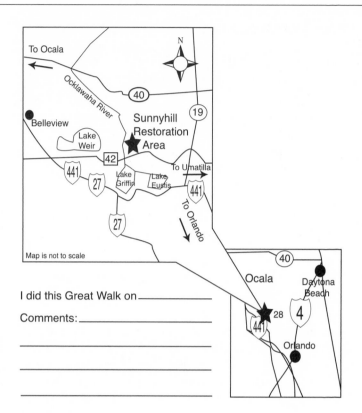

CENTRAL FLORIDA

I did this Great Walk on _____

Comments: _____

_____

_____

_____

it isn't every day you actually get to walk out into a marsh and be surrounded by it.

Trip Essentials

Name: Walking with Friends: Sunnyhill Restoration Area, St. Johns River Water Management District, Umatilla

Type of walk: Nature/birding

Length of walk: 2 miles for suggested walk

Time to finish: 1 to 2 hours, with many stops for bird watching

Difficulty: Easy. Dirt and grass surface. Wheelchair accessible.

Appeals to: Nature buffs, photographers, and birders (listed on page 11 of the East Section guide to the Great Florida Birding Trail)

Guides: Self-guided

Address: 19561 SE Highway 42, Umatilla, FL 32784

Phone: (352) 821-2066

Web site: www.sjrwmd.com

Cost: None

Getting there: Going south on U.S. 441 from Belleview, turn left onto County Road 42. Go through Weirsdale. Stay on C.R. 42. The entrance for the Blue House is on the north side of C.R. 42, 5.9 miles east of Weirsdale and just after you cross over a bridge.

GPS coordinates: (approximate) N 28° 59 36.7 W 81° 50 04.5

Hours: Daylight

Restrooms: Blue House and staff office just inside gate

Water/food: Bring water; no food available

Dogs: Leashed

Lunch ideas: American, at Duck's Dam Diner, 9685 Southeast Highway 464C, Ocklawaha, FL 32179, phone (352) 288-8332; American, at Billy's Cafe, 13752 North U.S. Highway 441, Lady Lake, FL 32159, phone (352) 259-8988

CENTRAL FLORIDA

29

Garden of Delights

Harry P. Leu Gardens, Orlando

Quick quiz: What is your first image of Orlando? Long lines of traffic? Your frazzled family waiting with ten thousand of your closest friends to get into a major attraction? True. All true. Been there. Done that.

There is another side to Orlando, another face. This one is gracious and leisurely, far removed from long lines and cartoon characters. If you are ready for a change of pace, and you like blooming landscapes, then it is time to discover the Harry P. Leu Gardens.

With the gardens tucked into an old Orlando residential area, getting there can be bit of a maze, turning left and right on unfamiliar city streets. But well-posted directional signs keep promising that Leu Gardens is up ahead. Trust the signs. You will get there.

In 1961, Harry and Mary Jane Leu gave the City of Orlando their home and the surrounding 50 acres. It is a gift that keeps on giving.

After parking in a shaded lot, go inside a white mansion, the Garden House, built in 2003. You'll be tempted right away to visit the botanical library and the gift shop. Resist. They will still be there when you get back from your walk.

Exit the Garden House through a side door on the left. Open up the free map you were given. Hold it flat in front of you so that the Garden House (on the north end) is next to your chest and the rest of the map points away from you. With this orientation, you can't get lost on the meandering paths.

A walkway leads down a slope from the Garden House to a tropical stream garden completed in 2000. Huge banana trees vie for space with gingers, ferns, lobster claws, palms, and bromeliads. Water from Lake Rowena circulates through a stream. It is shady, dense, and lush with tropical exuberance.

A terra-cotta pot and cactus plant in the home demonstration garden at Harry P. Leu Gardens, Orlando.

CENTRAL FLORIDA

Next, consult your map and make a choice—left to the demonstration gardens or straight ahead to the Leu House Museum (free tours available) and more gardens.

We turned left to the demonstration gardens. Opened in 2003, these gardens use plants and architecture, techniques, and materials that work in Central Florida.

One section has raised beds, really raised, to table height. This is for wheelchair gardeners or those who just don't want to bend over to the ground. Raised gardening makes so much sense. The pathways through the gardens are used to demonstrate different ways to lay brick and tile.

As you walk, good signage gives historical information and plant identification. The butterfly garden, next to the Florida Cracker homestead vegetable garden, is a must-see. A thick riot of color lines the pathways. Butterflies are everywhere. For those who are into the biggest and the best, Leu Gardens has the largest camellia collection in the South and the largest formal rose garden in Florida.

Benches are thoughtfully placed under trees, inviting you to sit and think about things. We thought about Mary Jane and Harry Leu, the final owners of this property. Buying the tract in 1936, they traveled the world, bringing back all sorts of plants. Those were the days before customs restrictions on living organisms.

These gardens are a blessing. The 50 acres could have been bull-dozed for a shopping mall. Thank goodness it was spared and that the City of Orlando is committed to its growth.

The Harry P. Leu Gardens, with their meandering paths and variety, will have their way with you quietly, and at moments dramatically. Savor them all.

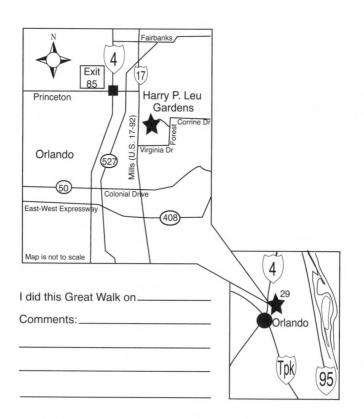

I did this Great Walk on _____

Comments: _____

_____

_____

_____

Bonus Points

After walking around the gardens, check your watch. The Leu House Museum is open from 10 a.m. to 4 p.m. Tours are given every 30 minutes on the hour and half hour. There is no charge. The last tour is 3.30 p.m. In July, the Leu House Museum is closed.

You can save money on Monday mornings from 9 a.m. to noon, when admission to the gardens is free.

Community education is a priority. After talking a walk through the gardens, consider coming back for a class. On their Web site, www.leugardens.org, click "Education" on the menu bar to find classes for all ages and interests.

A recent look at the site showed a children's class called "Critter Watch and Garden Projects." Children were advised to bring a jar if they wanted to make a terrarium. Gee, can adults come too? What fun. Under "Cooking Classes," we found a chance to make soup, create dishes from ingredients found in the gardens, and a lesson on Indian cuisine.

Trip Essentials

Name: Garden of Delights: Harry P. Leu Gardens, Orlando

Type of walk: Botanical

Length of walk: More than 3 miles of winding paths through 13 separate gardens

Time to finish: 2 to 3 hours

Difficulty: Easy, all pavement. Wheelchair accessible.

Appeals to: Gardeners, butterfly enthusiasts, and history buffs (Leu House Museum)

Guides: Self-guided. Guides available for 10 or more; book in advance; separate fee.

Address: 1920 N. Forest Avenue, Orlando, FL 32803

Phone: (407) 246-2620

Web site: www.leugardens.org

Cost: $5 adults; $1 grades K–12; free prekindergarten. Free on Mondays 9 a.m. to noon.

Getting there: From I-4, take exit 85, Princeton Street, and follow the signs. Princeton dead-ends at N. Mills Avenue (Highway 17-92). Turn

CENTRAL FLORIDA

right and go to second traffic light (Virginia Drive). Turn left onto Virginia and go about 1 mile, following curve to left. Main gate is on the left.

GPS coordinates: (Orlando) N28° 53806 W081°37944

Hours: Grounds, 9 a.m. to 5 p.m. every day except Christmas

Restrooms: In the Garden House at entrance; also near Leu House Museum

Water/food: 5 water fountains sprinkled along the paths; no food available

Dogs: No

Lunch ideas: Down-home cooking, at College Park Café, 2304 Edgewater Drive, Orlando, FL 32804, phone (407) 420-9892; American, Caribbean, and European, at White Wolf Café, 1829 North Orange Avenue, Orlando, FL 32804, phone (407) 895-9911

CENTRAL FLORIDA

30

Guided Nighttime Turtle Walk

Archie Carr National Wildlife Refuge, Vero Beach

She hears music in the night, an ancient song written over 200 million years ago. We strain to hear the words, but they elude us. But the primordial melody sings to a pregnant loggerhead sea turtle, as it has for generations. She cannot refuse the siren call even though it means abandoning the safety of her ocean world for several hours to enter an alien environment called land.

And leave she will, hauling her huge body weighing hundreds of pounds out of the water. Gravity takes over. The agile swimmer's shape becomes a dead weight she has to drag along the sand. Straining with each push, she uses flippers meant for swimming to propel her body up the beach. Her tracks look like a tractor passed this way.

Digging a shallow body pit, she settles into this space and then uses back flippers to dig a deeper cavity in the sand behind her. Next her rear flippers curl up with a contraction. She deposits 80–120 eggs. The look on her face as she lays her eggs is unfathomable, as if she is on another plane of existence. She doesn't care that you are there. She is on a mission and nothing will stop her. Loggerhead sea turtles are designated as a "threatened" species, while the other sea turtles that visit Florida's beaches—Kemp's ridley, hawksbill, green, and leatherback—are listed as "endangered."

Because the "threatened" designation denotes a less critical situation than the "endangered" label, groups with permits may organize guided nighttime turtle walks to view loggerheads during nesting season in June and July.

This is a walking experience where you can bring children and grandchildren. They should be old enough to stay up from past 9 p.m. to midnight and to follow directions such as only talking in whispers.

Children should also be able to walk without discomfort through soft beach sand.

On your walk you may or may not encounter a nesting loggerhead turtle. But even just being on the beach in the middle of the night, with the stars and the sand and the possibility of seeing a sea turtle, makes this a walk worth taking more than once.

To find groups in Florida that offer turtle walks, network with people who have taken a walk or research on the Internet (see Bonus Points). These nonprofit groups are licensed to guide walks during nesting season, and the number allowed on a guided walk is limited. Signup is imperative. Slots go fast.

I joined a weeknight tour organized by the Caribbean Conservation Corporation based in Gainesville. The location for the walk was the Archie Carr National Wildlife Refuge near Sebastian Inlet on the east coast. For the walk they suggest wearing dark clothing and shoes, bringing water and insect repellent, and leaving flashlights and cameras with flashes at home.

The tour leader wore rubber booties, the same kind worn by scuba divers. Tennis shoes will work too. Flip-flops do not. Some people wearing sandals took them off and walked barefoot. This is not a good idea. You can't see what you are stepping on in the dark, even with moonlight.

At 9 p.m., we all gathered in an auditorium for a slide presentation about sea turtles. For starters, I didn't know they were reptiles. Did you? They spend their lives in the ocean and can live seventy to eighty years. At about twenty-five years of age, the reproductive cycle kicks in. Reptiles lay eggs, so the female has to come on land to do this.

We head for a nearby county park in our own cars. Standing together on a boardwalk overlooking the beach, we wait while scouts walk the beach, looking for signs of nesting activity.

Here is something truly astonishing. The female loggerhead turtle will come back to nest at the beach were she was born. Think of it: mother deposits eggs and leaves. Eggs hatch in sixty days or so. Hatchlings boil up out of the sand at night and race to the sea, swimming fast to avoid predators. Years later, full-grown females born on this beach return to lay their eggs.

A loggerhead sea turtle laying eggs. Photo courtesy of the U.S. Fish and Wildlife Service.

CENTRAL FLORIDA

How do they find the place of their birth? Do they follow the stars? Is it the currents? Scientists have lots of theories, but they don't know. Perhaps it is the ancient melody that leads them, that song we cannot hear.

A scout calls on the portable radio to say a loggerhead has built a body pit and is about to lay eggs. We walk a fair distance down the beach. The sand is soft and the going tough for those out of shape. We walk single file, talking in whispers.

At the nesting site, the children are invited to come forward and make a circle behind the turtle. Lying on the sand, heads on hands, they watch the egg-laying process. The group leader shines a red light on the event, and the adults ring themselves behind the children. Not a word is spoken. We are stunned, all of us, even the children.

The calm, otherworldly look on her face was humbling. Do we think the sun rises and sets with us? Here is an ancient sea creature from the time of the dinosaurs whose ancestors did this very same thing. She knows much about longevity. We can learn from her.

Humans are a sea turtle's worst nightmare. Some countries allow consumption of sea turtles for food and shell products. Others ban sea-turtle food and products.

Beachfront property owners who leave lights on during nesting season disorient hatchlings; they go to the light instead of the bright horizon over the water—and they die. Plastic bags discarded on the beach become a death meal for sea turtles.

We leave reluctantly for the long walk back. The female loggerhead is throwing sand over her nest, slowly turning around, getting ready to go back to her ocean world.

It is midnight. We've had a life experience that will never leave us. It is our duty now to make other people care about sea turtles. Perhaps a child who comes on a turtle walk another night will grow up and find a way to save sea turtles. I hope so. Maybe someday we will finally hear their song and understand.

Bonus Points

Florida beaches have 90 percent of all nestings for loggerheads and all for the greens and leatherbacks. About 40 percent of the nestings in Florida for greens, loggerheads, and leatherbacks take place on the east coast from southern Brevard County to northern Indian River County.

The Archie Carr National Wildlife Refuge covers 20 miles of coastal dune habitat from Melbourne Beach to Wabasso Beach. It is the most important nesting area in the Western Hemisphere for loggerhead turtles.

The Bureau of Protected Species Management (BPSM) under the Florida Fish and Wildlife Conservation Commission permits organizations on the east and west coasts to offer public sea turtle watches. The group locations on the Atlantic Ocean stretch from Canaveral National Seashore to Miami. For a complete list of current permit holders and their contact information, call BPSM at (850) 922-4330 or (561) 575-5407 or go to this Web site: www.floridaconservation.org/psm.

Here are several suggestions: Sebastian Inlet State Park, 9700 South A1A, Melbourne Beach, FL 32951, phone (321) 984-4852, takes reservations for June turtle walks starting May 15. Reservations for July walks open up on June 15. Walks start at 9 p.m. five nights a week and generally last until midnight. Three different groups conduct walks on various nights of the week. All their reservations are made through Sebastian. The groups are the Caribbean Conservation Corporation, Archie Carr National Wildlife Refuge, and Sebastian Inlet State Park. Web site at www.floridastateparks.org.

Sea Turtle Preservation Society, P.O. Box 510988-0988, Melbourne Beach, FL 32951, phone (321) 676-1701, has turtle walks five nights a week in June and four nights a week in July. They ask for a $7 donation per person, and the maximum group size is 35.

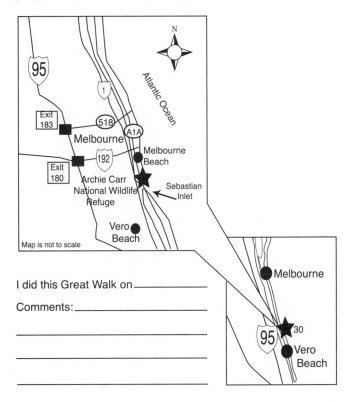

I did this Great Walk on _____

Comments: _____

_____

_____

_____

Reservations are taken starting May 1. Walks begin with a Power-Point presentation and then continue on the beach. The Web site is: www.seaturtlespacecoast.org.

Loggerhead Marinelife Center, inside Loggerhead Park at 14200 U.S. Highway One, Juno Beach, FL 33408, phone (561) 627-8280, takes reservations online for turtle walks in June and July. Walks are given on Tuesday and Wednesday nights. There is an $8 charge per person. Web site: www.marinelife.org.

John D. MacArthur Beach State Park, 10900 State Road 703, North Palm Beach, FL 33408, phone (561) 624-6952 (Nature Center), opens registration for turtle walks the day after Memorial Day. Cost is $5 per person, payable in advance. Nights for turtle walks in June and July are staggered. Park gates lock at 8:30 p.m.; plan to be at the park by 8:15 p.m. A slide presentation is given first at the Nature Center while scouts are on the beach looking for nesting activity. Then the group walks to the beach. If nothing happens by 11:30 p.m., they call it a night. Web site: www.floridastateparks.org.

Trip Essentials

Name: Guided Nighttime Turtle Walk: Archie Carr National Wildlife Refuge, Vero Beach

Type of walk: Nature

Length of walk: Depends on how far down the beach nesting activity is found. May be one-fourth to one-half mile one way.

Time to finish: 2 to 3 hours, depending on nesting activity

Difficulty: Moderate. Walking on sand. Not handicapped accessible.

Appeals to: Families, grandparents with grandchildren, nature buffs, and anyone wanting an experience of a lifetime

Guides: Required

Address: Three groups—Caribbean Conservation Corporation; Archie Carr National Wildlife Refuge; and Sebastian Inlet State Park—all use the same park phone number for turtle-walk reservations. Sebastian Inlet State Park, 9700 South A1A, Melbourne Beach, FL 32951

Phone: Sebastian Inlet State Park (321) 984-4852

Web site: www.floridaconservation.org/psm for complete list of permitted public sea turtle watches; www.cccturtle.org for turtle issues

Cost: Some turtle walk groups do have a requested donation; others are free.

Getting there: From I-95, take exit 183, Route 518, Eau Gallie Blvd. to Melbourne. Route 518 ends at A1A; turn right, go about 13 miles to sign that reads "State Park Marina." This is the location of Sebastian Inlet Administration Building, where the presentation is given if you are taking a walk with Caribbean Conservation Corporation. If you go over the Sebastian Inlet bridge, you've gone too far.

GPS coordinates: (Sebastian Inlet North Jetty Light) N 27° 86.167 W 080° 44.667

Hours: Usually 9 p.m. to midnight

Restrooms: Available where the slide presentation is given. None on the beach.

Water/food: Bring your own water; no food available

Dogs: No

Dinner ideas: American, at New England Eatery & Pub, 5670 South Highway A1A, Melbourne Beach, FL 32951, phone (321) 723-6080; American, at Surfin' Turtle Bar & Grill, 3830 South Highway A1A, Melbourne Beach, FL 32951, phone (321) 725-5900

CENTRAL FLORIDA

Part IV

Southwest Florida

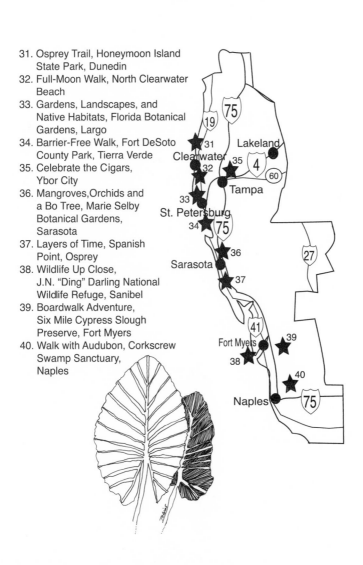

31

Count the Osprey

Honeymoon Island State Park, Dunedin

Wildlife is wild, which means unpredictable. Having said that, the Osprey Trail at Honeymoon Island State Park in Dunedin is aptly named.

There are no guarantees you will see osprey. It could be a vacation day for them. But chances are good you will see ospreys. Make that very good indeed. The Osprey Trail goes through one of the last remaining South Florida virgin slash-pine stands. Ospreys love using these trees as nesting sites.

The day my son Chris and I visited, we stopped at the trailhead to read the Osprey Trail sign. As we were reading, an osprey flew overhead, crying loudly. We thought this was a good beginning.

The kidney-shaped trail is 1 mile out and back. In addition to the slash-pine forest, you will see coastal communities including a mangrove swamp, sea-grass flats, marsh, tidal flats, and coastal strands.

Most of the trail is a good 8 feet wide, a sand trail covered with a carpet of pine needles. Dogs are allowed, and owners are advised to clean up after their pets.

One of the first kiosks we encountered on the trail is Kid's Corner. Local schoolchildren walked this trail and drew pictures of what they saw and found: a great horned owl, sea grapes, an osprey, poison ivy, a banana spider, and a Spanish bayonet. The text challenges us to see if we can find the same things.

This is a great trail for kids and for questions that will keep them going.

How many osprey nests can you find?

How many ospreys can you see?

Where are the sea grapes?

Dead trees, or snags, provide nesting areas for ospreys and other birds on the Osprey Trail, Honeymoon Island State Park, Dunedin.

The Osprey Trail is a testimonial to the value of dead trees, called snags. They are left standing in state parks to provide nests for birds of prey and other animals.

At one point, an osprey with a fish in its claws flew to a dead tree, landed on a limb, and began eating. Another osprey in a nearby dead tree started calling plaintively. But the osprey with the fish wasn't sharing. It was his sushi, and that was that.

As the trail gets closer to the end of the peninsula, vegetation thins out. The atmosphere is foggy, and we smell tangy salt water from the Gulf of Mexico.

Need to lose some stress in your life? The Osprey Trail is the place to come. The more we slow down, the more we appreciate what is around us. But just as we're appreciating wild Florida, along comes a walker with a cell phone in her ear. She is not looking around, fully intent on her conversation, talking, listening.

It is jarring. There should be a sign at every trail, wild place, garden, and historic walk that instructs: "Turn off your cell phone. Put it away.

You can't be in two places at once. If you are talking on the phone you will miss this moment. It is that simple."

Near the tip of the peninsula, you have a choice of staying on the Osprey Trail or taking the Pelican Trail, which runs closer to the water. We opt for the Pelican Trail. Soon we encounter deep puddles in the road. With the tide out, we saw hundreds of tiny fiddler crabs and the small holes that are their homes. It might be tempting to pick one up and put it in a jar. They live here. Removing them is illegal.

At one point, the trail turns to shell, and the going becomes tough. The shell is deep and soft. You really have to watch your footing.

Pelican Trail rejoins the Osprey Trail, and they both end at the trailhead. Next to the trailhead is a large picnic area with bathrooms, showers, water, and a playground. There is a designated swimming area farther down the road, closer to the ranger station. The wide sandy beach is on the Gulf of Mexico. A gift shop and snack bar are located at the swimming area.

On the other side of the road, across from the beach, a bird observation area is set aside overlooking St. Joseph Sound. Honeymoon Island also has a separate pet beach with showers. This is a place for all ages and all kinds of interests, from dog lovers to bird-watchers, beach walkers, and trekkers looking to discover wild Florida.

As islands go, Honeymoon Island is young, only seven thousand years old. The Tocobaga tribe lived here. Spanish explorers came and went. Some stayed. Hurricanes swept through and changed the shape of things. In 1921, the island was split by a hurricane, creating Caladesi Island to the south along with Hurricane Pass.

The Honeymoon phase started in 1939, when a New York entrepreneur bought the island and named it Honeymoon Isle. Palm-thatched bungalows were built. Newlyweds answering magazine ads could win a two-week Florida vacation on Honeymoon Isle.

But the honeymoon ended with World War II. The newlywed destination was requisitioned by the military as a Recreation and Relaxation (R&R) retreat for factory workers. Development took place until 1970, when environmental studies halted any further dredging and filling. In 1974, the state bought the last undeveloped 416 upland acres and 2,400 submerged acres of Honeymoon Island. Dunedin donated its 22-acre beach in 1982.

Bonus Points

Caladesi Island State Park is accessible by private boat or a pontoon ferry that departs from Honeymoon Island State Park.

The ferry is walk-on only. Cars stay in the Honeymoon parking lot. Weather permitting, ferries leave on the hour starting at 10 a.m. Visitors at Caladesi Island can stay 4 hours. The islands have white sand beaches. A 3-mile nature trail goes through the interior. Picnic tables, restrooms, a marina, cabanas for rent, a snack bar, and a gift shop are all on the island.

For those coming in by private boat, the admission fee to Caladesi Island State park is $4 for up to 8 people. Kayakers pay $1. Ferry fees from Honeymoon Island are $9 per adult; $5.50 for children 4–12; children under 4 are admitted free. Plus, the entrance fee to Honeymoon Island State Park is $5 per vehicle for up to 8 people.

The address for Caladesi Island State Park is: #1 Causeway Boule-

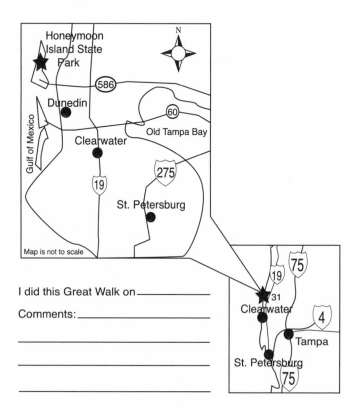

vard, Dunedin, FL 34698, phone (727) 469-5918. For ferry information, call (727) 734-5263.

Storms have changed the shape of the coastline. Maps do not show this, but it is possible to take a long walk onto Caladesi Island from the mainland. From North Clearwater Beach, it is a 4-mile walk to Caladesi. There is no charge for walking onto the island.

Trip Essentials

Name: Count the Osprey: Honeymoon Island State Park, Dunedin
Type of walk: Nature trail inside a state park
Length of walk: 2 miles
Time to finish: 1 1/2 to 2 hours
Difficulty: Easy. Dirt trails. Handicapped accessible.
Appeals to: Families with school-age children, photographers, and birders (listed on page 20, West Florida guide to the Great Florida Birding Trail)
Guides: Self-guided. Numerous signboards with good suggestions for activities.
Address: Honeymoon Island State Park, #1 Causeway Blvd., Dunedin, FL 34698
Phone: (727) 469-5942
Web site: www.floridastateparks.org
Cost: None for the walk. Park entrance fees are $5 per car for up to 8 people; $3 for car with 1 occupant; sunset fee of $3 per vehicle starting 1 hour prior to sunset.
Getting there: From Alternate 19 in Dunedin, take S.R. 586 west over Dunedin Causeway to Honeymoon Island.
GPS coordinates: N 28° 06.944 W 082° 83.056
Hours: 8 a.m. until sundown
Restrooms: Adjacent to trailhead
Water/food: Water at restrooms; food at Honeymoon Café inside the park
Dogs: Allowed on trail with 6-foot hand-held lead. Honeymoon also has a designated Pet Beach for dogs on 6-foot hand-held lead.
Lunch ideas: Varied, at Kellys for Just About Everything, 319 East Main Street, Dunedin, FL 34698, phone (727) 736-5284; Mexican and vegetarian, at Casa Tina's, 369 Main Street, Dunedin, FL 34698, phone (727) 737-9226

SOUTHWEST FLORIDA

32

Full-Moon Walk with T'ai Chi/Du Gong

North Clearwater Beach

"When the sun goes down, shorebirds morph into mystery silhouettes. We stand, breathing deep, raising our hands skyward, as waves wash over our feet. A full moon rises, huge and luminous, flooding the landscape with night knowledge."

These words, written when the sand was still between my toes, are my small attempt to capture a huge experience—walking on a Florida beach at night under a full moon.

We did just that at North Clearwater Beach. You can do a self-guided or a guided walk. We chose guided. Four of us joined Linda Taylor, an eco-guide who started moonlight walks ten years ago as a wellness/health walk.

Linda had her own life journey to get to the beach. She was the first woman regional salesperson for Stairmaster, traveling all over the country, making deals with gyms, working in a very competitive, fast-paced environment. When she realized climbing the corporate ladder was not living the life she really valued, Linda left. She started "It's Our Nature" tours, focusing on kayak and walking tours for women.

The moonlight walk was one of her first walks and has remained her most enduring. She conducts these walks once a month from November through April. The walk, originally started for women, supports wellness by empowering women to try things they have not tried before or would not try by themselves, like being out on a beach at night.

Linda quickly found that men also liked this moonlight walk, even preferred it to a gym workout. In the gym it is easy to let the body do the work and the mind drift off. All the surfaces, like the treadmill, are

A drawing of shorebird silhouettes, showing how birds appear at night. *Left*, great blue heron; *right*, black skimmer; *upper middle*, royal tern; *lower middle*, herring gull. Drawing by author.

smooth. Not so on the beach. You have to be connected to your surroundings as you walk on sand.

She soon opened the moonlight walk to everyone. On the night we went, it was a family affair with my son Chris, along with a writer friend and her seven-year-old granddaughter.

Perhaps because she wasn't as tall, our friend's granddaughter found shells and seaweed that the adults missed. We never could identify the birds looking for food along the shoreline. If you can find a silhouette guide to shorebirds, bring that with you. Like the beach, the birds lose their color at night.

Linda noted that more birds are feeding at night than in past years, and that may be a concern. Studies have yet to be done on why this is so. One theory: the increased use of Florida beaches by people and dogs is disturbing shorebird feeding routines. In fact, sometimes they can't even get to the water's edge, leaving them unable to feed during daylight hours.

Dogs are allowed on the beaches on retractable leads. Often people don't realize they are flushing birds' nests, as the nests are simple depressions in the sand. With all these stresses, birds have to wait until nightfall and the departure of humans to feed. This cuts back on their nesting time.

When walking on the beach, a rhythmic walking pace sets in. Plus, walking at night is a sensory experience that makes you use your ears, eyes, and sense of touch in different ways.

Smells we might have missed during the day, when our eyes were busy checking out the beach scene, begin to take center stage. A sharp, pungent tang emanates from seaweed drying on the beach. Salt air seasoned with marine life rolls in from the Gulf of Mexico. The offshore breeze is overlaid with subtle hints of flowers in full bloom or exotic spices, surely blown in from faraway places.

Looking up from the water's edge and over to where the land rises, we see sea oats silhouetted against the night sky. Sand dunes are building up nicely, a natural event and not the result of beach nourishment.

Beyond the dunes, the entire coastline of North Clearwater Beach is beset with condominiums, hotels, and private residences. Yet even with all that light shining from windows, streetlights, porches, and verandas, we still find Venus in the southwest sky. Linda tells us that how much you see in the sky is determined in part by humidity. As the weather cools and humidity disappears, the skies are clearer.

The full moon begins to rise in the east behind the buildings. The entire beach and the water become luminous with moonlight. We look at the moon through binoculars. It looks quite wonderful and incredibly large. Who would have thought to bring binoculars on a night walk? Linda did. It is a good recommendation, both for looking at the moon and the stars.

After about a mile, we stop at the water's edge to do Du Gong breathing exercises. By now our senses have adjusted to the night scene. We smell and hear and see things differently. Facing the water, we breathe in slowly through our noses, raise our arms, let the breath out through our mouths, and slowly lower our arms.

As anyone who has done yoga, Pilates, running, or swimming can attest, breathing is everything. We breathe some more, slowly, deeply, in resonance with the world around us.

Waves roll in, almost lapping at our feet, slowly, steadily, with a rhythm close to ours as we breathe in and out. We feel connected to the waves, the moon, the air, the stars, and the night. Everything seems simplified, clearer, and infused with energy.

The night deepens. It gets colder. We are glad we brought jackets. The return walk is quiet, slow, and meditative. We stop more than once to look at stars.

Our walk started on North Clearwater Beach at the intersection of Mandalay Avenue and Rockaway Street. A public parking lot is located here. A good starting point is the old fishing pier, now reduced to a piece of a pier that doesn't go all the way to the water. We walked north along the beach toward Caladesi Island for about a mile before turning around.

We had an excellent guide, but a moonlight walk could easily be self-guided. Children will find the after-dark experience exciting. This is a great time to pique their interest in stars and have contests to identify any shorebirds by their silhouettes.

Wear shoes to the site. Going barefoot on the beach is optional. We did, but be forewarned it is harder at night to see where you are stepping and what you are stepping on. Bring a flashlight just in case it is needed. We came early for dinner at a nearby beach restaurant and then started our walk as the sun went down.

Seeing the sunset and the moonrise on North Clearwater Beach was a deep, enriching, and energizing experience. The beach never sleeps. It has a whole different life at night, a life illuminated once a month by the full moon.

Bonus Points

Pier 60 Park in Clearwater Beach, at the foot of Memorial Causeway (State Road 60), has a nightly sunset celebration. Sunset at Pier 60 is a free, family event with artisans, crafters, and street performers; it includes a dog-trick show, face painting, and live music. Everything is weather permitting. Pier 60 has a large playground, a very long pier, the sunset, and the beach—all good reasons to celebrate. For more information, call their Festival Voicemail at (727) 449-6060.

If you want to know what is under the water, allow a good 2 hours to take in everything, including presentations, at the Clearwater Marine Aquarium, 249 Windward Passage, Clearwater, FL 33767, phone (727)

SOUTHWEST FLORIDA

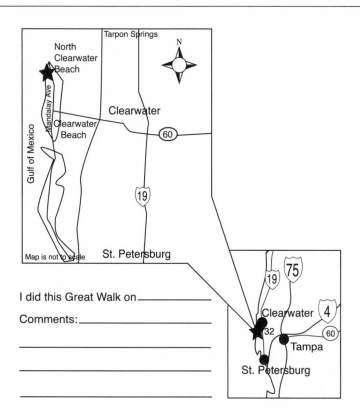

441-1790. Hours are Monday through Friday from 9 a.m. to 5 p.m.; Saturday 9 a.m. to 4 p.m.; and Sunday 11 a.m. to 4 p.m.

The staff gives a series of presentations every day on subjects ranging from sea turtles to stingrays to dolphins. Visit their Web site at www.cmaquarium.org to get the daily schedule.

The Suncoast Seabird Sanctuary, 18328 Gulf Boulevard, Indian Shores, FL 33785, phone (727) 391-6211, is open 365 days of the year from 9 a.m. to sunset. Admission is free. Donations accepted. Web site: www.seabirdsanctuary.org.

Its mission is rehabilitation and education. Public tours are given Wednesday and Sunday at 2 p.m. The facility is both wheelchair and stroller accessible. Do bring your camera. If you missed bird photos while walking along the beach, the sanctuary is the place to get that brown pelican up close and personal.

Trip Essentials

Name: Full Moon Walk with Tai Chi/Du Gong: North Clearwater Beach

Type of walk: Beach walk at night from sunset to a rising full moon

Length of walk: Approximately 2 miles

Time to finish: 1 1/2 hours

Difficulty: Mildly moderate. Trail is beach sand. Not wheelchair accessible.

Appeals to: Families, birders, beachgoers who want to see a different side of the beach

Guides: "It's Our Nature" guide or self-guided

Address: Walk begins on North Clearwater Beach at the old pier.

Phone: It's Our Nature, Inc., (888) 535-7448 (toll-free) or (727) 441-2599

Web site: For the guide, Linda Taylor, www.itsournature.com; for the Clearwater area, www.floridasbeach.com.

Cost: $10 per person if guided; none if self-guided

Getting there: From downtown Clearwater, take State Road 60 west over the Memorial Causeway; turn right on Mandalay Avenue.

GPS coordinates: (Clearwater Beach Island) N 27° 98972 W 082° 82667

Hours: After the sun sets and the moon starts to rise

Restrooms: At public parking lot

Water/food: Water at restrooms; restaurants nearby

Dogs: Not advised for a night walk

Dinner ideas: American, at Frenchy's Rockaway Grill, 7 Rockaway Street, North Clearwater Beach, FL 33767, phone (727) 446-4844; American, at Britt's Beach Café, 201 South Gulfview Blvd., Clearwater Beach, FL 33767, phone (727) 461-5185

SOUTHWEST FLORIDA

33

Gardens, Landscapes, and Native Habitats

Florida Botanical Gardens, Largo

A Great Walk can happen where you would least expect it. Florida Botanical Gardens in Largo is such a place. Located off a busy highway lined with commercial development, you'd never guess a natural masterpiece thrives here, and you are welcome to visit.

The gardens are part of Pinewood Cultural Park, which also includes a living-history museum called Heritage Village and the Gulf Coast Museum of Art.

The gardens' welcome center is inside the Pinellas County Extension Office of the University of Florida's Institute of Food and Agricultural Services (IFAS). A free Pinewood Cultural Park brochure is available and contains an excellent map showing a loop trail (nine-tenths of a mile) going through all three parts of the park.

You may end up making your walk longer, as we did, by detouring through the native habitat and the Shirley McPherson Nature Trail. Also, side paths radiating from the loop trail lead to various gardens such as the Tropical Fruit Garden.

Florida Botanical Gardens excels in education. Signs give a plant's common name, Latin name, and information describing the amount of water and light needed for its propagation. You might want to bring a notebook and take notes.

Crossing a bridge over McKay Creek, we see a wood stork. On the other side of the creek, the whole landscape becomes lush and tropical. At McKay Creek Plaza and Pavilion there is a large courtyard flanked with huge planters containing the largest geranium I've ever seen.

A great egret checks out the signs at Florida Botanical Gardens, Largo.

SOUTHWEST FLORIDA

Inside the pavilion is an interactive video center. You can learn about the Florida Yards and Neighborhoods program. FYN was developed by the Institute of Food and Agricultural Sciences at University of Florida to enlist homeowners in addressing the problems of pollution and loss of natural habitats.

In addition, one wall in the pavilion is covered with a large butterfly display, Wings of Wonder, showing the life cycle of butterflies and the kinds of plants they need.

The plaza has restrooms and places to sit. Chairs are painted lavender, fitting right in with the tropical look. Just past the plaza is a large curved bench decorated with patterns of koi in tile—funky and fun. This bench is a creative prelude to the outdoor sculptures you will find farther down the pathway at the Gulf Coast Museum of Art.

To get to the Native Ecosystem Demonstration and Education Area, a separate walk from the looped trail, go between the Kiln House and the Studio Classrooms at Gulf Coast Museum of Art. The demonstration area entrance is across the parking lot behind these two buildings.

Here is wild Florida, tangled and untamed. We find it to be quite a contrast to the arranged gardens and displays. In this natural habitat, vines move in, climb up trees, and form umbrellas over bushes. Dead trees simply fall over, becoming shelter for wildlife and food for the next generation of plants and tree. Blackberry bushes flourish. A native plant guidebook would be helpful to have along on this trail.

Not to put too fine a point on it, but this is what your backyard would look like if you let it go. Perhaps a good idea, at least letting part of it go wild. It is acknowledging we are part of a chain of life that is more than manicured lawns and flowerbeds.

Back on the loop trail, we walk into the Bromeliad Garden with brick pathways, sculptures, and plants in a rainbow of colors. Crossing back over McKay Creek, you enter Heritage Village. The historic buildings here were transported to this site from different parts of Pinellas County. Exhibits, house tours, and the museum are open every day except Monday, but even the walk alone is informative. Near a lamppost in the village is the start of the Garden for the Blind. A parking lot with handicapped access is located near the garden exhibit. There is a fence at hand height, flat on top, with signs in English and Braille describing the nearby bushes.

As it winds through Heritage Village, the walk loop heads to the starting point at the Pinellas County Extension Office. On one side of Heritage Village, the Shirley McPherson Nature Trail is a short but sweet walk, less than a quarter of a mile. People have lived here for thousands of years. All relied on the land for the basic needs—food, shelter, water. The environment provided them with what they needed, and so their lives were intertwined with their surroundings. Walkers are encouraged to see the connections with these words: "As you walk the trail, understand the relationship of people with their environment. We hope you will gain a respect and appreciation for Florida's native plants and wildlife and their value for the past and the future."

Bonus Points

All three parts of Pinewood Cultural Park have special events, classes, workshops, and demonstrations.

Heritage Village is open Tuesday through Saturday from 10 a.m. to 4 p.m.; Sunday from 1 p.m. to 4 p.m.; closed on Monday. Admission is free. Donations are welcome. The address is: 11909 125th St. North, Largo, FL 33774, phone (727) 582-2123. The Web site is: www.pinellascounty.org/heritage.

The buildings have stories to tell. A group of St. Petersburg women drove livestock and wildlife from a city park and then raised funds to build the original Williams Park bandstand in 1894. The one you see today in Heritage Village is a replica.

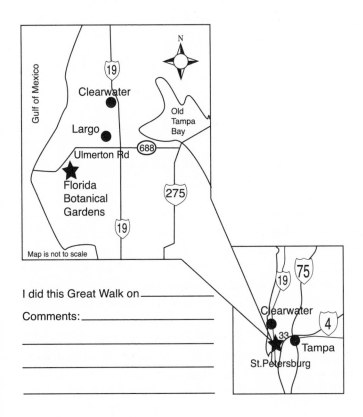

SOUTHWEST FLORIDA

On the day we walked the loop trail, children were coming to Heritage Village for a winter day-camp experience. A reenactor in period pioneer dress stirred cast-iron Dutch ovens suspended over a fire. Homemade pea soup was simmering in one pot; bread was being made in another. Two other pots held herbs in water. When cooked, black tea and onions turn different colors used to dye fabrics.

The Gulf Coast Museum of Art, the third part of Pinewood Cultural Park, features contemporary art by Florida artists and southeastern crafts. There are sculpture gardens, classrooms, a museum store, and nine galleries with both permanent and changing exhibits.

Admission is $5 for adults; $4 seniors; $3 students; children under 10 admitted free. The art museum is open Tuesday through Saturday, 8:30 a.m. to 4:30 p.m.; Sunday noon to 4 p.m.; closed on Monday.

On Saturday from 10 a.m. to 12 p.m., admission is free. The address is: 12211 Walsingham Road, Largo, FL 33778, phone (727) 518-6833. Web site: www.gulfcoastmuseum.org.

Trip Essentials

Name: Gardens, Landscapes, and Native Habitats: Florida Botanical Gardens, Largo

Type of walk: Botanical

Length of walk: .9-mile loop through Pinewood Cultural Park, including Florida Botanical Gardens, Heritage Village, and Gulf Coast Museum of Art

Time to finish: 45 minutes to 1 hour

Difficulty: Easy. Pavement, some dirt trails. Wheelchair accessible.

Appeals to: Homeowners, novice and experienced gardeners

Guides: Self-guided. Guided tours available by appointment, with a minimum of 20 people

Address: 12175 125th Street North, Largo, FL 33774

Phone: (727) 582-2100

Web site: www.flbg.org

Cost: Free

Getting there: Take Ulmerton Road (S.R. 688) going west. At 121st Ave., turn left into Pinewood Cultural Park.

GPS coordinates: (Largo) N 27° 90917 W 082° 7875

Hours: Gardens open 7 a.m. to 7 p.m.; Pinellas County Extension Office
  open 8 a.m. to 5 p.m. Monday through Saturday
Restrooms: At extension office building and Tropical Courtyard
Water/food: Water at restrooms; no food
Dogs: No
Lunch ideas: Florida Botanical Gardens is located in a commercial/indus-
  trial area. Recommend a brown bag lunch. Picnic tables with umbrel-
  las near the Palm Garden & Pavilion.

34

A Walk for Everyone

Fort DeSoto County Park, Tierra Verde

Imagine a coastal island trail where you can go if you are visually impaired and not have to worry about reading signs because information is on tape. Imagine a trail where you don't have to worry if you are physically challenged because the trail is barrier free.

There is such a trail at Fort DeSoto County Park in Tierra Verde. The Friends of Fort DeSoto first imagined it in 1997. Volunteer groups built the trail. The Barrier-Free Nature Trail, 2,200 feet long, begins alongside park headquarters.

All ages will find good vibes on this trail. It is a compressed shell trail with raised timbers placed 8 feet apart to mark the trail edges. There are rest areas with benches and water fountains. Six interpretive stations have boxes with two buttons each. You push a button to hear a tape. I know it can't be true, but the narrator sounds just like my political science professor in college.

The trail entrance has a number of cabbage palms, Sabal palmetto, a native of Florida's coastal regions and the Florida state tree. Sabals have tall, straight trunks and a huge crown of fronds. When breezes blow off Tampa Bay, the palm fronds rustle in the wind.

Strangler figs like sabal palms, and that is not good for the palm. The fig grows on the trunk or in the crown of the palm, then sends its root system down and around the trunk. It is strangling the palm, and, yes, the palm dies. Then the fig uses the decaying tree for food. Birds eat the fruits of the strangler fig, eject the seeds somewhere else, and the strangling goes on.

While all this natural drama slowly unfolds, human presence has been at work too. People have been part of this island's history for over five hundred years. The Tocobaga Indians were here. Then Spanish explorers passed through. The U.S. Army Corps of Engineers began surveying the area in the mid-1800s for possible use as coastal defense.

As a response to conflict with Cuba in 1898, Fort DeSoto was built on this barrier island and began operation in 1900. A military post, Fort Dade, was also built on nearby Egmont Key.

Picture what it was like being stationed here before air-conditioning, wearing wool uniforms with full-length trousers and long-sleeved shirts. Then add heat, rain, and mosquitoes.

One mosquito solution uses fish. The U.S. Army Corps of Engineers built a number of mosquito-control ditches. A ditch is alongside the Barrier-Free Nature Trail. Mosquito fish in the ditches act as natural insect control.

Along the sides of ditches are mangroves with roots anchoring the muddy bottom. Their leaves turn into organic matter called detritus, and a whole food chain depends on this detritus. Mangrove roots also provide nursery areas for young fish such as grouper.

The trail turns away from the mangroves and enters the dune area. Life is harsh here. Plants and animals have to be specialized to put up with sun, salt spray, blowing sands, flooding, and wind.

Over 290 different kinds of birds have been seen in the Fort DeSoto area. Sitting on a bench facing Tampa Bay is an easy way to start your bird count. The months of March through mid-May bring thousands of birds migrating to northern breeding grounds. Fort DeSoto and the long Bayway leading to it are favorite stopovers.

The barrier-free walk is on Mullet Key, only three thousand years old, quite young in the geologic scheme of things. The park has five islands or keys including Madelaine Key, St. Jean Key, St. Christopher Key, Bonne Fortune Key, and Mullet Key. Barrier islands and keys change daily as tides come in and go out.

Coming back to the trailhead and its canopy of sabal palms, turn right to visit the park headquarters adjacent to the Barrier-Free Nature Trail.

Look for free brochures on birds, shells, and self-guided walks at Fort DeSoto, on the beach, and at Arrowhead Nature Trail. There is a

SOUTHWEST FLORIDA

Looking down the barrel of a 12-inch M 1890-M1 mortar, Fort DeSoto Historic Area, Fort DeSoto County Park, Tierra Verde.

laminated guide to Tampa Bay birds. It is free. The guide can be used for a good project for children. Challenge them: How many birds in the guide can you find while we are here in the park?

Also inside the park headquarters there is a hands-on table. Pick up the skull of a dolphin, bird bills, or shells. Both children and adults will like examining this collection.

The park keeps a log of bird sightings. If you've seen a bird they don't have on their list, and have written or photographic evidence, they have an address for the Archbold Biological Station, and the biologists there will want to hear from you.

Consider bringing a picnic lunch and staying for a half day or more. A suggested plan would be to take the barrier-free walk and then visit Fort DeSoto. Move on to check out the Quartermaster Storehouse Museum and walk the beach on the self-guided tour that starts just below the fort. A brochure at the trailhead gives you beach background.

Note for beach walkers: be on the lookout for nesting birds. A beach is not like your backyard, where birds nest off the ground in trees.

Waterbirds make a small cavity right in the sand and lay eggs. The nests and the eggs are often hard to see. Disruption of nesting activity means those eggs won't hatch. Future generations of birds are then lost.

What can you do? Keep your distance. If birds appear agitated, move away. Terns and skimmers, for example, need a good 600-foot comfort zone during nesting season. Since the birds have to share the beach with humans, proximity is a problem. Don't let your children run at birds and make them fly.

After the beach visit, have lunch at one of the many picnic areas, go swimming, or take the Arrowhead Nature Trail. Sunscreen, hats, and water are all important. Remember to bring them.

Dog owners are welcome to take their dogs to a 2-acre fenced leash-free Paw Park. It has separate areas for big dogs and little dogs.

Bonus Points

In 2005, the park's North Beach area was voted the best beach in North America by Dr. Stephen Leatherman at Florida International University, also known as "Dr. Beach." The North Beach area has showers in the restrooms and also outdoor showers. North Beach is wide with an inlet of water that is warm and shallow. This is a great place for wading and swimming.

History buffs will love climbing around Fort DeSoto. Families with young children are also going to find it fascinating. At the park headquarters and the fort there are free brochures describing the Fort DeSoto Historic Trail and the Quartermaster Storehouse Museum. The trail has numbered stations that identify twenty-nine original buildings and structures.

Fort rooms are labeled over the doorways. When you are inside the Battery Room, you will realize quickly that it is a good place to let loose and yell. It is a great echo chamber. Kids will like this. My son Chris and I gave the chamber a good yelling workout. You are never too old to be a kid.

Arrowhead Nature Trail is 1.5 miles long and across from North Beach. There is a shortcut that can make the walk about a half mile long. A free brochure at the trailhead gives station numbers and explains the changing environment. Heed the advice to stay on the trail.

SOUTHWEST FLORIDA

SOUTHWEST FLORIDA

The historic Snell Arcade, built in 1928, is reflected in the windows of a modern office building on Central Avenue in St. Petersburg.

Not only does going off the trail disturb fragile ecosystems, but the area has abundant poison ivy.

Egmont Key National Wildlife Refuge and State Park can be accessed by boat only. The Fort DeSoto ferry leaves twice a day for Egmont, at 10 a.m. and 11 a.m., departing from the Fort DeSoto Bay Pier. Returns are at 2 p.m. and 3 p.m. Cost is $15. Check schedules as they change during the year. You walk onto the ferry and leave your car at the pier. For information, call (727) 867-6569 or visit this Web site: www.hubbardsmarina.com.

Bicyclists, inline skaters, walkers, and joggers find Fort DeSoto to be a little piece of heaven. Seven miles of wide, paved trails link North Beach, East Beach, the boat ramp, and the camping areas of the park. In addition, paved trails parallel much of the Pinellas Bayway leading to Fort DeSoto County Park.

Downtown St. Petersburg has history on every block. St. Petersburg was incorporated in 1903. Northerners flocked to St. Petersburg in the wintertime. The city was selling sunshine then, and it still does today. In the early 1900s, visitors stayed in small apartments, so small that a Murphy bed folded out in a combination living room/bedroom. Many people spent their time outdoors. Early city planners reflected this lifestyle by building wide streets, wide sidewalks, and city parks all along the bayfront.

Saint Petersburg Preservation Inc. does occasional downtown historic walking tours. Contact SPPI at P.O. Box 838, St. Petersburg, FL 33731, phone (727) 824-7802. The Web address is: www.stpetepreservation. org.

Bob Jeffrey, assistant development director for the City of St. Petersburg, is leading a project to put a historic downtown St. Petersburg walking tour in cyberspace. Anyone can download the brochure at

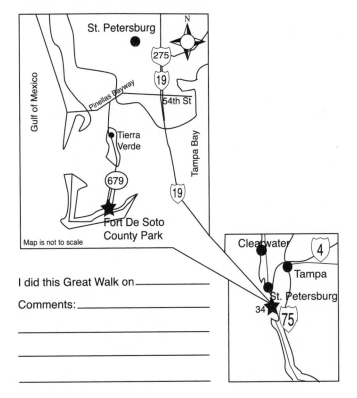

SOUTHWEST FLORIDA

www.stpete.org. On the menu, go to "City Departments," "Development Services."

M. C. Bob Leonard, a professor of history at Hillsborough Community College, maintains a Web site, www.floridahistory.org, with detailed information about Florida's West Coast. He has an excellent St. Petersburg guide, complete with directions (turn left, turn right), and the tour can be done by car or walked in 2 hours. His starting point is the St. Petersburg Pier.

At the pier entrance is the St. Petersburg Museum of History, 335 2nd Avenue Northeast, St. Petersburg, FL 33701, phone (727) 894-1052. Hours are noon to 7 p.m. on Monday; 10 a.m. to 5 p.m. Tuesday through Saturday; and noon to 5 p.m. on Sunday. Admission is $7 adults; $5 seniors; $3 children 7–17; children under 6 admitted free. See their Web site at www.spmoh.org.

Trip Essentials

Name: A Walk for Everyone: Fort DeSoto County Park, Tierra Verde
Type of walk: Nature
Length of walk: 2,200 feet
Time to finish: 30 to 40 minutes
Difficulty: Easy. Compacted dirt and shell trail. Handicapped accessible.
Appeals to: Children (who will like pushing the buttons to hear the tapes), photographers, families, nature lovers, anyone physically challenged, and birders (Fort DeSoto County Park is a designated Gateway on the Great Florida Birding Trail; see page 22 of the West Florida guide.)
Guides: Self-guided
Address: Fort DeSoto County Park, 3500 Pinellas Bayway South, Tierra Verde, FL 33715
Phone: (727) 582-2267
Web site: www.pinellascounty.org
Cost: Two toll booths on the Bayway, one for 50¢; one for 35¢
Getting there: Going south on I-275 in St. Petersburg, take exit 17 going west onto Pinellas Bayway (State Road 682). At second traffic light, turn left (south) onto Pinellas Bayway (State Road 679). Park is at the end of the road.
GPS coordinates: N 27° 61.944 W 082° 72.778

Hours: Park headquarters are open from 8 a.m. to 5 p.m. seven days a
   week. Park closes at sundown. Fishing pier and boat ramps open 24
   hours a day.
Restrooms: At park headquarters, Fort DeSoto, and North Beach
Water/food: Water fountains on the trail; food at fort snack bar
Dogs: Dogs on 6-foot hand-held lead. Not allowed on beaches or in
   picnic areas. There is a 2-acre fenced leash-free Paw Park.
Lunch ideas: Shaded picnic areas and shelters at East Beach and North
   Beach. Suggest bringing a picnic lunch.

SOUTHWEST FLORIDA

35

Celebrate the Cigars

Historic Walk, Ybor City

Carmen gently slips the ebony castanets over her fingers. The right hand is female and does all the talking. She raises her right hand. The castanet rips loose with a volley of sound. The left hand is male. His job is to say "yes, dear," "yes, dear." She clicks the castanet in the left hand, once, twice.

Her castanets are more than sixty years old. Carmen Morales Cares, born and raised in Ybor City, brings them out of her coat pocket reverently. They gleam with the patina of age and great care. Ybor City is a lot like Carmen and her castanets, aging with a patina of great care that spans the years.

This is a city with a passionate past. A good place to start inhaling the past is at the Ybor City Museum State Park. It is located on a historic block that includes a museum housed in the 1926 Ferlita Bakery, a renovated casita that is a museum store, several restored houses used by cigar workers, and a Mediterranean garden.

On Saturday mornings, for a fee, you can team up with a guide for a historic walking tour of the museum and a renovated cigar worker's home, as well as a stroll through the Ybor City's National Historic Landmark District.

No reservations taken. Sign up and pay the $6 fee at the museum store next to the museum. The store opens at 10 a.m., and the tour starts at 10:30 a.m. (see Trip Essentials). This fee also entitles you to come back the same day (to visit the museum only) for free. Museum entrance fee alone is $3.

Carmen was our guide the day my son Chris and I signed up for the tour. Leading us first to the walled Mediterranean garden next to

The museum at Ybor City Museum State Park was originally a bakery. Photo by
Christopher Tobias.

the museum, she stops next to a white marble bust of Don Vicente
Martinez Ybor, founder of Ybor City.

It is hard for us in the twenty-first century, standing before a cold
marble statue with sightless eyes, to get a feeling for this man born in
the nineteenth century. Carmen and the other guides come close to
making the connection because they were born in Ybor City and know
the stories firsthand. These are the children of parents who worked in
the cigar factories and related trades.

Cuba in the nineteenth century was still a Spanish colony. Born
in Valencia, Spain, in 1816, Don Ybor immigrated to Cuba at the age
of fourteen. He learned to make cigars and was a tobacco broker. In
1885, the Cuban push for independence from Spain got serious. Ybor
moved to Key West, a sleepy fishing village, because he opposed Spain.
He opened a cigar factory. Labor unrest made him look for a new location.

A friend of his was looking for guava and found both the guava and
the perfect place for making cigars—Spanish Town, a small fishing
village of seven hundred people on the west coast of Florida (the name

was changed to Tampa in 1835). Ybor came and liked what he saw. There was a railroad and a deep-water port. The humidity, so disliked by today's residents and tourists, suited him just fine. It kept the cigars moist.

He bought 40 acres of wetlands in 1885, dispatched the alligators without the slightest hint of a permit, and filled in the land. Ybor Cigar Factory was opened in 1886. Then he bought more land and called the area Ybor City. The truth is, Ybor City is not a separate city and never has been. Ybor City is a part of Tampa.

Within a few years of the first cigar factory opening, more than three thousand people lived in Ybor City. Cigar making reached its peak by 1900. Ybor City, having more than two hundred cigar factories, became the "cigar capital of the world."

A radical thing happened inside those factories, and it changed the future of Ybor City. Workers wanted to be educated. Using their own money, they hired a lector, *el lector* in Spanish, who read newspapers to them in the morning and novels in the afternoon. A lector had to be passionate, with a voice that could carry without a megaphone. He translated English newspapers into Spanish.

In 1931, worker unrest led management to declare the readers off-limits because management feared workers were getting too smart.

In the late 1800s, cigar factory owners noticed that workers who went home to Cuba for the holidays were reluctant to return to work. So casitas were built. "Casita" means "little house," and they were reasonably priced from $400 to $900. The whole family could live in Ybor City.

Casitas were built shotgun style—with a long hallway that ran from the front to the back door. Rooms led off to each side. It is said a man could stand in the front door of a shotgun house and shoot a bullet out the back door.

After the museum and casita, we walk along 7th Avenue, look up, and see the names of the buildings' owners carved into the fronts. Seventh Avenue survived the urban-renewal destruction of the 1960s that leveled large areas of Ybor City. It is now lively with art galleries, restaurants, nightclubs, and a vintage clothing store that has been there longer than most businesses.

During the heyday of cigar making, many nationalities contributed to the vibrancy of Ybor City. Among the cultures having mutual-aid clubs were the Cubans, Spanish, Italian, German, Jewish, and Afro-Cubans. These clubs were not just a place for the men to play dominos and dances to be held. The mutual-aid clubs took care of everything in their members' lives, including hospital care and burials. As a member of a mutual-aid club, you could get womb-to-tomb care for 25 cents a week.

Some of the clubs still survive. Walk to 1731 East 7th Avenue to see L'Unione Italiana. Entering the Italian club, you will encounter a rarity right away. The cantina, where men once played dominos, is a good half floor below street level. It is a cellar, practically a basement, or the closest you'll get to one in Florida.

Women were not allowed in the cantina. They had to stand on the first floor, look over the railing, and call for their husbands.

A different view of Ybor City happens when you stand on the third floor of this building. It is easy to see some of the large brick cigar factories that are still standing. Notice the factories have observation decks on top. This was so manufacturers could send someone up to keep a lookout for ships. When they arrived in port, then it was time to go unload the tobacco.

The Cuban club, another one of mutual-aid clubs, is enfolded in a modern and upscale shopping, dining, and entertainment area called Centro Ybor. What used to be the upstairs ballroom, where dances were held on Sunday afternoon, is now a restaurant.

The walking tour ends at the visitor information center at Centro Ybor. We watch a video about Ybor City's history. After soaking up all the history, all the changes, we are more than ready for lunch.

Bonus Points

Should you take the museum walking tour on Saturday morning, a nice bonus is the Ybor City Fresh Market from 9 a.m. to 3 p.m. in Centennial Park directly across from the museum. The location is 8th Avenue and 19th Street. There's fresh bread, café con leche, crafts, arts, plants, and vegetables.

SOUTHWEST FLORIDA

Remember those lectors? The education they imparted helped seal immigrants' determination that their children should have a future of hope. They did not pass on the cigar trade but worked instead to send their children to school.

Coming full circle, some of those children would eventually return to Ybor City as doctors, lawyers, architects, and more. In the 1970s and 1980s, they purchased decaying cigar factories to keep them from demolition. After renovations, the old buildings have new life today as offices, artists' lofts, and shopping centers. At its height, Ybor City's two hundred cigar factories turned out 700 million cigars a year. Cigar making lives on in Ybor City with the local specialty of hand-rolled cigars. You can watch them being made at a number of stores.

Get the free brochure "Ybor City: The City with a Past," available everywhere, and use the map inside to find some of the old cigar factories converted to new uses.

One side of Centennial Park hosts a Saturday market. The other side has the Ybor Art Studio, with a full schedule of classes for adults and children. It is part of the City of Tampa's Parks and Recreation Department. Perhaps you will meet Roby Robwski. "Roby" is "Ybor" spelled backwards. The staff at the Ybor Art Studio adopted the stray, a small, black female cat. Or was it the other way around—did she adopt them?

In addition to the museum tours, there is a good guide on the Web that can be printed out. It has directions, photos, and addresses for a walking or driving tour. The Web address is: www.floridahistory.org/westcoastfla/yborcity.htm.

You can view the inside of a cigar worker's home without taking the Saturday museum tour. The museum gives guided tours of a casita, a cigar worker's home, on the hour from 11 a.m. to 3 p.m. Monday through Saturday.

After walking Ybor City and soaking up its history, you may be inspired to experience more of Tampa. This is possible without getting back in your car. Streetcars connect historic Ybor City with downtown Tampa and the Channelside area, which includes the Florida Aquarium.

A one-way fare is $1.50. Unlimited rides for the day are $3. Seniors 65 and older, those 17 and younger can get a discount one-day unlim-

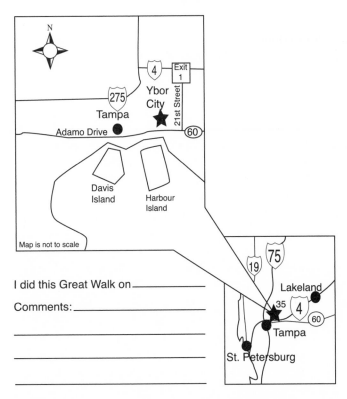

I did this Great Walk on _____

Comments: _____

_____

_____

_____

ited pass for $1.50. To know more, call the HARTinfo line and streetcar information at (813) 254-4278. Their Web site is: www.hartline.org.

Trip Essentials

Name: Celebrate the Cigars: Historic Walk, Ybor City

Type of walk: Historic

Length of walk: About 1 mile

Time to finish: 1 1/2 hours

Difficulty: Mildly moderate. Pavement. Some high curbs not wheelchair accessible.

Appeals to: History buffs, photographers, and families

Guides: Historic tour, Saturdays at 10:30 a.m. Starts at Ybor City Museum State Park.

Address: Ybor City Museum State Park, 1818 East 9th Ave., Tampa, FL 33605

Phone: (813) 247-6323

Web site: www.floridastateparks.org and www.floridahistory.org

Cost: Historic walking tour $6 for adults. Walks are on Saturday morning starting at 10:30 a.m. Price includes walk plus museum admission. Buy tickets at museum store next to the museum. Store opens at 10 a.m.

Getting there: From I-4, take exit 1 and turn south onto 21st Street. Turn right onto Palm Avenue and take second left onto 19th Street. The next right is 9th Avenue.

GPS coordinates: N 27° 96139 W 082° 43833

Restrooms: Inside museum

Water/food: Numerous restaurants and cafes along the way

Dogs: Leashed on the street and well behaved. No dogs allowed inside buildings.

Lunch ideas: Cuban, at La Tropicana Café, 1822 East 7th Ave., Tampa, FL 33605, phone (813) 247-4040; Spanish/Cuban cuisine, at Columbia Restaurant, 2117 East 7th Avenue, Tampa, FL 33605, phone (813) 248-4961

SOUTHWEST FLORIDA

36

Mangroves, Orchids, and a Bo Tree

Marie Selby Botanical Gardens, Sarasota

Marie Selby Botanical Gardens in Sarasota knocks your socks off as soon as you step on the garden path. After you pay the admission fee, a docent gives you a guide sheet and then motions to a door on the right. Open this door and enter the Tropical Display House.

Tropical plants crowd the floor and even hug the ceiling. Orchids, bromeliads, hanging baskets of gesneriads, air plants, along with palms and aroids are all exuberant and in full bloom.

Orchids are the supernovas of the collection. They hang from the ceiling, overflow from pots on the ground, and even trail across high wires. Everywhere you turn there is another surprise. There is nothing simple about an orchid. They are almost haughty in their elegance, rather like a Persian cat sitting in a sunny window.

Mist is everywhere. Water flows softly from a dozen different waterfalls. This is a place to walk gently and look closely. Cameras click. It is hushed. People whisper. The Tropical Display House has the feel of a cathedral.

The map shows gardens to the left of the Tropical Display House, including a cycad display, a fernery, and an epiphyte garden-oak grove. My son Chris and I turn instead to the right. We follow our own advice for most walks—when in doubt which path to choose, go right and stay right. Eventually you will go completely around the loop.

We walk into a children's activity area. A large children's book, at least 4 feet high, has pages that turn. Both parents and children can go through a maze made of trimmed hedges about 4 feet high. The day we were there, two children made it through the maze easily while, to their delight, their parents were still stuck inside.

A bench beneath the bo tree at Selby Botanical Gardens, Sarasota.

SOUTHWEST FLORIDA

Next is a cluster of gardens including a bromeliad display, an azalea garden, and a butterfly garden loaded with bees. In this area you will see and smell a fragrance garden of plants in huge clay pots.

A two-story white house called the Mansion is at the end of the path. The Paynes, neighbors of Bill and Marie Selby, owned the home. When Marie Selby died in 1971, she willed her peninsula property as a botanical garden. In 1973, the Paulks, then the current owners of the Payne House, sold it to the gardens.

Going back to the children's area, we turn right onto a walkway that takes us toward a mangrove forest on Sarasota Bay. Mangroves are the first line of coastal defense against storms. Their curving roots stake out territory, firming up the shoreline.

You will come to a bo tree. Buddha came to enlightenment while sitting under a bo tree. It was not a blinding flash while on a lunch break. Buddha sat under the bo tree for six years before enlightenment arrived. What makes a bo tree special? A sign tells us it is the sound that the leaf tips make rustling in the breeze. It sounds like gentle rain on a tin roof.

This bo tree at Selby Gardens has a dedicated group of admirers, including couples that married and pledged lifelong commitment to one another under its spreading branches.

On September 14, 2001, Tropical Storm Gabriel came ashore and wreaked havoc on the south end of Selby Gardens. The bo tree was uprooted. In a desperate attempt to save the tree, a 50-foot crane was floated up to the water's edge at high tide. Then ropes were looped around five of the tree's six trunks. Ever so carefully, the crane hoisted the tree for ninety minutes, until it was upright. Volunteers shoveled tons of soil around the tree. Staff watered the tree daily. After six weeks, new growth appeared. The bo tree was saved.

Beyond the bo tree, the path winds through a succulent garden, then past hibiscus in bloom. Farther along, in a banyan grove, there is an elevated walkway. It is called the Canopy Walkway of the World, and it is ADA accessible. The boardwalk will have you 10 feet up in the air, right in the branches and leaves of banyan trees. Children love this place, running up and down the walkway.

Near the banyan trees is the Selbys' former home, now a café and host to rotating exhibits of artwork. The path winds past a koi pond and into a bamboo garden. Here is the humming stone. You put your head into the opening and hum. It causes a cranial resonance.

Count on a good hour or more to do the entire half-mile walk, especially with children, who will want to stop and play. The banyan grove might be their favorite spot, or maybe the maze.

Bonus Points

What started out in 1981 as one man's effort to rehabilitate seabirds has turned into a full-feathered facility treating five thousand injured, orphaned, and sick birds each year. The Pelican Man's Bird Sanctuary, Wildlife Hospital and Education Center is located 1 mile north of St. Armands Circle on City Island. Their address is: 1708 Ken Thompson Parkway, Sarasota, FL 34236, phone (941) 388-4444. Hours are 10 a.m. to 5 p.m. every day except Christmas and Thanksgiving. Admission is $6 adult; $4 children 12–17; and $2 children 4–12. The Web site is: www. pelicanman.org.

SOUTHWEST FLORIDA

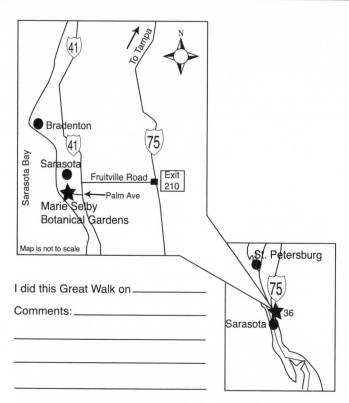

I did this Great Walk on _____

Comments: _____

_____

_____

_____

Mote Marine Laboratory and Mote Aquarium are right next door to the Pelican Man's Sanctuary. Mote's address is: 1600 Ken Thompson Parkway, Sarasota, FL 34236, phone (941) 388-4441. Hours are 10 a.m. to 5 p.m. every day. Admission is $15 for those 13 and up; $10 children 4–12; children under 4 admitted free. The Web address is: www.mote. org.

The John and Mable Ringling Museum of Art is situated on 66 acres facing Sarasota Bay. Give yourself a good 3 hours to take in the Museum of Art, the former Ringling residence called Ca d'Zan, the Circus Museum, and the museum grounds.

Their address is: 5401 Bay Shore Drive, Sarasota, FL 34243, phone (941) 359-5700. Web site: www.ringling.org. Admission is $15 adults; $13 seniors and active military; $5 students and Florida teachers; children under 5 admitted free. Hours are 10 a.m. to 5:30 p.m. every day.

The Sarasota Bay National Estuary Program has, as part of wetland enhancement projects, helped complete a number of nature walks in the Sarasota area. Among them are the Sarasota Baywalk at City Island and the Bayfront Baywalk at 6th Street. They also have free brochures on the Sarasota Bay Blueways and the Gulf Coast Heritage Trail. Their address is: 111 South Orange Avenue, Suite 200W, Sarasota, FL 34236, phone (941) 955-8085. The Web address is: www.sarasotabay.org.

Trip Essentials

Name: Mangroves, Orchids, and a Bo Tree: Marie Selby Botanical Gardens, Sarasota

Type of walk: Botanical

Length of walk: Approximately one-half mile

Time to finish: 1 to 3 hours

Difficulty: Easy. Paved walkways. Wheelchair accessible.

Appeals to: Gardeners, photographers, and families

Guides: Self-guided. Guides are available for groups of 10 or more with 2 weeks' notice; no extra cost.

Address: 811 South Palm Ave., Sarasota, FL 34236

Phone: (941) 366-5731

Web site: www.selby.org

Cost: $12 adults; $6 children 6–11; children 5 and under admitted free with paying adult

Getting there: From I-75, take exit 210. Go west 7 miles to the end. Turn left onto U.S. 41. After three lights, turn right onto Palm Avenue just after large curve. Entrance to gardens is at the end of the block on the right.

GPS coordinates: (Sarasota Bay) N 27° 35028 W 082° 57222

Hours: 10 a.m. to 5 p.m. daily, closed on Christmas.

Restrooms: At welcome center and the Museum Gallery Store

Water/food: Two water fountains; food at Michael's in the Garden, an al fresco café

Dogs: No. Only guide dogs for the physically challenged are permitted.

Lunch ideas: Bistro style, at Michael's in the Garden Cafe, located in the historic Selby House, phone (941) 302-4762; American, at Citrus Café, 543 S. Pineapple Avenue, Sarasota, FL 34236, phone (941) 957-0432

SOUTHWEST FLORIDA

Layers of Time

Spanish Point, Osprey

Spanish Point has nothing to do with Spanish history. Ponce de León did not stop by looking for the Fountain of Youth. In fact, volunteers, who deeply love this place, often think that people pass by Spanish Point and don't turn into the driveway because they think it had something to do with conquistadors, with blood and guts spilled on the sand.

If you are one of those people, it is time to turn around and discover the true story of Spanish Point, located in Osprey, about 15 miles south of Sarasota.

A walk through Spanish Point is a Great Walk through time. Two different groups of prehistoric Indians lived along the shoreline. Each group disappeared for reasons unknown. After the Civil War, John and Eliza Webb came from New York in 1867 to homestead, putting down roots. The nearest white settlement was two days away by boat.

Bertha Mathilde Honore Palmer, widow of Potter Palmer of Chicago, bought Spanish Point in 1910 from a Webb family member. She called it Osprey Point. Each one of these cultural eras left behind remnants of the lives lived there.

Literally a point of land thrust into Little Sarasota Bay, this is prime waterfront development property that easily could have disappeared under the weight of condominiums and concrete. In 1980, Spanish Point was saved from that fate. The 30-acre site was donated by a grandson of Mrs. Potter Palmer to the nonprofit Gulf Coast Heritage Association, Inc.

A 1-mile walk around Spanish Point takes about 2 hours. You can do it yourself, but you'll miss going inside several locations, including a historic home, because guides are the keeper of the keys. They literally wear them around their neck on a lanyard, and only they can unlock the doors. Fortunately, guided walks are offered three times a day at no extra charge. Call ahead to make sure of the times. There are also tram tours.

Plan to arrive at least a half hour before the walk. Turn into Spanish Point at the sign on U.S. 41. Drive past the small building that serves as a guard post, go to the left, and park in front of the old Osprey School, now a visitor center for Spanish Point. Pay your admission inside and keep your stub where you can find it. A short video is played continuously in one of the classrooms. This tells the history of Spanish Point and is a good orientation.

Then get back in your car, because you will drive to the start of the walk. As you pass behind the guard post, a volunteer will ask to see your ticket stub. Drive through the entrance gates behind the guard post to the parking lot on the left. The walk starts at a large white garden gazebo next to the parking lot.

We come first to a burial mound. Archaeologists digging in 1959 and 1960 uncovered four hundred skeletons. Half were shipped to the Florida Museum of Natural History in Gainesville. The other half went to the Smithsonian in Washington, D.C. These Indians with no known name lived here from AD 300 to 1000. No Indian tribe has ever claimed them.

John and Eliza Webb and their five children came to Florida after the Civil War from Utica, New York. Arriving in Key West, they met a Spanish-speaking person who suggested an area on the water south of Sarasota. Those were homesteading days. You could have 160 acres if you did a few things—lived on site five years, built a house, and planted crops.

The Webbs named their point of land Spanish Point after the unknown Spanish-speaking person in Key West who gave them advice.

John Webb planted citrus and sugar cane. Then, as a third industry, he invited winter visitors to come and stay at Webb's Winter Resort. During the winter, the family moved out of their house, visitors moved in, and the Webbs lived in small quarters in the building that contained the kitchen.

The Indians had their burial mounds. The pioneers had a cemetery.

Bertha Palmer had this classic portal built at Spanish Point, Osprey.

It is set back on a side path behind the packinghouse. Three genera-tions of Webbs are buried here. A long branch of a live-oak tree arches over several gravestones. After a rain, resurrection ferns spring to life and turn green along the top of the tree branch.

Next to the cemetery is a reconstruction of Mary's Chapel, finished in 1986. The stained-glass windows are original, and so is the chapel bell. Mary Sherrill died here while vacationing at Webb's Winter Re-sort.

The walk continues on a dirt roadway called Guptill Road. A long, manicured lawn runs from the road down to Webb's Cove. Near the top of the lawn is the classic portal. Mrs. Palmer had it built so it framed a view of Webb's Cove. It is easy to wonder what the Indians might have thought if they stumbled upon such a structure.

Frank Guptill, a boatbuilder, married Webb's youngest daughter. When she died, Frank married her sister. Guptill built a house on a high mound at Spanish Point, a mound that is actually a prehistoric Archaic Period midden. Next to his home, Frank built a boatyard. The boats you see under construction are modern-day versions of the boats Frank built.

Perhaps it is the way of gardeners. They must rearrange Mother Nature. Mrs. Palmer was no exception. In the woods behind the Guptill House, she created what she called a Jungle Walk. Lots of tropical plants give the jungle feel, and dirt paths meander through the landscape. She also had a small aqueduct installed. Water flows down the aqueduct and ends up flowing out of a large cascade made of conch shells.

Out of the garden jungle, you cross a footbridge called Cock's Footbridge. Our guide tells us that one morning he saw a bobcat on the bridge looking at the water, perhaps getting an early start on fishing. Anchored off the bridge are several boats built by volunteers, including a traditional sharpie named *Lizzie G.*

Over the footbridge and through the woods is an archaeological exhibit, A Window to the Past. Behind a glass wall is a shell midden that has been sliced from top to bottom. A Palmer relative wanted to build a car garage here, so he brought in a bulldozer and started removing the shell midden. Archaeologists managed to get that project stopped. The result is a slice of Indian life you can't see anywhere else in Florida.

The midden was created about one thousand years ago. From examining the layers, archaeologists know the Indians ate clams, oysters, shellfish, and thirty-seven different kinds of fish including sharks. They used hooks, lines, and spears for fishing. Women collected blueberries and acorns. They made and wore jewelry.

Near the shell midden is another Palmer garden. This one is called the Pergola and Sunken Garden. Beyond that is the White Cottage. Webb's Winter Resort once housed guests here. There is a room dedicated to Mrs. Palmer and her life in Florida. Another room shows her life in Chicago. A screened porch has tables for public use, a good place to have a picnic lunch. This is the official end of the guided walk.

Bringing a brown bag lunch is highly recommended. In addition to the porch at the White House, the picnic tables under old oak trees near the Visitor Gazebo and Water Garden are recommended. These are right next to the parking lot, where the walk began.

Bonus Points

Living history reenactments are given at Spanish Point from January through April. Call (941) 966-5214 for times.

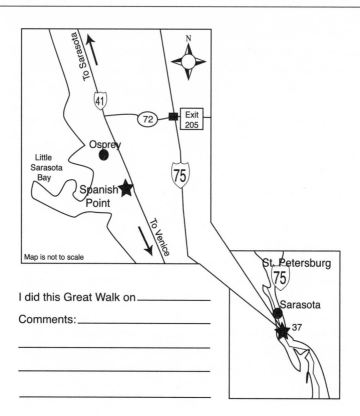

I did this Great Walk on _____

Comments: _____

_____

_____

_____

Two state parks are near Spanish Point.

Myakka River State Park, one of the oldest and largest state parks, is located at 13207 S.R. 72, Sarasota, FL 34241, phone (941) 361-6511. Admission is $5 per vehicle for up to 8 people. Myakka has log cabins and campsites. For an extra fee, take a daily tram tour given from mid-December through May.

The Myakka River is designated as a Florida Wild and Scenic River. The park has two lakes available for boating, fishing, canoeing, and kayaking. You can walk a boardwalk at Upper Myakka Lake.

Oscar Scherer State Park has lots of scrubby flatwoods, making it attractive to Florida scrub jays. Located at 1843 S. Tamiami Trail, Osprey, FL 34229, it is literally down the road from Spanish Point. Entrance fee is $4 per vehicle for up to 8 people. Phone (941) 483-5956 for information on canoe and kayak rentals to paddle along South Creek. Both walkers and bicyclists use some 15 miles of hiking trails.

Both parks have Web sites at www.floridastateparks.org.

Trip Essentials

Name: Layers of Time: Spanish Point, Osprey
Type of walk: Historic
Length of walk: 1 mile
Time to finish: Allow 2 hours, includes going inside structures
Difficulty: Easy. Shell and dirt roads. Most areas wheelchair accessible.
Appeals to: History buffs, gardeners, boatbuilders, and photographers
Guides: Guided walks at 10:30 a.m., 12:30 and 2:30 p.m. No fee.
Address: 337 North Tamiami Trail, Osprey, FL 34229
Phone: (941) 966-5214
Web site: www.historicspanishpoint.org
Cost: $9 general admission; $8 Florida residents; $8 seniors 65 and over; $3 children 6–12; children under 6 admitted free
Getting there: Located 10 miles south of Sarasota on U.S. 41
GPS coordinates: (Osprey) N 27° 19583 W 082° 49056
Hours: 9 a.m. to 5 p.m. Monday-Saturday; noon to 5 p.m. on Sunday
Restrooms: At visitor center at Osprey School, also White House and Guptill House
Water/food: Water at restrooms; no food sold inside Spanish Point
Dogs: No
Lunch ideas: Bring a brown bag lunch and eat at tables on the porch at White Cottage or at picnic tables under live oak trees near gazebo; Florida laidback food, at Spanish Pointe Pub & Restaurant, 135 Bay Street, Osprey, FL 34229, phone (941) 966-5746

SOUTHWEST FLORIDA

38

Wildlife Up Close

J. N. "Ding" Darling National Wildlife Refuge, Sanibel

What is Wildlife Drive doing in the middle of *Great Walks*? Should you leave your walking shoes at home?

No, not at all. You need your walking shoes. A vehicle gets you onto Wildlife Drive, but you'll be spending most of your time out of the car along the 4-mile, one-way drive.

Plan your visit around a low tide. At the refuge, tide changes are 1 to 2 hours later than the times listed on island tide charts. Call the refuge at (239) 472-1100 for more information. When the tide is out, supper is in, and birds congregate on the flats.

Park the car. Walk along the roadside. Be amazed, totally and completely amazed, at the abundance of wildlife. The best months for birding are December through March. Migrating songbirds such as prairie warblers and red-eyed vireos come from March through May. Even when wildlife is scarce, the mud flats flanked by mangrove islands are a wonder worth seeing.

The very sight of wildlife promotes instant camaraderie. When approaching a group where everyone is looking through binoculars, simply ask what's happening and someone will probably hand you a pair of binoculars.

Volunteer naturalists patrol the drive. They set up spotting scopes and invite anyone to have a look. Volunteers are knowledgeable about the ecosystems and wildlife.

On the day we visited, white pelicans filled a tidal flat, roseate spoonbills were spotted in a pond, and, farther down the drive, an American crocodile was sunning herself less than 10 feet from the road. White ibises, ducks, brown pelicans, and yellow-crowned night herons were all in view, either up close or through spotting scopes. A naturalist vol-

White pelicans preening at J. N. "Ding" Darling National Wildlife Refuge, Sanibel.

unteer said they'd been on Wildlife Drive for 2 hours and had traveled less than one-quarter of a mile—there was that much to see.

Two refuge employees and a group of people were looking down an embankment at an American crocodile, about 15 feet long, sunning on a mud bank.

This crocodile is a female. She arrived sometime in the 1980s and every year faithfully produced eggs. They were infertile due to the lack of a Mr. Crocodile. Thinking she'd have a better chance of meeting a mate somewhere else, the staff trapped her, put her in the back of a vehicle, and transported her about 80 miles south to Collier-Seminole State Park on the edge of the Everglades.

Within six months she was back at the refuge. Somehow she found her way through swamps, shorelines, backyards and golf courses, and over asphalt. Did she travel at night, avoiding humans? Was there a scent, a yearning, a piece of primordial lodestone inside her that kept her going north and gave her the endurance to make such a long journey?

When she returned, the staff threw in the towel and gave up their romance plans. They think she is the northernmost American crocodile to be found in Florida.

Either before or after a trip along Wildlife Drive do plan to visit the Education Center, which doubles as the refuge's visitor center. There is no charge to come inside the main entrance to the refuge and see the Education Center. Fees apply only when you go onto Wildlife Drive or walk the Indigo Trail.

Inside the center are interactive exhibits on refuge ecosystem, explainers about migratory flyways, a bookstore, and a hands-on area for children. You will also find history on "Ding" Darling, whose real name was Jay Norwood Darling. He signed his political cartoons "Ding," a short version of his last name. These cartoons often had an environmental bite and raised American consciousness about issues such as deforestation and loss of habitat for migrating birds.

Darling became head of the U.S. Biological Survey, the early version of the U.S. Fish and Wildlife Service. On December 1, 1945, more than 6,400 acres were established as the Sanibel National Wildlife Refuge. In 1967, the refuge was renamed the J. N. "Ding" Darling National Wildlife Refuge, part of the U.S. Fish and Wildlife Service. More than 850,000 visitors find their way here every year.

Bonus Points

Tarpon Bay Nature Tours and Rentals has a kiosk in the main refuge parking lot in front of the Education Center. Rentals include kayaks, canoes, bicycles, and boats. They give guided tours on pontoons, kayaks, and trams and also offer fishing tours. Especially popular are their sunset tours in boats or kayaks to sit and watch birds coming back to roost for the night.

The Indigo Trail is 2 miles out and 2 miles back. Once the trail crosses Wildlife Drive and becomes a shell-compressed road, there is a $1 trail access fee, payable at Wildlife Drive's pay station.

Shell Mound Trail, located just past the end of Wildlife Drive, is one-third of a mile long on elevated boardwalks. A small trailhead provides parking space.

The Sanibel-Captiva Conservation Foundation has a Nature Center at 3333 Sanibel-Captiva Road, Sanibel, FL 33957, phone (239) 472-2329. Hours are 8:30 a.m. to 4 p.m. Monday through Friday from October through May; 8:30 a.m. to 3 p.m. from June through September.

SOUTHWEST FLORIDA

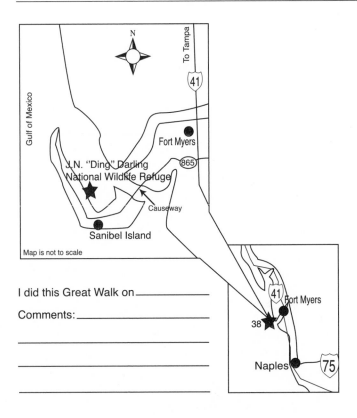

I did this Great Walk on _____

Comments: _____

_____

_____

_____

SOUTHWEST FLORIDA

Saturday hours from December through April are 10 a.m. to 3 p.m.; from May through November, they are closed Saturdays.

You can walk 4.5 miles of trails and visit an enclosed butterfly habitat. They also have an education center, nature shop, and bookstore and conduct estuarine research. One of the exhibits in the Nature Center is a marine-life touch tank. Admission for the trails, education center, nature shop, and bookstore is $3 for adults; children under 17 admitted free. SCCF has an extensive schedule of walks, talks, and events—everything from sea-grass wading trips to stargazing. Visit the Web site: www.sccf.org.

SCCF has a native-plant nursery right next to the Nature Center. For information about the nursery, phone (239) 472-1932.

Trip Essentials

Name: Wildlife Up Close: J. N. "Ding" Darling National Wildlife Refuge, Sanibel

Type of walk: Wildlife walk or drive through a national refuge

Length of walk: 4 miles one way. More if you add foot trails such as the 1/3-mile Shell Mound Trail or 2-mile Indigo Trail

Time to finish: 3 to 4 hours on Wildlife Drive

Difficulty: Easy. Wildlife Drive is pavement. Wheelchair accessible.

Appeals to: Wildlife watchers, families, photographers, and birders (listed on page 10, South Florida guide to the Great Florida Birding Trail)

Guides: Self-guided. Volunteer naturalists patrol Wildlife Drive. They carry spotting scopes and guidebooks. Their cars are clearly marked, and they wear vests with patches.

Address: 1 Wildlife Drive, Sanibel, FL 33957

Phone: (239) 472-1100

Web site: www.fws.gov/dingdarling

Cost: Wildlife Drive costs $5 for motorized vehicles; $1 for hikers/bikers. Crossing the Causeway to Sanibel costs $6.

Getting there: Located about 15 miles southwest of Fort Myers on Sanibel Island; must use Sanibel Causeway. The refuge is located on Sanibel Captiva Road.

GPS coordinates: (Sanibel Island) N 26°44 W 082° 11389

Hours: Wildlife Drive is open 7:30 a.m. to sunset, Saturdays through Thursdays; closed Fridays. Refuge visitor center hours vary by season.

Restrooms: At education/visitor center

Water/food: Water at visitor center; no food

Dogs: No

Lunch ideas: American, at Amy's Over Easy Café, 630-1 Tarpon Bay Road, Sanibel, FL 33957, phone (239) 472-2625; American and Italian, at Sanibel Bean, 2240 Periwinkle Way, Sanibel, FL 33957, phone (239) 395-1919

39

Boardwalk Adventure

Six Mile Cypress Slough Preserve, Fort Myers

Lynette Brown's children went on a wet walk at Six Mile Cypress Slough Preserve south of Fort Myers. They came home from their school field trip raving about the slough.

Brown came to the slough to see what was exciting her children. She got involved and took a class to be a volunteer naturalist. That was ten years ago. Her children are now in college. They gave her a pair of binoculars so she could keep on discovering new things at the slough.

You don't have to get wet to get excited about the slough. You and your family can stay dry walking on an elevated boardwalk and still see it all.

The slough is a 2,200-acre wetland ecosystem about 9 miles long and one-third of a mile wide. A boardwalk trail, more than a mile long, loops past ponds, a lake, and cypress stands, giving a full view of the wetlands in action.

An "Explorer's Companion Guide" is available for self-guided walks. They ask that you return the guide to its box when you are done so others may use it. Plus, guided walks are given daily. There is no charge. Guided walk times vary according to the season (see Trip Essentials). We choose to go on a guided-walk tour.

A woman on the tour has a list of things she wants to see in her lifetime. On her list—some kind of Florida panther. Are they here? Yes, our guide says, there were sightings a long time ago. Other sightings include bears, otters, and bobcats. The guide saw three otters a year ago, a big surprise, but she cautions that sometimes when you are looking for something, you won't see it.

The slough is a linear corridor for wildlife, practically a superhighway compared to the urban areas around it.

Cypress trees reflected in the slough at Six Mile Cypress Slough Preserve, Fort Myers.

SOUTHWEST FLORIDA

The "Explorer's Companion" has tips for spotting wildlife while walking on the boardwalk, good for any wild Florida walk. It suggests being quiet, walking slowly and looking for movement, keeping your head and eyes moving in all directions, standing or sitting still for a while, and taking time to look at ordinary things.

Our guide stops by a tree and points to a line of holes made by a yellow-bellied sapsucker. First the sapsucker bores the holes, and when sap runs out of the tree, bugs get stuck in the sap. The bird comes back later and has dinner.

We come to the central wet area of the slough, the Flag Pond Community, named after the alligator flag plants—tall with broad, green leaves—that grow everywhere. Towering cypress trees cast mirror images on the smooth water surface.

The water may look still, but it is moving like a wide stream, especially in the wet season. The slow pace lets sediments settle out, cleaning the water before it moves on. The slough collects water runoff from a 57-mile watershed. During the wet season, from June to October, water flows through the slough and heads southwest to the Estero Bay Aquatic Preserve. From there it empties into the Gulf of Mexico.

There is no charge to visit the slough, but a $3 parking fee is assessed for the day. You'll need coins or bills to feed the machine that gives you a ticket to put on your dashboard.

Guides tell you that even visiting in the summertime is bearable. The slough has two kinds of fish that eat mosquitoes. So the bug situation is not nearly what you might imagine when you hear the word "wetlands."

The slough is a Lee County Regional Park/Preserve and a Florida Greenway. There is enough variety to keep children interested and having the "Explorer's Companion" guide is helpful.

Bonus Points

The Edison and Ford Winter Estates in Fort Myers are located at 2350 McGregor Boulevard, Fort Myers, FL 33901, phone (239) 334-7419. The Web site is: www.edison-ford-estate.com.

Hours are 9 a.m. to 5:30 p.m. Monday through Saturday; and noon to 5:30 p.m. on Sunday. The grounds are closed on Thanksgiving and Christmas. There are guided tours of the homes and gardens every half hour. Separate botanical tours are given on Thursday and Saturday mornings.

The homes and gardens tour costs $16 for nonresidents and $14 for Florida residents 13 and over. Other tours—including a Sunday Stroll in the Garden, Holiday House, laboratory and museum only, and the in-depth botanical tour—have separate fees. Parking is free.

Edison and Ford were great friends. The two homes, as you will see, are mirror images of each other and were built in 1886. One home was originally built for a business partner, the other for the Edison family. When that business relationship dissolved, the partner left. In fact, Edison left too and did not return until 1901. Henry Ford purchased

Thomas Edison had this long fishing dock built at his Fort Myers winter estate on the Caloosa-hatchee River.

the property in 1916. A fence used to divide the two properties. There was a friendship gate. It is said the gate was never closed.

Edison liked to fish. He also liked to sit and think about his inventions. To further both ends, he built a long dock going out into the Caloosahatchee River. Protocol says you don't disturb a fisherman. So, the story goes, Edison would sit at the end of the dock, fishing pole in hand, undisturbed by either man or fish.

After taking the guided house and garden tour, take time to walk along the shoreline. You might see Mr. Edison's electric launch on the water. It still works. Boat cruises are given on weekdays. An electric launch ride costs $7.

An Estates' Works ticket is available for a one-time visit. It includes the homes and gardens tour, the museum, laboratory, and a boat ride.

The cost is $20 for an adult nonresident; $18 for adult Florida resident; and $11.50 for a child.

The Southwest Florida Museum of History, 2300 Peck Street, Ft. Myers, FL 33901, phone (239) 332-5955, gives walking tours from December through April. Web site: www.cityftmyers.com/museum.

Their Historic Downtown Walking Tours are Wednesday and Saturday at 10 a.m. Walking tour cost is $5 adults; $3 children. Call for reservations.

Museum hours are 9 a.m. to 4 p.m. Tuesday through Saturday; and Sunday noon to 4 p.m. Admission is $9.50 adults; $8.50 seniors; and $5 for children 3–12.

Museum Mania is a City of Fort Myers program to encourage visiting museums. At any museum site, ask for a Museum Mania Passport. It comes with discounts to the Imaginarium, Edison and Ford Winter

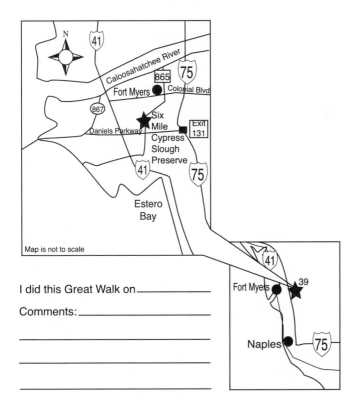

SOUTHWEST FLORIDA

Estates, and Calusa Nature Center and Planetarium. To know more, visit: www.cityftmyers.com/museum.

Trip Essentials

Name: Boardwalk Adventure: Six Mile Cypress Slough Preserve, Fort Myers

Type of walk: Nature walk on elevated boardwalk

Length of walk: 1.2 miles

Time to finish: 1 hour

Difficulty: Easy. Wood boardwalk and dirt trail. Wheelchair accessible.

Appeals to: Nature buffs, photographers, families, and birders (listed on page 14, South Florida guide to the Great Florida Birding Trail)

Guides: Self-guided, or guided walks given 9:30 a.m. on Wednesdays from May through October; daily at 9:30 a.m. during April, November, and December; daily at 9:30 a.m. and 1:30 p.m. during January, February, and March.

Address: 7751 Penzance Boulevard, Ft. Myers, FL 33912

Phone: (239) 432-2042

Web site: www.leeparks.org

Cost: None for walk

Getting there: Located at Penzance Crossing along Six Mile Cypress Parkway between Colonial Boulevard and Daniels Parkway (exit 131 off I-75)

GPS coordinates (Six Mile Slough parking lot) N 26° 34 M 16.7308 S W 081° 49 M 34.6669 S

Hours: 8 a.m. to sunset

Restrooms: At trailhead

Water/food: Water at restrooms; no food available

Dogs: No

Lunch ideas: Recommend the picnic area next to trailhead and parking lot

40

Walk with Audubon

Corkscrew Swamp Sanctuary, Naples

On Saturday, January 14, 2006, Corkscrew Swamp Sanctuary became a designated Gateway to the South Florida section of the Great Florida Birding Trail. It was standing room only as birders from around the state came for the dedication ceremony and crammed together on a porch at the Blair Audubon Center.

One speaker noted that too many young people today suffer from nature-deficit disorder, or NDD. The cure is to get out and observe wildlife.

Adults can also suffer from NDD. Symptoms include an inability to push the "off" button on the remote, an indentation on the couch from sitting too long, and an incapacity to name birds by their songs or identify animal tracks.

Going to Corkscrew Swamp Sanctuary is a great way to get well. Start the cure by walking the 2.25-mile boardwalk loop through four different ecosystems: a pine flatwoods, wet prairie, marsh, and cypress forest.

The boardwalk is accessed through the Blair Audubon Center. This is a good time to buy the "Corkscrew Swamp Sanctuary Companion Field Guide." The cost is $2. Carry it with you on the walk to help identify plants, mammals, birds, reptiles, and amphibians, even fish and insects. There is a trail map in the center.

Note: During wood stork nesting season, certain sections of the boardwalk are closed to the public. Notices are posted in the center.

The walk starts in a pine flatwood. Slash pines are common here. They got their name from early settlers who slashed the pine tree to get sap that was used to make pine tar and oil for disinfectant and turpentine. American Indians used the inner bark, which contains vitamin C, to make a paste for wounds.

Interpretive signs along the way are of two kinds: large ones giving an overview, such as the role of water in the ecosystems, and small signs that describe specific things, like apple snail eggs.

On the big signs, have your children or grandchildren look for the teaser questions in the lower right-hand corner. One question: In the swamp, does the air smell fresh and clean?

From the start of the walk, breezes have moved through the young cypress and the pine trees, making a light, rustling sound. Then we enter the Bald Cypress area, where the trees are ancient, some up to six hundred years old. Here the sounds change. The wind in the trees sounds deeper, more resonant, like tenor or bass notes.

While walking the boardwalk, make note of the wildlife you see along the way. At the walk's end, just outside the center, there is a blackboard. You or your children can write down what you saw, like a black-crowned night heron and an anhinga.

Since 1912, the National Audubon Society has protected wading birds nesting within the area. Swamps were favorite logging places during the 1800s, with heavy logging in the 1930s. During the 1940s and 1950s, a push was on to level all cypress forests in Florida for their lumber. The largest forest of ancient bald cypress in North America is right here.

Fourteen conservation groups plus individuals formed the Corkscrew Cypress Rookery Association. An acquisition program was worked out with forest owners, and Audubon agreed to manage the area. Corkscrew Swamp Sanctuary was acquired in 1954.

You go to Corkscrew to be awed and to pay your respects to the bald cypress, the marsh, the prairie, and the pine flatwoods. Inside Corkscrew is a cycle of life that has gone on for generations. To survive, it needs both our attention and our respect.

Bonus Points

As part of the Gateway dedication ceremony, a new South Florida section guide to the Great Florida Birding Trail was introduced. Birders cheered when a mock-up of the cover was unveiled. The Great Florida Birding Trail is a program of the Florida Fish and Wildlife Conservation Commission.

The boardwalk at Corkscrew Swamp Sanctuary, Naples.

SOUTHWEST FLORIDA

There are four section guides in all: West Florida; the East Section; Panhandle Florida; and South Florida. Birding guides are free. You'll find them at state parks, sanctuaries, state forests, and national wildlife refuges. Guides can also be downloaded or ordered from this Web site: www.floridabirdingtrail.com.

The Blair Audubon Center has a nature store with books, binoculars, and all things birding. A yearly schedule of programs offered at Corkscrew is available at the center or visit www.corkscrew.audubon. org.

To get a good taste of the Greater Everglades ecosystem, visit Collier-Seminole State Park, located 15 miles south of Naples on U.S. 41 (Tamiami Trail). The address is: 20200 Tamiami Trail East, Naples, FL 34114, phone (239) 394-3397. Web site address: www.floridastateparks. org. Admission is $4 per vehicle for up to 8 people. Hours are 8 a.m. to sunset. Campsites are available.

Once occupied by the Calusa and Tequesta Indians and Spanish explorers, this area was the last refuge for the Seminoles. The park has a tropical hammock and is one of the few places where rare Florida royal palms thrive.

Royal Palm Hammock Nature Trail goes nine-tenths of a mile through the hammock. The loop trail, on both dirt and boardwalks, includes an observation deck overlooking a salt marsh.

Warning: sections of boardwalk along the trail are old and covered with mold and mildew. The surface is slippery. Footwear with good traction is recommended.

The entrance to this trail is across from the boat/canoe basin on Blackwater River. The basin is a good place for a family picnic. Benches are situated facing the river. Picnic tables are scattered on a grassy knoll, along with a playground, jungle gym, a park store, and restrooms.

At an informational kiosk next to the walking dredge used to help build the Tamiami Trail, look for a free brochure about the Everglades

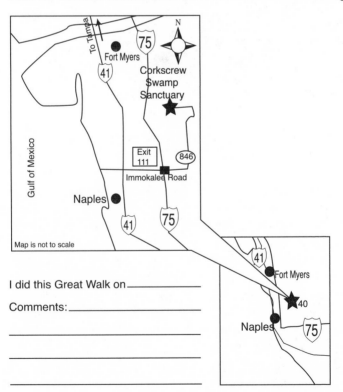

SOUTHWEST FLORIDA

I did this Great Walk on _____

Comments: _____

_____

_____

_____

Trail. Former Florida governor and U.S. senator Bob Graham helped start this trail. A map shows twenty places to see, self-guided, in no particular order. A narrated CD about the trail is available at the park visitor center.

Trip Essentials

Name: Walk with Audubon: Corkscrew Swamp Sanctuary, Naples
Type of walk: Nature
Length of walk: 2.25 miles on raised boardwalk
Time to finish: 1 to 2 hours
Difficulty: Easy. Dirt trail. Wood boardwalks. Wheelchair accessible.
Appeals to: Families, photographers, nature buffs, and birders (Corkscrew is a designated Gateway on the Great Florida Birding Trail; see page 15, South Florida guide to the trail.)
Guides: Self-guided. Companion field guide costs $2. Audubon programs, including guided walks both day and night, are scheduled from November to May. Fee and preregistration required.
Address: 375 Sanctuary Road, Naples, FL 34120
Phone: (239) 348-9151
Web site: www.corkscrew.audubon.org
Cost: $10 adults; $6 full-time college students; $5 Audubon members; $4 children 6–18; children under 6 admitted free
Getting there: From I-75, take exit 111 and go east on Immokalee Road/County Road 846 for 15 miles. Turn left on Sanctuary Road. The road makes a 90-degree bend left. Stay on paved road to Sanctuary sign on the right.
GPS coordinates: N 26° 39056 W 081° 62
Hours: 7 a.m. to 7:30 p.m. from April 11 through September 30; 7 a.m. to 5:30 p.m. from October 1 through April 10. Closed during severe weather.
Restrooms: At Blair Audubon Center
Water/food: Small selection of bottled water and food available at Blair Audubon Center Tea Room.
Dogs: No
Lunch ideas: Bring your own. Picnic areas adjacent to the parking lot.

Part V

Southeast Florida

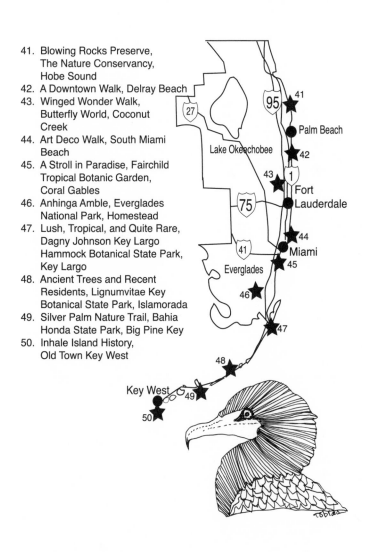

41

Into the Sea Grapes

Blowing Rocks Preserve, The Nature Conservancy, Hobe Sound

Pick a label: Native Florida habitat, restoration project in progress, a safe place for plants and animals. Blowing Rocks Preserve on Jupiter Island is all of these things and more.

There's a shoreline walk along Indian River Lagoon, a boardwalk going through mangroves, a native plant nursery, a butterfly garden, an exhibit center, and a dune walk that goes through an arbor of sea grapes.

The 73-acre barrier-island sanctuary, owned and managed by The Nature Conservancy, was not supposed to exist at all. A developer planned to build high-density homes right here. But a funny thing happened on the way to concrete and construction. The residents of Jupiter Island rose up to protest, took the developer to court to stop the project, and won. Then they bought the land and gave it to The Nature Conservancy in 1969.

You will find the beach entrance to the preserve on the ocean side of South Beach Road. After paying an admission of $2 per person (children under 12 admitted free), a pathway to the beach goes immediately into a tropical hardwood hammock, with sea grapes and gumbo-limbo trees forming a canopy.

Just a short distance along the hammock the path dead-ends at a beach crossover. An overlook platform gives a good view of the limestone rocks lining the beach like a long, low shelf. This is Anastasia limestone, and the outcropping you see is the largest on the Atlantic coast.

The rocks look pretty tame when the tide is out. These are the famous blowing rocks. When winds and high tides come together, incoming salt water gets forced through holes in the rocks, and huge sprays of water shoot up into the air, an impressive sight.

To the left there is an archway made by human hands carefully sculpting sea grapes. A path goes straight along the top of a sand dune with the sculpted sea grapes providing an arbor overhead.

The morning I walked the dune path, the Atlantic Ocean was a spectacular blue green. It was so calm that waves barely rippled when they came ashore. The sky glowed a soft blue like the color of blue hydrangeas. Puffy clouds trailed long, wispy ends as though cotton candy strands had been twirled off into space.

Whenever you visit, the beach scene is changing. In the summertime, the north end of the beach is where three species of sea turtles—loggerhead, green, and leatherback—lumber ashore in the night hours to lay their eggs.

A sign tells you that turtle nesting season is June to September and to refrain from digging or sticking fishing poles or umbrellas into the sand during those months as you might hit a nest. Also, carry out your trash or put it in receptacles. Turtles are not too particular about what they eat. If a plastic bag is ingested, it won't be digested. The bag becomes an obstruction, and the turtle dies from starvation.

Walking on the wide sandy path, it doesn't seem possible that these dunes were once part of A1A. But it is true. This was A1A before road planners realized it made more sense to move the road away from the shifting dunes and the high tides. The road was moved inland in the 1950s.

Take time to contemplate sea grapes, native to South Florida and the Caribbean. Their green pie-shaped leaves have lighter veins inside the leaves. The veins look like bare trees. In their display of fall color, sea grape leaves turn from green to a lovely, deep, red brown. When they fall on the ground, the colors change again to tans and ochres.

The sand dune trail ends unceremoniously. You leave the sea-grape arbor and then step into a small clearing with a trail roundabout and a path to the right that leads down the dune to the beach. My suggestion is to walk the beach on the way back. If you do that, now is a fine time to take off your shoes and walk close to the water.

Once you are back at the beach overlook, take a look back at where you have been and give yourself a pat on the back. Congratulations.

PVC pipe used to anchor young mangroves in a shoreline restoration project at Blowing Rocks Preserve.

SOUTHEAST FLORIDA

You have just walked the best of two worlds—sand dunes and the beach.

There are more trails on the lagoon side of Blowing Rocks Preserve. Take the Restoration Trail to the left of the Hawley Education Center. It is a loop trail one-third of a mile long. The elevated path you walk along near the water's edge didn't exist decades ago. Wakes caused by passing boats in the lagoon threw up small amounts of sand that eventually made a berm and then a shallow lagoon. Wetlands became isolated from tidal ebb and flow.

After finishing the Restoration Trail, go to the other side of Hawley Education Center and walk the lagoon boardwalk. Right across from the lagoon boardwalk is a demonstration butterfly garden, a small area totally packed with plants and yet with room enough for several benches so you can sit and watch the butterflies.

After walking on both sides of the road, stand a moment and enjoy the fact that this safe haven for natural beauty exists and will be there when you come back one day with your grandchildren.

Bonus Points

Loggerhead Park has free admission. Located at 14200 U.S. Highway I, Juno Beach, FL 33408, the Palm Beach County park lives up to it name. Inside the park you will find the Loggerhead Marinelife Center, phone (561) 627-8280. The Web site is: www.marinelife.org.

The center hours are 10 a.m. to 4 p.m. Tuesday through Saturday; 1 p.m. to 3 p.m. Sunday; closed Monday. No admission fee; donations requested. A sea turtle hospital operates at the rear of the center.

The sea turtle hospital is a great place to bring children and grandchildren. In addition to the center, the park has numerous picnic pavilions. Beach access is across the street from the park and involves crossing a road.

John D. MacArthur Beach State Park, the only state park in Palm Beach County, encompasses 317 acres of uplands and another 120 acres of submerged lands on the north end of Singer Island. The location is 10900 State Road 703 (A1A), North Palm Beach, FL 33408, phone (561) 624-6950. Web address is: www.floridastateparks.org.

Admission is $4 per vehicle for up to 8 people. Hours are 8 a.m. to sunset. Their nature center, inside the park, has a gift shop and interpretive displays. The center hours are 9 a.m. to 5 p.m. daily, phone (561) 624-6952.

MacArthur functions as a community gathering place, a public beach access point, and an education hub with summer camps, guided snorkeling trips, kayak tours, sea turtle information, guided walks, and birding opportunities. The park is listed on page 22 of the South Florida guide to the Great Florida Birding Trail.

On a Sunday afternoon, you may find a bluegrass band playing at the nature center. Kayaks will be pulled up on shore as some folks

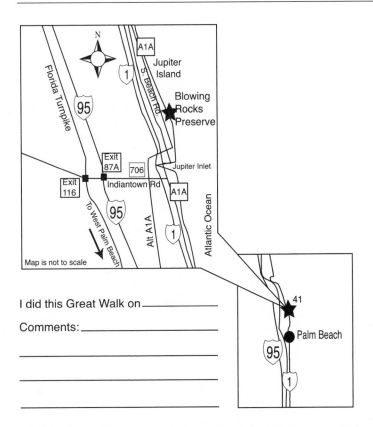

I did this Great Walk on _____

Comments: _____

_____

_____

_____

arrive at the concert by water. Kayaking and canoeing are popular in Lake Worth Cove, as is going over to Munyon Island, accessible by boat only. Check with the park for upcoming events.

Lake Worth Cove, a mangrove-lined estuary, runs up the middle of the park. A 1,600-foot-long boardwalk goes over the cove to the beach. The boardwalk is adjacent to the nature center and parking lots.

For a faster trip across the long boardwalk, especially appreciated after a day of sun and fun at the beach, a free tram service runs back and forth along the boardwalk from 10 a.m. to 4:30 p.m. Ask for free brochures, including a park birding checklist and a self-guided walking tour of park plants.

Both Loggerhead Marinelife Center and John D. MacArthur Beach State Park offer guided turtle walks at night during June and July (see chapter 30).

Trip Essentials

Name: Into the Sea Grapes: Blowing Rocks Preserve, The Nature Conservancy, Hobe Sound

Type of walk: Nature/beach

Length of walk: 1 mile round trip, plus one-third mile if also doing the Restoration Trail

Time to finish: 1 to 1 1/2 hours

Difficulty: Easy. Sand and pavement trail. Not handicapped accessible.

Appeals to: Nature buffs, gardeners, photographers, families, and birders

Guides: Self-guided. Free brochure. Some guided walks scheduled; see Web site.

Address: Blowing Rocks Preserve, 574 South Beach Road, Hobe Sound, FL 33455

Phone: (561) 744-6668

Web site: www.nature.org/florida. Click on "Blowing Rocks."

Cost: $2 per person for beach access; children 12 and under admitted free

Getting there: Coming from the south on I-95, take Jupiter exit 87A (Indiantown Road) and go east on Indiantown to U.S. 1. Turn north (left) onto U.S. 1 at Jupiter Inlet. Right after crossing the bridge, turn right on South Beach Road (C.R. 707). Go 2 miles and look for preserve sign. Parking is 1/2 mile ahead.

GPS coordinates: (Jupiter Island) N 27° 03.139 W 080° 10.083

Hours: 9 a.m. to 4:30 p.m. every day except major holidays

Restrooms: Inside Hawley Education Center on the lagoon side

Water/food: Water inside center; no food. No picnicking allowed.

Dogs: No

Lunch ideas: Seafood and American (and a great view of Jupiter Inlet and the lighthouse), at the Crab House, 1065 North Highway A1A, Jupiter, FL 33477, phone (561) 744-1300; barbecue at Park Avenue BBQ & Grill of Tequesta, 236 South U.S. Highway 1, Tequesta, FL 33477, phone (561) 747-7427

SOUTHEAST FLORIDA

42

Vanishing Florida

A Downtown Walk, Delray Beach

As cities go, Delray Beach, founded in 1895, ranks as a new kid on the block, especially when compared with an ancient city like St. Augustine, founded in 1565.

Age is relative. Anything over fifty years old is considered historic. We're talking buildings here, not people. What were YOU thinking?

In 1894, African-American families from the Panhandle, Georgia, and South Carolina arrived, followed the next year by white homesteaders from Michigan. William S. Linton, postmaster of Saginaw, Michigan, bought lands and solicited settlers and named the town Linton for himself. The name changed to Delray in 1900.

Atlantic Avenue became the main thoroughfare, and, like many small-town main streets all over America, it became comfortable and familiar. Combining with a small community east of the canal that sat on the Atlantic Ocean, the whole area became Delray Beach in 1927.

The first elementary and high schools, built in 1913, shared the same building. A separate high school was built in 1925, followed by a gymnasium in 1926. All were constructed in diverse styles including masonry vernacular and Mediterranean revival.

In the 1980s, no longer used for education, the schools were scheduled for demolition. Local citizens balked. They saw a new life for the buildings as a cultural arts center, and Delray's preservation movement began.

At the intersection of Swinton and Atlantic Avenues you will find the Old School Square Complex, with all the restored buildings now listed as a National Historic Site.

A free brochure, "Downtown Delray Beach, Florida: Village by the Sea," available at many businesses, lists places of historical inter-

The Old School is part of the Old School Square Cultural Arts Center in Delray Beach.

est along with all the municipal parking lot locations. Or, before you leave home, download the "City of Delray Beach Historic Architecture Walking Tour" from: www.mydelraybeach.com (look under "Planning & Zoning").

The Old School Square is part of a historic district that covers fifteen blocks of what used to be the center of town. Leaving Old School Square, go north on Swinton to the next block, NE 1st Street. The Delray Beach Historical Society has its offices and a small museum in Cason Cottage and a bungalow that was moved to this corner site in 2002 to save it from demolition. History covered in the museum exhibits spans 1915 to 1936.

One block north on Swinton is Banker's Row, where many town leaders built Mediterranean revival and frame vernacular homes during the 1920s and 1930s. Today the area is both residential and commercial. You are in a city section with two designations—Pineapple Grove Main Street along with the Old School Square Historic District.

A suggested route at this point would be to turn right (east) onto NE 3rd Street and walk toward the railroad tracks. Once you reach the tracks, turn right (south) onto Railroad Avenue. You soon come to a small complex of shops and businesses between NE 1st Avenue and Atlantic Avenue.

Delray Beach is very good at making new things look old, and they outdo themselves here. Modern shops have old facades. Some walls are covered with bougainvillea vines that look like they've been there a long time. On one building, there is a mural of eighteenth-century people waving from the back of a train, but the historic 1896 train station itself was destroyed by fire. The only thing left is a 40-foot freight building tucked into the complex of new buildings.

Back on Atlantic Avenue, if you're up for a 1-mile stroll to the beach, turn left and begin your promenade. The wide sidewalks invite outdoor dining. On the morning we took this walk, we observed a waiter spreading out white linen tablecloths, then setting a vase with a fresh red rose in the center of each table. Parts of historic Delray Beach may be vanishing, but touches of the old elegance live on.

Even the bridge over the Intracoastal Waterway is historic, built in 1951. Three blocks past the Intracoastal is the Atlantic Ocean. At the water's edge, turn right onto Ocean Boulevard. The Sandoway House at 142 South Ocean Boulevard was built in 1936 and is one of the last frame vernacular style homes on the beach.

Bonus Points

Five historic districts make the list in the Local Register of Historic Places in Delray Beach: Old School Square, Nassau Park, Del-Ida Park, Marina, and West Settlers. Individual district maps can be downloaded from www.mydelraybeach.com.

The stroll we took does not go through all five historic districts but takes you on a walk through a mixture of old and new Delray Beach. History buffs can download the tour map and/or the individual maps. You can easily walk or drive to every district.

Those wanting to see the inside of the art museum need to plan a visit around the museum's hours. The Cornell Museum of Art & History, 51 North Swinton Avenue, Delray Beach, FL 33444, phone (561) 243-7922, is open 10:30 a.m. to 4:30 p.m. Tuesday through Saturday; 1 p.m. to 4:30 p.m. on Sunday; closed Monday and major holidays; closed Sunday from May 1 through September 30. Admission is $6 adults; $4 seniors and students 14–21; children 13 and under admitted free. Web site: www.oldschool.org.

The Cason Cottage Complex, 5 NE 1st Street, Delray Beach, FL 33444, phone (561) 274-9578 or (561) 243-2577, has a museum that displays local history from 1915 to 1936. The museum is open for tours by request. Donations are appreciated.

Sandoway House Nature Center, 142 South Ocean Boulevard, Delray Beach, FL 33483, phone (561) 274-7263, is open 10 a.m. to 4 p.m. Tuesday through Saturday; and noon to 4 p.m. on Sunday; closed Monday and major holidays. Admission is $3. Web site: www.sandowayhouse. com.

Check their schedule on the Web site. Sandoway has a lot going on each month such as nature walks, astronomy nights, turtle walks, and butterfly garden demonstrations.

The Morikami Museum and Japanese Gardens are at 4000 Morikami Park Road, Delray Beach, FL 33446, phone (561) 495-0233. Hours are 10 a.m. to 5 p.m. daily except Monday and major national holidays. Admission is $10 plus tax for adults 19–64; $9 plus tax for those 65 and up; children 6–18 and college students pay $6 plus tax; while children under 6 are admitted free. Morikami has a café that is open from 11 a.m. to 3 p.m. Tuesday through Sunday. Web site: www. morikami.org.

The Japanese Gardens are designed for their beauty. There are no signs with names of plants and trees. The visitor center has a sign saying plants are not identified because Morikami seeks ambiance rather than horticulture knowledge.

An audio guide can be rented for $3, and many visitors take advantage of the extra learning opportunity. The gardens are grouped around a lake. The complete circle around the lake is seven-tenths of a mile.

For a walk on the wild side, go to Arthur R. Loxahatchee National Wildlife Refuge, 10216 Lee Road, Boynton Beach, FL 33437. The phone number for the visitor center is (561) 734-8303. Reach the administrative office at (561) 732-3684. Web site: www.loxahatchee.fws.gov/ home.

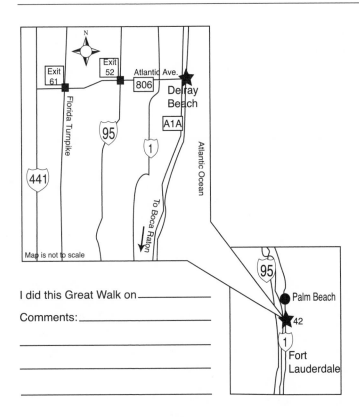

I did this Great Walk on_____

Comments:_____

_____

_____

_____

Refuge hours are 6 a.m. to 8:30 p.m. every day of the year. Public access by two entrances: the headquarters area, off U.S. 441; and the Hillsboro area at the west end of Loxahatchee Road.

An entrance fee of $5 per vehicle is charged. America the Beautiful, Golden Access, Golden Eagle, and Duck Stamp annual passes get in free. At the headquarters area is a visitor center open 9 a.m. to 4 p.m. Monday through Friday; and 9 a.m. to 4:30 p.m. Saturday and Sunday. These hours are good from mid-October through April. The rest of the year hours are 9 a.m. to 4:30 p.m. Wednesday through Sunday.

Even if the visitor center is closed when you visit, you will enjoy walking the cypress swamp boardwalk, a quarter-mile loop that starts behind the center. The South Florida guide to the Great Florida Bird-

SOUTHEAST FLORIDA

ing Trail recommends birding on the boardwalk and even in the visitor center parking lot.

The refuge is a designated Gateway for the Great Florida Birding Trail; see page 26 of the South Florida guide to the trail.

Trip Essentials

Name: Vanishing Florida: A Downtown Walk, Delray Beach
Type of walk: Historic
Length of walk: About 1.2 miles from Old School Square on Swinton down Atlantic to the beach. More to walk the separate historic districts. There are five districts in all.
Time to finish: 2 hours
Difficulty: Easy. Pavement. Wheelchair accessible.
Appeals to: History buffs, photographers, vacationers, and families
Guides: Self-guided. Delray Beach Historical Society gives occasional walking and trolley tours. Call (561) 274-9578 for schedule.
Address: Begin historic walk at Old School Square, 51 North Swinton Ave., or at Cason Cottage, 5 NE 1st Ave., Delray Beach, FL 33444
Phone: Delray Old School Square (561) 243-7922; Delray Beach Historical Society (Cason Cottage) (561) 243-0223
Web site: www.mydelraybeach.com
Cost: None
Getting there: Delray Beach is south of West Palm Beach. From I-95, take exit 52B (State Road 806) going east. S.R. 806 is Atlantic Avenue, which leads to downtown Delray Beach.
GPS coordinates: (Delray Beach Public Library) N 26° 27.15 W 080° 04.15
Hours: Walking tour best during daylight hours
Restrooms: Public restrooms at Sandoway parking lot next to Sandoway Nature Center and Anchor Park
Water/food: Drinking fountain at Anchor Park; numerous restaurants
Dogs: Leashed on the street, none allowed in buildings. No dogs allowed east of Ocean Boulevard (on the beach).
Lunch ideas: American, at City Oyster, 213 East Atlantic Ave., Delray Beach, FL 33444, phone (561) 272-0220; Italian and American, at Luna Rosa Cafe, 34 South Ocean Blvd., Delray Beach, FL 33483, phone (561) 274-9404

43

Winged Wonder Walk

Butterfly World, Coconut Creek

Music wafts through the air as you approach the entrance to Butterfly World. It's light and lilting, a fitting prelude to what you are about to see.

Inside Butterfly World, hundreds of butterflies flutter from one nectar flower to another. The first part you enter is called Paradise Adventure, and the name fits. The flowers are brilliant colors, with lots of red, a favorite butterfly color. Lush tropical foliage drapes over waterfalls that flow into ponds. Even the soft piano music in the background is beautiful.

The whole life cycle of butterflies and moths is lived out here inside screened domes connected to one another by doorways and walkways. All butterflies are hatched at Butterfly World's butterfly farm, not captured in the wild. Caterpillars eat leaves, and butterflies emerge from the chrysalis stage and get to work eating and reproducing.

Winding paths inside the domes make you slow down to a meandering pace, all the better to see more butterflies. Volunteers are stationed along the paths, ready to answer questions. My son Martin and I are rather shocked to learn that the Atlas moth hasn't got a mouth and lives only about two days. Its sole purpose is to reproduce. It seems regrettable that something so beautiful has such a short life span.

The largest enclosure is the Tropical Rainforest, with over five thousand butterflies. The 8,000-square-foot screened enclosure reaches 30 feet in height. This open-air environment is billed as the world's single-largest butterfly habitat.

Hanging gardens and the butterfly emerging garden are where caterpillars turn from mean leaf-eating machines into beautiful butterflies. Metamorphosis—the process of turning from a pupa into a

Can you see two snakes on the Atlas moth? The design works to scare away predators.

caterpillar into a nectar-eating winged wonder—could take days or weeks, even years. Butterfly World releases up to thirty-five pupae each week from their butterfly farm.

Outside the domed enclosures, the walkway continues through Grace Gardens, a flowering botanical garden with a large pond. Native Florida butterflies are flying wild here.

The nifty Secret Garden has long walkways landscaped with arbors. All are overflowing with passion-flower vines and other butterfly-friendly plants. The English Rose Garden adds to the overall beauty.

The Tinalandia suspension bridge crosses over the pond. It actually sways. Children like to run across it. Adults prefer to walk. On the other side of the bridge are macaws and parrots. Then it is back into another screened enclosure. This one is the Jewels of the Sky Hummingbird Aviary.

For such small birds, they have a large number of enemies including birds, frogs, wasps, snakes, lizards, praying mantises, and spiders. For their size, hummingbirds have the largest heart and brain of all animals.

The walkway winds down at the end by taking you through an outdoor display of butterfly plants for sale; then you enter a gift shop complete with books on hummingbirds and butterflies, coloring books, puzzles, T-shirts—the whole gamut.

Bonus Points

Butterfly World has a campaign called "Bring Back the Butterflies." It is a call to people in the continental United States and Canada to counteract butterfly-habitat destruction by starting a small garden with host and nectar plants for local butterflies. The Web site www.butterflyworld.com has lists of plants for different areas of the country.

For young children, the Web site has several resources, including a sweet little booklet about colors. Each color is illustrated with a butterfly. For example, a blue morpho is pictured for the color blue. The booklet can be downloaded at no cost.

Butterfly World, a private facility, is located inside Tradewinds Park, a Broward County park. In addition to picnic tables and walkways, Tradewinds Park has a multitude of sport activities. Fees are charged for different tours, guided trail rides, educational farm tours, and rentals including large picnic shelters and lake-house boats.

For their schedule and fees, call (954) 968-3880. There is no admission fee to the park on weekdays. There is a $1 per person admission fee on weekends, with children under 5 admitted free.

Fern Forest Nature Center, 201 South Lyons Road, Coconut Creek, FL 33063, phone (954) 970-0150, has free admission. There are nature

Schoolchildren enjoy crossing the suspension bridge at Butterfly World, Coconut Creek.

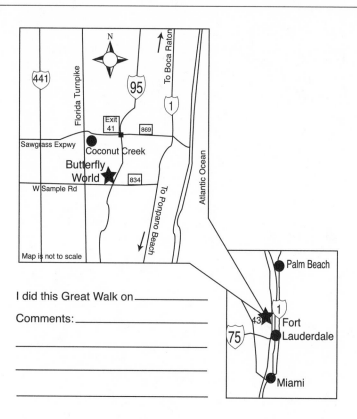

I did this Great Walk on _____

Comments: _____

_____

_____

_____

walks, including a half-mile boardwalk through hammock, and a sensory garden. Web site: www.broward.org.

Trip Essentials

Name: Winged Wonder Walk: Butterfly World, Coconut Creek
Type of walk: Nature, botanical
Length of walk: Not measured
Time to finish: 2 to 3 hours
Difficulty: Easy. Pavement. Wheelchair accessible.
Appeals to: Gardeners, families, children, photographers, and nature buffs
Guides: Self-guided. Volunteers are situated throughout the facility to answer questions.

Address: Butterfly World is a private facility inside Tradewinds Park, a Broward County Park at 3600 West Sample Road, Coconut Creek, FL 33073

Phone: (954) 977-4400

Web site: www.butterflyworld.com

Cost: $18.95 adults and seniors; $13.95 children 3–11; children under 3 admitted free

Getting there: Located 10 miles north of Ft. Lauderdale. From I-95, exit at Sample Road, head west, enter at Tradewinds Park. Butterfly World is straight ahead about 1/3 of a mile

GPS coordinates: (Coconut Creek Park) N 26° 24167 W 080° 1825

Hours: Monday through Saturday, 9 a.m. to 5 p.m.; Sunday 1 p.m. to 5 p.m. Admission gate closes at 4 p.m.

Restrooms: In the entrance area

Water/food: Water at restrooms; no food allowed.

Dogs: No

Lunch ideas: Lakeside Café inside Butterfly World. Or pack a cooler and use the picnic areas in Tradewinds Park.

44

The Delight of Deco

Art Deco Walk, South Miami Beach

Sun and fun. That's why people go to Miami Beach. Even the buildings get in the mood.

South Beach, the twenty-three blocks of lower Miami Beach that locals call Sobe, delights in art deco architecture. To learn more about the Art Deco District in South Beach, and have fun doing it, take a guided tour offered several times a week through the Miami Design Preservation League. This district has the largest collection of art deco architecture in the world.

Twenty blocks of Miami Beach—a square mile of hotels, apartments, and other buildings built between 1923 and 1946—comprise the Art Deco District, listed in the National Register of Historic Places since 1979. It's the first historic district to recognize twentieth-century architecture. You will see art deco plus Mediterranean revival and MiMo (Miami modern) styles.

The walk starts just outside the Art Deco Welcome Center, a small building with a gift shop located next to Lummus Park on Ocean Drive. The day my son Martin and I took the tour, Matt Ruiz was our guide. He tells us the only natural things to be found here are sky and water. That's it. Everything else is imported, even the sand.

John Collins, a Quaker farmer from New Jersey, tried in 1896 to grow coconuts here but that didn't work. By 1907, he found success growing mangos, avocados, tomatoes, and potatoes.

He discovered freshwater and had designs on land development. Collins started building the Collins Bridge, a wooden bridge 2.5 miles long, over Biscayne Bay to connect Miami Beach with Miami, but he ran out of money. The bridge stopped a half mile short of Miami.

Elongated eyebrows over the tops of windows are a common feature on art deco buildings, Miami Beach.

SOUTHEAST FLORIDA

What Collins lacked in currency he made up for in land. Carl Fisher gave Collins $50,000 to finish the bridge; in return, Fisher got 200 acres of land north of Lincoln Road facing Miami on the bay side. He became known as Mr. Miami Beach because he began building hotels for a resort town.

Hotels made of wood sprang up at the southern end of the beach and moved northward. The hurricane of 1926 demolished most of them. Then came the stock market crash and the Great Depression. Before the hurricane of 1926, much of the architecture was Mediterranean revival.

Art deco architecture arrived in earnest after the 1926 hurricane and took on the influences of sun and fun. One old building that tied itself into its surroundings is the Main Post Office on Washington Avenue and 12th Street. Built in 1939 as a Works Project Administration in the deco Federal style, the steps were made of pink marble to match the sidewalks. There is a city decree, Ruiz tells us, mandating that sidewalks in South Miami Beach will always be red, as in roll-out-the-red-carpet-for-our-visitors red.

The tour covers about a mile, and the route is roughly a rectangle. Fossilized coral was used to front many of the buildings. It was dug up right on the beach. Buildings that had been nautical white and off-white were painted shades of aqua and peach. Coral rock faces were covered with siding, stucco, or paint. When uncovered years later, the lovely coral was still there.

No Art Deco Walk is complete without going inside some of the old hotels. For example, go inside the Victor to see an original mural. Be sure to look down at the floors in these hotels, such as the one in the Sagamore, to see the art deco patterns in the terrazzo floors.

Walk north to see the interiors of the Royal Palm, the San Moritz, the Sagamore, and the National hotels. These hotels are part of the North Beach Resort Historic District, a recent designation.

The basic Art Deco Walk will orient you to the highlights of the district. Come back again, perhaps this time with an art deco book in hand. One book suggestion, available at the Art Deco League gift shop: *Deco Delights: Preserving the Beauty and Joy of Miami Beach Architecture*, by Barbara Baer Capitman (Dutton, 1988).

Bonus Points

We chose the art deco guided tour offered four times a week. There is a second option, a good one for those whose timelines don't mesh with scheduled tours.

The Miami Design Preservation League also has Art Deco District self-guided audio tours. The tapes are in English, Spanish, Portuguese, German, and French. They are available 7 days a week from 10 a.m. to 4 p.m. at the Art Deco Welcome Center, 1001 Ocean Drive, Miami Beach, phone (305) 531-3484.

Other tours offered by the league are titled "Deco to MiMo," "North Beach Tour," "World War II Revisited Tour," and a "Deco Underworld

Tour," all scheduled by appointment. To learn more about these tours, or to arrange a private tour for a minimum of 25 people, call Sheldon S. Brown, tour coordinator, at (305) 672-2014.

In North Miami Beach, there is a piece of history quite different from the Art Deco District. Long before art deco was even a gleam in an architect's eye, the Monastery of Our Lady, Queen of Angels was built in Sacramenia, in the province of Segovia, Spain.

Construction of the monastery took place between 1133 and 1144. Cistercian monks lived in the monastery cloisters for almost seven hundred years. When a famous Cistercian monk, Bernard of Clairvaux, was canonized, the monastery was renamed the Monastery of St. Bernard de Clairvaux.

Following a revolution in the 1830s, the monastery was seized, the monks evicted, and the building used as a granary and stable. In 1925, William Randolph Hearst bought the monastery. It was dismantled piece by piece, and the stones were packed in hay, put in numbered boxes, and shipped to America.

Unfortunately, an outbreak of hoof-and-mouth disease in Segovia had agricultural inspectors in this country afraid of contamination. They opened every box, burned the straw, and never replaced the stones in their numbered boxes.

The monastery stones sat in a warehouse. After Hearst died in 1952, two men purchased the rocks. Their plan was to rebuild the monastery and open it as a tourist attraction in North Miami Beach. Over a period of nineteen months, at a cost of $1.5 million, the monastery was put back together—almost. There is still a pile of unmatched stones.

You can see the Cloisters of the Ancient Spanish Monastery at 16711 West Dixie Highway, North Miami Beach, FL 33160, phone (305) 945-1461. Their Web site is: www.spanishmonastery.com.

Admission is $5 adults; $2.50 seniors; and $2 for children under 12. Hours are Monday through Friday 9 a.m. to 5 p.m.; Saturday 10 a.m. to 5 p.m.; and Sunday 2 p.m. to 5 p.m.

Because it is a church, St. Bernard de Clairvaux Episcopal Church, as well as a cultural heritage, the monastery may close to the public without notice for private events. It is best to call ahead before you visit.

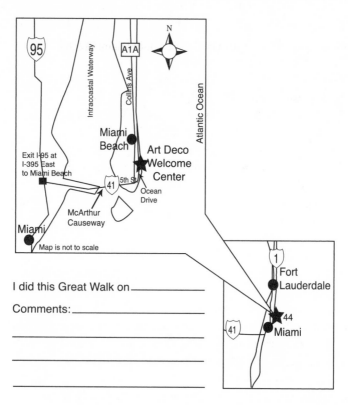

I did this Great Walk on _____

Comments: _____

_____

_____

_____

Oleta River State Park is located nearby at 3400 NE 163rd Street, North Miami Beach, FL 33160, phone (305) 919-1846. Admission is $5 per vehicle for up to 8 people; $3 for a vehicle with 1 person,; $1 for pedestrians and bicyclists. Web site: www.floridastateparks.org.

This is an immensely popular destination for off-road bicycling, with over 10 miles of trails. The paved trails are also good for roller-blading, jogging, and walking. Other activities are picnicking, fishing, kayaking, and swimming. With 1,043 acres, Oleta is the largest urban park in Florida. Located on Biscayne Bay, it is named after the Oleta River.

The Blue Moon Outdoor Center, phone (305) 957-3040, operates inside the park. Kayaks, canoes, and mountain bikes can be rented. Blue Moon organizes outings such as sunset kayak trips and mountain bike events. Their Web site is: www.bluemoonmiami.com.

Trip Essentials

Name: The Delight of Deco: Art Deco Walk, South Miami Beach
Type of walk: Historic
Length of walk: 1 mile
Time to finish: 1 1/2 to 2 hours
Difficulty: Easy. Pavement. Wheelchair accessible. Some hotel entrances
   are not wheelchair accessible.
Appeals to: History buffs, artists, and architecture aficionados
Guides: Guided walking tours by Miami Design Preservation League.
   Self-guided audio tours also available.
Address: Walking tour starts at Art Deco Welcome Center, 1001 Ocean
   Drive, Miami Beach, FL 33139.
Phone: (305) 531-3484
Web site: www.mdpl.org
Getting there: Exit I-95 to Miami Beach, go east on McArthur Causeway,
   exit at the end (Causeway becomes 5th Street). Continue on 5th and
   turn left onto Ocean Drive
Cost: Guided walking tours $20 adult; $15 seniors and students; children
   admitted free
GPS coordinates: (Miami Beach) N 25° 79028 W 080° 13028
Hours: Tours Wednesday, Friday, Saturday, and Sunday at 10:30 a.m.;
   Thursday at 6:30 p.m.
Restrooms: At Lummus Park and public beach next to Art Deco Welcome
   Center
Water/food: Numerous drinking fountains and restaurants at Lummus
   Park
Dogs: Leashed. None allowed in buildings; some restaurants allow pets
   at outdoor seating.
Lunch ideas: Cuban and Spanish, at Puerto Sagua, 700 Collins Ave., Mi-
   ami Beach, FL 33139, phone (305) 673-1115; Deli-style/comfort food, at
   Jerry's Famous Deli, 1450 Collins Ave., Miami Beach, FL 33139, phone
   (305) 532-8030

45

A Stroll in Paradise

Fairchild Tropical Botanic Garden, Coral Gables

In South Florida, Miamians feel about the Fairchild the way Parisians feel about the Eiffel Tower. It is their treasure, and they are proud of it.

Tucked into a residential section of Coral Gables, the main Fairchild entrance is located on Old Cutler Road. Access to the gardens is through a visitor center. The magnitude of the garden is surprising—83 acres with ten ponds and just under 2 miles of pathways.

Allow yourself at least 3 hours, more if you stay for lunch at the café. Wear good walking shoes. Don't worry about walking so far it will be hard to get back. Little electric-powered shuttles, driven by volunteers, will zip by and offer to take you anywhere.

The Fairchild opens at 9:30 a.m. On the hour, starting at 10 a.m., a free tram tour goes all around the garden with stops to let riders off and on. The last tram leaves at 3 p.m. Tram tours last about 45 minutes.

With your admission, you get a free map and visitor guide. From mid-November through April, volunteers give free guided walking tours through the following areas: the Richard H. Simons Rainforest, McLamore Arboretum, Montgomery Palmetum Native Plants, and the Vine Pergola. Times vary for the guided tours. There is no extra charge.

We opted for the free guided walking tour through the western end of the garden. It takes about an hour and covers just under a mile. The Tropical Flower Garden is the first area you walk through. White ibis stride across the walkway. They fan out in the manicured grass, putting red curved beaks into the grass, searching for bugs. Photogra-

Trumpet flowers in the Richard H. Simons Rainforest at Fairchild Tropical Botanic Garden, Coral Gables.

phers quickly adjust to taking pictures of wildlife as well as flowers in bloom.

If your time is limited, definitely include the Windows to the Tropics Conservatory, the Arid Garden, and the Richard H. Simons Rainforest.

In the Rainforest, narrow walkways wind past streams, under trumpet flowers that were blooming the day we visited. It is a short, memorable walk and a highlight of the Fairchild.

The Fairchild opened its doors to the public in 1938. It is the oldest cultural destination in Miami-Dade County. Started by Col. Robert H. Montgomery, an attorney, it is named for Dr. David Fairchild, a botanist who founded the U.S. Department of Agriculture's Foreign Plant Introduction Section.

Botanically, this location is unique. The Miami area is the only region in the United States where tropical and subtropical plants can be grown outdoors all year long. As you walk the pathways, the biodiversity of their collection is evident. Ancient cycads, found with dinosaur fossils on all continents, grow in many sizes and shapes. There are some 200 species of cycads. The Fairchild has about 180 of them.

SOUTHEAST FLORIDA

The lighthouse built in 1825 and reconstructed in 1846, at Bill Baggs Cape Florida State Park, Key Biscayne.

Visiting the Fairchild is a unique experience, but it can be a bit overwhelming. One suggestion: combine a walking tour with a tram tour.

Every day a large army of volunteers descends on the Fairchild. They give guided tours, are available to answer questions, and can be found doing chores throughout the grounds.

It began raining the day my son Martin and I visited, the first rain for that area in thirty days. A volunteer magically appeared with a tray full of ponchos and began handing them out to visitors. We felt welcomed. You will too, rain or shine.

Bonus Points

The Cape Florida lighthouse, built in 1825, is the oldest standing structure in Miami-Dade County. It stands inside Bill Baggs Cape Florida

State Park, 1200 South Crandon Boulevard, Key Biscayne, FL 33149, phone (305) 361-5811.

The park is at the end of a peninsula called Key Biscayne. Going over the Rickenbacker Causeway to the peninsula costs $1.25 per car.

Park admission is $5 per vehicle for up to 8 people. The park overlooks Miami and Biscayne Bay. There are nature trails, a bike trail, a playground, showers, and concessions including two places to eat. You'll also find areas for swimming, picnicking, and fishing. Canoes and kayaks can be launched over the sea wall at No Name Harbor.

Tours of the lighthouse are given at 10 a.m. and 1 p.m. Thursday through Monday. No extra charge for a tour. The lighthouse, still in operation, is automated.

There are 109 steps up to the lighthouse watchroom. You can count them going up or coming back down. I chose not to count steps and

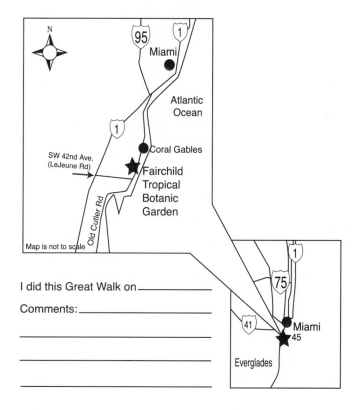

concentrated on two things: breathing and not thinking about the height or the narrow space that gets narrower as you ascend.

Trip Essentials

Name: A Stroll in Paradise: Fairchild Tropical Botanic Garden, Coral Gables

Type of walk: Botanical

Length of walk: Just under 1 mile to walk the east side of the garden. Just under 2 miles if you walk the entire trail through the garden.

Time to finish: 2 to 3 hours

Difficulty: Easy. Pavement. Wheelchair accessible.

Appeals to: Families, gardeners, photographers, and nature lovers

Guides: Self-guided. Volunteers offer guided tours from November 1 to April 30. Schedule varies. No extra charge for guided tour.

Address: 10901 Old Cutler Road, Coral Gables, FL 33156

Phone: (305) 667-1651

Web site: www.fairchildgarden.org

Cost: Entrance fee $15 adults; $12 seniors; children 10 and under admitted free

Getting there: Take I-95 south to U.S. 1 (also called South Dixie Highway). Go south on U.S. 1 to Southwest 42nd Avenue (LeJeune Road). Turn left. Drive south to roundabout. Enter and take the second right onto Old Cutler Road. Fairchild is 2 miles from the roundabout. Entrance is on your left.

GPS coordinates: (Coral Gables Wayside Park) N 25° 73778 W 080° 28667

Hours: 9:30 a.m. to 4:30 p.m. every day except Christmas

Restrooms: At visitor center, Garden House, and across from the Windows to the Tropics Conservatory

Water/food: 5 water fountains along the paths; food at Garden Café

Dogs: No

Lunch ideas: Garden Café. Consider taking a walking tour, have lunch, then take a tram tour.

46

Anhinga Amble

Everglades National Park, Homestead

The environmental writer Marjory Stoneman Douglas lived to be 108 and always championed the Everglades. I interviewed Douglas at her Coconut Grove home when she was ninety-nine. Her eyes saw the world faintly through glasses as thick as the bottom of a glass soda bottle. But her memory was in perfect focus as though everything from long ago had just happened yesterday.

She and her family and friends would drive out to where the road came to a dead end at the edge of the Everglades. That was sixty years before I met her. They would spread out a picnic lunch and enjoyed the view.

While having lunch, they saw wildlife, birds in abundance, and miles of yellow-green grass that swayed in the slight breeze. The grass was dotted with small islands of trees. Marjorie loved those family outings and the Everglades. Little did she know that she would become the "mother of the Everglades."

In 1947, Douglas wrote *The Everglades: River of Grass* (Rinehart). The book forever changed the world's perception of this vast and amazing place.

Congress named the Everglades a national park in 1934. It took thirteen more years to get additional land and funds. The same year Douglas published her book, 1947, Everglades National Park was opened. It covers 1,508,570 acres.

Since those family picnics decades ago and even with the park in place, the Everglades are deeply diminished by drainage and alterations. For every one bird you see today, there were two hundred more back in 1930. Yet it is still possible to see some of what Douglas saw and to feel the same awe at the enormous scale of the Everglades.

Alligators sunning themselves along the route of the Anhinga Amble, Everglades National Park.

To get to the main park entrance from Miami, take the Florida Turnpike south to the last exit, then follow the signs to Everglades National Park. The fee station is just past the Ernest F. Coe Visitor Center. There is one road that goes to the Flamingo Visitor Center, with access to Florida Bay. Your admission is good for seven days, including the day you paid.

From the Coe Visitor Center to the end of the road and Flamingo Visitor Center is a 38-mile drive. Along the way are walking trails, more visitor centers, and overlooks.

Royal Palm is a visitor center 4 miles inside of the park. It is an excellent place to see wildlife. The Anhinga Amble guided walks, done on a half-mile loop of paved trail and boardwalks, are regularly scheduled. Or do your own walk.

As we waited for people to gather for a guided Anhinga Trail walk, a woman walked up to the volunteer guide and wanted to know if the alligator on the bank was real. Yep. Real. What part of the word "wildlife" don't people understand? Do they think the alligator sitting immobile on the bank is a prop they can sit on to pose for a photograph? People have tried that.

Reality check: There is a reason for the retaining wall along the Anhinga Trail. It separates wildlife from people. Life in the wild is a daily round of finding things to eat and sometimes being eaten. Anyone who does not appreciate this fact of life, and treats alligators as toys, could end up as sushi. The best way to view all wildlife is not to invade their space but observe them from a distance through binoculars or a camera lens.

The Anhinga Trail follows part of the old Ingraham Highway completed in 1916. It is a paved walkway with some boardwalks as overlooks. There is an unscripted agreement between people and wildlife. People walk slowly or stand still and take pictures. Wildlife goes about its business as though all the people were not there.

Wood storks shuffle their feet on the marsh bottom, stirring things up, grabbing their prey. Anhingas and cormorants dive for fish, come up, flip the fish down their throats head first, then retreat to a tree limb to spread their wings and let them dry.

Along the trail is an overlook that offers a fabulous view of the vast sea of yellow-green grass, swaying gently in a breeze.

The seasons here in Everglades National Park are quite simple—wet and dry. As the wet season ends and the dry season begins, the water levels drop. Fish become more concentrated and draw a concentration of predators. For photographers and nature buffs, this is a golden wildlife viewing time. The best months are December through April.

The Royal Palm area got its name from trees and a park. Royal Palm State Park, formed in 1916 with 4,000 acres, was given to the nation and became the nucleus of Everglades National Park. The royal palms are still here. They can grow up to 100 feet tall and live one hundred years. A beautiful royal palm is located in a grassy area right at the beginning of the Anhinga Trail. Six of the fourteen kinds of palms native to the United States thrive right here.

Bonus Points

To the right of the Anhinga Trail is the Gumbo Limbo Trail, a half-mile loop through a dense hardwood hammock reshaped by Hurricane Andrew in 1992 but still dense, lush, and tropical.

The trail is aptly named. Gumbo-limbo trees have their red, peeling limbs stretched across the trail. Those peeling limbs give this tree the nickname "tourist tree," as in red and peeling from too much sun. In places, you have to duck under the limbs. One gumbo-limbo tree grows right in the middle of the paved walkway.

The trail goes past a wetland section. This is where you will be glad you wore bug repellent. Surely you have your mosquito stories. We all do. Here is one:

A photographer friend grew up in South Florida. One day in August he and some high school buddies decided they had to go see the Everglades. Arriving at the park, they looked around and said: "Cool, nobody here. We have the place to ourselves."

As they got out of the car, mosquitoes immediately descended in dark clouds all around them. They all screamed, jumped back in their car, and left. He has never been back.

The moral of this story: From May through September, mosquitoes rule.

For an interactive education on the Everglades and its challenges, go to the Ernest F. Coe Visitor Center, the park headquarters at 40001 State Road 9336, Homestead, FL 33034-6733, phone (305) 242-7700.

Coe Visitor Center hours are 8 a.m. to 5 p.m. December through April; and 9 a.m. to 5 p.m. May through November. There is no charge to visit the center. It is located just before the park entrance fee station. A regular schedule of ranger-led walks and talks, at no extra charge, can be found at the Web site: www.nps.gov/ever.

In the Everglades, water and life go hand in hand. Historically, rainwater flowed from the Kissimmee River basin south to Lake Okeechobee. From there, the water moved into the shallow, 50-mile-wide River of Grass—the Everglades—flowing south at the rapid rate of 100 feet a day and ending up in Florida Bay.

Hurricanes in the 1920s led to dike building at Lake Okeechobee. Then a series of channels were built and freshwater diverted. Much of it goes out to tides, into oceans, and never makes it to Florida Bay. Restoration projects are under way, but the four factors of management—quality, quantity, timing, and distribution of water—remain the subject of intense debate.

An interactive exhibit at the Coe Visitor Center has cutouts of different people involved in water issues. There is a housewife, a farmer, a water manager, a fisherman, a ranger, and an environmentalist. You can pick up the telephone on a table, push a button, and hear each one's comments on water and the Everglades. It is a good way to present many sides of the water issue.

Hurricanes continue to change the Everglades landscape. In 2005, Hurricanes Katrina, Rita, and Wilma delivered storm surges that required massive recovery efforts.

On Highway 41 (Tamiami Trail), some 30 miles west of the Florida Turnpike, is the Shark Valley Visitor Center, another entranceway into Everglades National Park. The phone number is (305) 221-8776. Hours are 8:30 a.m. to 4:45 p.m. December through April; and 9 a.m. to 4:30 p.m. from May through November. Admission is $10 per vehicle.

The Tram Trail is 15 miles long, and wildlife viewing is often excellent. A tram tour provides a good introduction to the Everglades. Reservations required. Call (305) 221-8455. The cost is $14 adults; $13 seniors 62 and older; $8.50 children 12 and under.

The Tram Trail is popular with walkers and bicyclists. Bicycles can be rented at Shark Valley. For a short walk, take the Bobcat Boardwalk, a quarter-mile round-trip walk through a saw-grass marsh. It starts at the Shark Valley Visitor Center. Also starting at the visitor center is the Otter Cave walking trail, a 1-mile round trip through a hardwood hammock.

When you look at a Florida map, you quickly appreciate how big the Everglades are, extending almost coast to coast. The Gulf Coast Visitor Center is 3 miles south of Highway 41 (Tamiami Trail) on Highway 29, south of Everglades City, phone (239) 695-3311. This is a favorite boat-launching point for visits to mangrove estuaries and the Ten Thousand Islands.

Daily boat tours are offered to both the estuary and Ten Thousand Islands. For schedule and fees, call (239) 695-2591.

The Everglades is the only national park to be designated an International Biosphere Reserve, a World Heritage Site, and a Wetland of International Importance.

Marjory Stoneman Douglas said it all in the first sentence of her book. She wrote: "There are no other Everglades in the world."

SOUTHEAST FLORIDA

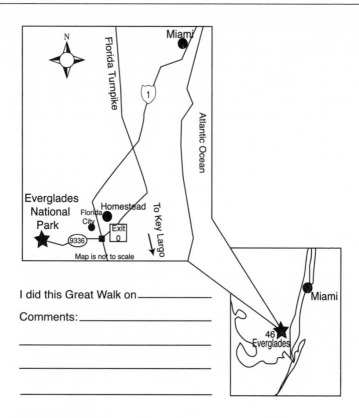

I did this Great Walk on _____

Comments: _____

_____

_____

_____

Trip Essentials

Name: Anhinga Amble: Everglades National Park, Homestead

Type of walk: Nature

Length of walk: Half-mile loop trail

Time to finish: 1 hour

Difficulty: Easy. Pavement, wood boardwalk, dirt trail. Wheelchair accessible.

Appeals to: Families, nature lovers, photographers, and birders (Several parts of Everglades National Park are part of the Great Florida Birding Trail; see page 25 of the South Florida guide to the trail.)

Guides: Weather permitting, the Anhinga Amble is a ranger-guided walk at 10:30 a.m. daily. Schedule subject to change. Check at Coe Visitor Center, phone (305) 242-7700, to confirm time and days.

Address: Everglades National Park, 40001 State Road 9336, Homestead, FL 33034

Phone: (305) 242-7700

Web site: www.nps.gov/ever

Cost: Entrance fee $10 per vehicle; $5 walk-in or bicycle. Fees good for 7 days. Holders of Golden Eagle passports and America the Beautiful passes get in free. No charge for guided walks.

Getting there: From Miami, take the Turnpike south until it ends and merges with U.S. 1 at Florida City. Turn right at first light onto State Road 9336 (Palm Drive). Follow the signs to Everglades National Park

GPS coordinates: N 25° 3125 W 080° 9375

Hours: Main park entrance at Homestead open 24 hours a day. Ernest F. Coe Visitor Center open 8 a.m. to 5 p.m. December through April; 9 a.m. to 5 p.m. May through November.

Restrooms: At all the visitor centers: Ernest F. Coe, Royal Palm, and Flamingo

Water/food: Water at restrooms; no food

Dogs: Not allowed on any trail

Lunch ideas: Picnic areas inside the park at Long Pine Key, Nine Mile Pond, and Flamingo

Lush, Tropical, and Quite Rare

Dagny Johnson Key Largo Hammock Botanical State Park, Key Largo

You are forgiven if you drive right by the entrance to Dagny. Everybody does. A massive archway looks like the front of a California mission or an entranceway to a residential development. As you drive along County Road 905 you see the arch, then wonder where the park begins. The address says it should be right here.

And it is. The grand entrance was made long ago for a condominium development that never happened. The entrance has a new lease on life, recycled as the grand gateway to Dagny Johnson Key Largo Hammock Botanical State Park.

A paved driveway leading from the entrance to an old plaza has become a favorite nature stroll for both locals and visitors fortunate enough to find their way here. Going there and back is just over a mile.

When you go through the archway, you step into the largest remaining fragment of West Indian tropical hardwood hammock in the United States. The entire hammock would have been lost to concrete.

This is wild Florida at its wildest, so dense with tropical trees and vines that you can't see past 10 feet on either side of the trail. It is a jungle in here. Three kinds of ironwood, Jamaica dogwood, sabal palm, wild coffee, mahogany mistletoe, poisonwood—and that is just the tip of the list!

Indians must have found a way through the tropical maze because shell middens exist within the park. Although it looks original to us, and we think the first explorers had the same view we do, what you see today is all second growth. This area was timbered right up until the 1950s. What makes the island hammock seem timeless is the rich-

Elevated board-walk through the mangroves at John Pennekamp Coral Reef State Park.

ness and diversity of the dense jungle growth. If it is tropical, it thrives here.

The denseness that is daunting to humans works well for plants and animals. Dagny has eighty-four protected species of plants and animals, including seven endangered species. Information signs are set along the walkway, helpful in untangling some of the mystery of this tropical hammock.

A word about poisonwood—this tree is aptly named. Dagny has a lot of it. Stay on the trail. Read the signs explaining what poisonwood is and its toxic effects. Some people have allergic reactions to even breathing the tree's odor.

As we walked along, having chosen a day when there was a guided walk, our guide asked why we were here instead of at Pennekamp snor-

SOUTHEAST FLORIDA

keling, because the warm water and lure of coral reefs get all the pub-
licity.

Everyone, all ages, from teenagers to grandparents, said they'd been
to Pennekamp and wanted to see this botanical park. It may be second
growth, but Dagny is as close as you'll get to what the Upper Florida
Keys looked like originally before paradise was paved over to make a
parking lot.

At the end of the half-mile trail, a round plaza that used to have a
large water fountain has been filled in. Picnic tables are here. This is the
turnaround point if you are doing the half-mile Nature Trail only.

Trails continue past the plaza area. In addition to the paved trail,
Dagny has 6 miles of backcountry trails requiring a backcountry per-
mit, which is free. You can get one at John Pennekamp Coral Reef State
Park in Key Largo.

Bonus Points

John Pennekamp Coral Reef State Park is oceanside too, located north
of Key Largo at Mile Marker 102.5, phone (305) 451-1202. Their mailing
address is: P.O. Box 487, Key Largo, FL 33037.

Hours are 8 a.m. to sundown. Admission fees are on a sliding scale.
Every fee has the 50¢ Monroe County fee added to it. Pedestrians/bi-
cyclists pay $1.50; a single-occupant vehicle is $3.50; 2 people pay $6
plus 50¢ cents for each additional occupant up to 8 people.

Covering 70 nautical square miles, Pennekamp has the honor of
being the first underwater park in the United States. John Pennekamp
Coral Reef State Park is next to the Florida Keys National Marine Sanctuary. Together they cover about 178 nautical miles of coral reefs, sea-
grass beds, and mangrove swamps.

For information on boat tours and reservations, phone (305) 451-
6300.

To get you ready for the underwater world, the park's visitor center
has a 30,000-gallon saltwater aquarium, and nature videos are played
constantly. A concession rents everything you need from fins to snor-
kels along with paddleboats, canoes, and kayaks.

Avoid the crowds waiting to go out on the reef by taking a sweet,
and at times impressive, walk through a mangrove swamp. The Mangrove Trail, about eight-tenths of a mile long, winds along an elevated

boardwalk through thick stands of red, black, and white mangroves. At one point, as far as the eye can see, mangroves are everywhere.

Not many trees can stand a saltwater environment. Mangroves can. Worldwide, there are fifty species of mangroves. Florida has three.

An observation tower affords a full landscape view. Red mangroves grow at the water's edge, easily identified by the tangled reddish-colored roots that make it seem as if the tree is walking. Hence the nickname "walking tree."

Black mangroves, with rough pencil-like roots, grow a little farther inland. White mangroves, with flat oval leaves rounded on both ends and large prop roots, grow in the uppermost zone.

If you are all mangroved out, try the Wild Tamarind Trail, which goes inland through a hardwood hammock. It is a quick walk, a little less than a third of a mile.

Some suggestions for planning a Pennekamp visit: Walk the Mangrove Trail first, followed by a boat ride to see the reef (reservations required). Come back, have a picnic lunch at a table near the water, and then enjoy the beach.

Dagny was established in 1982, purchased through Florida's Conservation and Recreational Lands program. The park has 2,400 acres set aside on the north end of Key Largo to protect its ecosystems.

Also purchased to protect ecosystems are the adjacent John Pennekamp Coral Reef State Park and Crocodile Lake National Wildlife Refuge, right across the street from Dagny. Contact: Crocodile Lake National Wildlife Refuge, P.O. Box 370, Key Largo, FL 33037, phone (305) 451-4223. Set aside in 1980, Crocodile Lake has 6,700 acres. It was slated to be a residential development complete with canals.

The Florida Keys are a series of coral rock formations, some big, some small, all strung together by bridges. Once you are in the Keys, it helps to know the local lingo in order to get around. Here are some Key terms:

- "Bayside" means Florida Bay.
- "Oceanside" means Atlantic Ocean.
- U.S. 1 becomes the Overseas Highway in the Keys.
- Mile Markers are small green signs with white numbers.
- Places have street addresses and Mile Marker locations.

SOUTHEAST FLORIDA

- Mile Markers run north to south.
- Mile Marker 112 is north of Key Largo.
- Mile Marker 0 is in Key West.
- Cities cover more than one Key. For example, Islamorada addresses include Long Key, Lignumvitae Key, Lower Matecumbe Key, Indian Key, Upper Matecumbe Key, Windley Key, and Plantation Key.

Dagny, for example, is oceanside. It is located one-half mile north of the intersection of County Road 905 and U.S. Highway 1 at Mile Marker 106, north of Key Largo.

See how easy it is? You will be speaking like a Conch in no time. Conchs were immigrants to Key West from the Bahamas. Conch is a local term used today for a Key West native while Fresh Water Conch applies to people who have moved and lived for more than seven years in Key West.

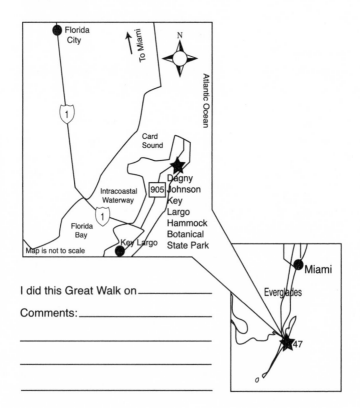

SOUTHEAST FLORIDA

Florida City

To Miami

N

Atlantic Ocean

1

Card Sound

Dagny Johnson Key Largo Hammock Botanical State Park

Intracoastal Waterway

905

1

Florida Bay

Key Largo

Map is not to scale

Miami

Everglades

47

I did this Great Walk on _____

Comments: _____

_____

_____

_____

Trip Essentials

Name: Lush, Tropical, and Quite Rare: Dagny Johnson Key Largo Hammock Botanical State Park, Key Largo

Type of walk: Nature

Length of walk: 1 mile round trip

Time to finish: 45 minutes

Difficulty: Easy. Pavement and dirt trail. Wheelchair accessible.

Appeals to: Nature lovers, plant enthusiasts, photographers, and birders (listed on page 34 of the South Florida guide to the Great Florida Birding Trail)

Guides: Self-guided, or guided walks given at 10 a.m. on Thursday and Sunday. No charge.

Address: Dagny Johnson Key Largo Hammock Botanical State Park, P.O. Box 487, Key Largo, FL 33037. The park is near Mile Marker 106.

Phone: Dagny is administered by John Pennekamp Coral Reef State Park, phone (305) 451-1202.

Web site: www.floridastateparks.org

Cost: $1.50 at self-pay station

Getting there: In the Upper Keys. One-half mile north of the County Road 905 intersection with U.S. Highway 1 at Mile Marker 106.

GPS coordinates: N 25° 28056 W 080° 29722

Hours: 8 a.m. to sundown

Restrooms: Halfway down the Nature Trail

Water/food: Bring your own.

Dogs: Well-behaved and leashed on a 6-foot hand-held lead

Lunch ideas: Seafood, at the Fish House Restaurant and Seafood Market, 102401 Overseas Highway, Mile Marker 102.4, Key Largo, FL 33037, phone (305) 451-4665; American and seafood, at Fish Tales Café, 103400 Overseas Highway, Mile Marker 103, Key Largo, FL 33037, phone (305) 451-0507

SOUTHEAST FLORIDA

48

Ancient Trees and Recent Residents

Lignumvitae Key Botanical State Park, Islamorada

Some things never change. In the 1800s, the only way to reach Lignum-vitae Key was by boat. The same is true today. You get there by private boat, kayak, or canoe. Other choices are to rent a boat or use a charter boat from a nearby marina.

Park rangers, who also arrive by boat, give guided house and hammock tours year-round at 10 a.m. and 2 p.m. Tour days are Thursday through Mondays, weather permitting. Tours last about an hour and a half, and that includes a house tour plus a walk through the hardwoods.

Lignumvitae Key Botanical State Park is located bayside. If you arrive at the island on your own and it is not a tour time, the house will not be open. Visitors are welcome to walk around the grounds (the grassy areas around the house) but are not allowed to go on the trails into the hardwood hammock without a guide. There are more than 4.5 miles of trails on the island, and signs warn that the trails are restricted to tours only.

Getting the most from a visit and a walk in the woods takes some planning to arrive on a tour day (Thursday through Monday) and at the right time (10 a.m. or 2 p.m.).

One example: Robbie's Marina provides tour-boat service to the park. The cost is $20 per adult, plus tax; children 12 and under $12, plus tax. Call ahead to make sure boats are running. The phone number is (305) 664-9814. The tour boat departs for Lignumvitae a half hour before tour time.

If you arrive early at Robbie's for the tour boat, your family will not be bored while waiting to depart. You can purchase fish food and feed huge tarpon that hang around underneath the docks. Their size is amazing. Or you can feed the pelicans. The seabirds will treat you as their newest best friend if you have food.

Lignumvitae Key can actually be seen from U.S. 1. It is located at Mile Marker 78.5. The boat trip takes about 10–15 minutes.

For some people, owning an island is a dream. In 1919, William J. Matheson made it a reality. The Miami chemist bought Lignumvitae Key. A coral rock house, built by Matheson for his full-time island manager, occupies the top of a hill on the island.

Unlike other keys that have been stripped of their trees by development, the 280-acre Lignumvitae has a thriving tropical hardwood hammock growing on an ancient coral reef, complete with ancient examples of its namesake—lignumvitae. The trees were saved in part because no bridge was ever built to the island.

The island became a state park in 1970. When you arrive at the island, you step off the boat onto a floating dock. Next is a walk down a pier toward a grassy, cleared slope. It is a surprise to find six cannons lying on the grass, spaced evenly apart with their barrels facing the water. What are they doing here?

Matheson lived on the mainland at Key Biscayne, not on the island. He used the island as a place to grow exotic plants and raise animals. His wife wanted to redecorate, and she said the cannons on their Key Biscayne lawn had to go.

The cannons, recovered from a British warship that ran aground several centuries ago, were moved to Lignumvitae Key, where they still stand today.

The tour starts on the second floor, inside the home that now serves as the park's visitor center. The living room is furnished as it might have been in the 1930s. A breeze blows through the open windows. Around the outside of the house at the roofline are copper gutters to catch the rain, which was then funneled into a cistern. A windmill provided electricity but it no longer exists. Food came from vegetable gardens and the sea. Life was simple and self-sufficient.

Lignumvitae stayed relatively undisturbed and independent, a genuine West Indian hardwood hammock in a sea of development. Caretakers came and went. Charlotte and Russ Niedhauk stayed the longest, even riding out the 1935 hurricane. Later Charlotte wrote a

SOUTHEAST FLORIDA

Pelicans begging at Robbie's Marina, Islamorada.

SOUTHEAST FLORIDA

book about the adventure called *Charlotte's Story: An Undated Florida Key Diary, 1934–1935* (Exposition Press, 1973).

The Matheson family sold the island in 1953. In the 1960s, condominiums were proposed for the island. The Nature Conservancy stepped up and bought the land, which in turn was purchased by the state in 1970.

We leave the house, and the ranger leads us into the woods. He stops to show us a tree that is about 8 feet tall. It has a number of scrawny limbs, not very many leaves, and looks like it has seen better days. Perhaps it has. This is a lignumvitae tree, and the ranger says it may be many hundreds of years old.

A lignumvitae tree may not look grand, but it is one of the densest woods known. People on the tour are surprised. They thought an ancient lignumvitae would look, well, grand, like a redwood or a cypress. Instead it is a humble tree and quite a survivor.

Along the hammock trail, gumbo-limbo trees are plentiful, as are buttonwood. Closer to shore, black mangroves form a natural barrier between land and sea. The ranger tells us that Key deer lick the leaves of black mangroves because the leaves excrete salt.

If you arrived by tour boat, the ranger will make a call on a cell phone to alert them when the walk is almost over, and the boat will return for you.

Bonus Points

Indian Key Historic State Park is located oceanside at Mile Marker 78.5, almost directly across from Lignumvitae. You may need to know

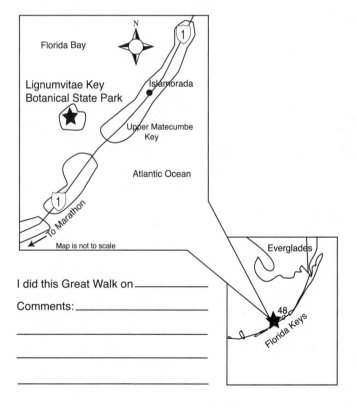

I did this Great Walk on _____

Comments: _____

_____

_____

_____

SOUTHEAST FLORIDA

this next fact for a trivia quiz someday—in 1836, Indian Key was the first county seat for Dade County. Is it weird to have an island as a county seat? Not in the Keys, especially not at a time when Indian Key was doing a thriving business salvaging cargo from shipwrecks.

Due to storm damage, the pier at Indian Key has been inaccessible. Guided tours were not being given. Call to see if Indian Key is open again. Public access is only by canoe or kayak. The address is: Indian Key Historic State Park, P.O. Box 1052, Islamorada, FL 33036, phone (305) 664-2540.

Bicyclists and hikers find the Keys to be close to heaven on earth. Many Keys have an excellent paved pathway separated from the roadway. On both sides are views of beautiful blue-green water that stretches to the horizon. This is the essential thing about the Keys. The water swallows you up and makes you dream, even when you have both feet on dry land.

Trip Essentials

Name: Ancient Trees and Recent Residents: Lignumvitae Key Botanical
    State Park, Islamorada
Type of walk: History and nature
Length of walk: The park has 4.5 miles of trail. Use of the trails is restricted
    to tours only. The tour walk is about a half mile.
Time to finish: 1 1/2 hour for tour of the house and walk in the hammock
Difficulty: Easy. Dirt trails. Wheelchair accessible.
Appeals to: Nature lovers, history buffs, photographers, and birders
Guides: Rangers give tours Thursday through Monday at 10 a.m. and 2
    p.m. Tour includes the Matheson House and walking in the hard-
    wood hammock.
Address: Lignumvitae Key Botanical State Park, P.O. Box 1052, Islamorada,
    FL 33036, Phone: (305) 664-2540
Web site: www.floridastateparks.org
Cost: $1 park entrance fee; children under 6 admitted free.
Getting there: One mile west of U.S. 1 at Mile Marker 78.5. Access by pri-
    vate boat, canoe, kayak, or charter boats (at nearby marinas).
GPS coordinates: N 24° 9 W 080° 7
Hours: 8 a.m. to 5 p.m. Thursday through Monday
Restrooms: Behind the Matheson House

Water/food: Water at restroom; no food available

Dogs: No

Lunch ideas: American, at Mangrove Mike's Café, 82200 Overseas Highway, Mile Marker 82.2 Bayside, Islamorada, FL 33036, phone (305)
664-8022; seafood, at Squid Row Restaurant, 81901 Overseas Highway,
Mile Marker 81.9, Islamorada, FL 33036, phone (305) 664-9865

49

A Silver Lining

Silver Palm Nature Trail, Bahia Honda State Park, Big Pine Key

Silver palms are short, slender, and grow 20–35 feet tall. Capped with a small frond chapeau, they look like elongated feather dust mops. In their own quiet way, silver palms are very classy trees.

A great place to get acquainted is along the Silver Palm Nature Trail at Bahia Honda State Park, located oceanside at Mile Marker 37 on Big Pine Key in the Florida Keys. Bahia Honda State Park, famous for its beaches, snorkeling, and sunsets, is long and narrow, with a 3.5-mile paved road running end to end.

Sandspur Beach is the largest and most popular beach. At the very end of the parking lot, you will find the trailhead for Silver Palm Nature Trail. The loop trail, one-fourth of a mile long, follows the shore of a tidal lagoon and also goes along the beach. Free self-guided brochures are in a holder at the trailhead.

This trail has one of the largest concentrations of silver palms left in the state. Silver palms are a threatened species. Most are found at the beginning of the trail. Look for them dotted here and there among other trees like cabbage palms and Jamaica dogwood.

Over time, lots of time, a mature hardwood hammock will take over this area. The process is called succession. In the natural process of change, bigger hardwoods like gumbo-limbo and poisonwood will eventually shade out silver palms.

But not to worry, silver palms will be here for a while, quietly waiting for you to visit and admire them. The clock ticks slowly when it comes to change. It took thousands of years for the beach to form after water receded from covering Florida. Soil had to take hold, but it is not

A section of the Old Bahia Honda Bridge.

the black soil you may have in your backyard. This is white sand, made up of tiny broken shell particles, ground-up coral and algae.

Then plants arrived, carried by the wind or seeds dropped by birds. Some drifted in with the tides. Others were carried from the Caribbean and South America by the Gulf Stream.

A strong current, the Gulf Stream carries drift seeds ashore when the wind blows from the southeast. Unlike botanical gardens, where everything is planned, much of what grows along the Silver Palm Nature Trail is opportunistic. What comes ashore stays ashore only if it can survive. Only the tough survive.

Bahia Honda is an Ellis Island for plant and animal immigrants. Biologists have been coming for over fifty years to study the diversity of plants found here. On the walk, you go from hardwood hammock to mangroves and a lagoon.

Suddenly, it seems, the elevation rises as you turn away from the lagoon and crest a sand dune. Sea oats anchor the sand and signal that the plant community is changing once again. Gone are the silver palms; gone are the mangroves. At the edge of the salt water are plants and animals that can tolerate a lot of salt water and the direct assault of tides and changing weather.

SOUTHEAST FLORIDA

The Atlantic Ocean laps at your feet. Africa and Europe are due east over the horizon. To the south lie the Caribbean and South America, and, to top it off, you are standing on a world-class beach.

Once you are hooked on Florida natural habitats, there is no turning back. You start to care about silver palms and their environment. And that is a good thing.

Bonus Points

During winter months, guided nature walks are given Tuesday at 11 a.m. at the Silver Palm Nature Trail. Sign up at the ranger station.

Also in winter months the story of the Overseas Railway is told Thursdays at 11 a.m. on the old Bahia Honda Bridge, part of the Overseas Railway. During September, the bridge is the location of a local hawk watch.

Henry Flagler built the East Coast Railway and in 1905 began extending all the way to Key West. The project was called "Flagler's Folly." The original Bahia Honda Bridge is part of that project. A short section remains.

Inside the park are six different habitats: lagoon, beaches/dunes, mangroves, coral reef, hardwood hammock, and gulfside. To see paintings of all six habitats, visit the Sand and Sea Nature Center inside the park at the end of the Calusa swimming area parking lot.

The center is small but packed with goodies. Pick from a number of nature videos. Children will like putting together a sea turtle puzzle or trying Mystery Boxes. You reach inside and try to discover what's in there by touch alone. Staff can answer all those questions you came up with while walking on the Silver Palm Nature Trail. During winter months, the center hosts illustrated talks. Their phone number is (305) 872-9807. Check with them for the current program schedule.

The National Key Deer Refuge has fragmented tracts of land on twenty-five islands in the Lower Keys. Key deer, tiny when born and diminutive as adults, are the smallest members of the Virginia white-tailed deer family. They are cute, but off-limits. Look from a distance. Feeding or enticing them is illegal. Key deer are seen mainly on Big Pine Key and No Name Keys in the refuge.

From Mile Marker 33 to Mile Marker 30, a slow-speed zone is in place to protect the endangered Key deer.

SOUTHEAST FLORIDA

Places to visit at National Key Deer Refuge include the Blue Hole, the Jack Watson Wildlife Trail, and the Fred Mannillo Wildlife Trail. All three are accessed from Key Deer Boulevard, Mile Marker 30.5 on Big Pine Key. Most of Big Pine Key is refuge property.

A paved walkway from the parking lot of the Blue Hole provides handicapped access to a water overlook. The rest of the trail around the Blue Hole is a dirt pathway. The Blue Hole is a deep sinkhole with steep sides, filled with freshwater.

Dogs are allowed on a leash. Both hikers and bicyclists use this trail.

The Fred Mannillo Wildlife Trail and the Watson Trail share the same trailhead. The Mannillo Trail, about one-fourth of a mile long, is totally handicapped accessible. A number of signs explain history and habitat.

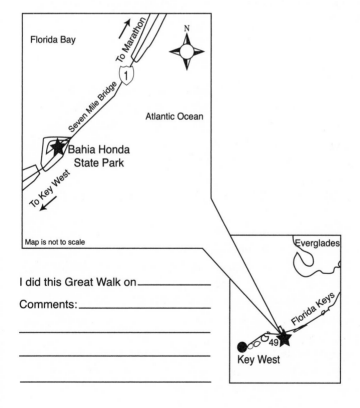

SOUTHEAST FLORIDA

The Watson Trail right next door is about seven-tenths of a mile and has fewer information signs. Bicycles are not permitted on either trail. Dogs are allowed on a leash.

In addition to the Key deer, this national wildlife refuge and three others throughout the Keys, provide habitat for twenty-two threatened or endangered species.

A visitor center in Big Pine Key Plaza, Mile Marker 31.5, serves as a good orientation for National Key Deer Refuge, Crocodile Lake National Wildlife Refuge, Key West National Wildlife Refuge; and Great White Heron National Wildlife Refuge. The address is: 179 Key Deer Blvd., Big Pine Key Plaza, Big Pine Key, FL 33043, phone (305) 872-2154. Web site: www.fws.gov/nationalkeydeer.

Trip Essentials

Name: A Silver Lining: Silver Palm Nature Trail, Bahia Honda State Park, Big Pine Key

Type of walk: Nature

Length of walk: One-fourth of a mile

Time to finish: 30 to 40 minutes

Difficulty: Easy. Dirt and sand trails. Handicapped accessible except for beach portion.

Appeals to: Nature buffs, photographers, gardeners, and birders (listed on page 35, South Florida guide to the Great Florida Birding Trail)

Guides: Self-guided. In winter months, guided walks offered on Tuesdays at 11 a.m.

Address: Bahia Honda State Park, 36850 Overseas Highway, Big Pine Key, FL 33043

Phone: (305) 872-2353

Web site: www.floridastateparks.org

Cost: $5 per car, plus 50¢ additional per person inside the vehicle

Getting there: Bahia Honda State Park is 12 miles south of Marathon in the Florida Keys at Mile Marker 37, oceanside.

GPS coordinates: N 24° 66278 W 081° 26389

Hours: 8 a.m. until sundown

Restrooms: At Sandspur Beach, Calusa Beach

Water/food: Water fountains at restroom; café concession at Calusa Beach

SOUTHEAST FLORIDA

Dogs: Not allowed in cabins, bathhouses, pavilions, the concession
   building, on beaches, or in the water.
Lunch ideas: Café concession has sandwiches, salads, and snacks. Sandspur Beach area has picnic tables. The Calusa area has small picnic
   shelters with barbecue grills.

SOUTHEAST FLORIDA

50

Inhale Island History

Old Town Key West

U.S. 1 runs out of gas at Mile 0 in Key West. The road ends. Let the celebration begin. Upon arrival, throw away your watch. You're on mañana time. Have to look at e-mail? Mañana. Need to check with the office? Mañana.

Take your walking clues from local animals. Roosters strut around Mallory Square claiming they own the place. Their days may be numbered, though, as the Key West City Council in April 2006 passed a chicken eviction notice.

It won't be easy. Roosters and cats are revered in Key West, so why not walk like the local animals? Lounge along with a strut. Start your new stride by taking a promenade along the Historic Seaport Harbor Walk that begins at the Ferry Terminal near the Old Town Parking Garage. The garage is a good alternative to scarce street parking.

Harbor Walk is about one-third of a mile long. Boats on the right, stores and restaurants on your left make for an interesting stroll. Marinas, accessible by owners only, showcase mega powerboats and yachts. In between are day-trippers—water rides for those currently footloose and yearning to be at sea.

At one intersection, a bronze salver statue shows Henry C. Singleton Sr. dressed for salvage work, a lucrative job paying more than fishing ever did. Shipwreck salvers and pirates, their maritime bad cousins, lost ground in the early twentieth century with the arrival of better navigation aids, stiffer laws, and an increased military presence at Fort Zachary Taylor.

Harbor Walk ends at Front Street. Keep walking two more blocks to Mallory Square. The distance from the parking garage to Mallory Square is a half mile.

Statue of a salver
on the Harbor
Walk, Key West.

Mallory Square has a split personality. The place seems tame in the daytime. Tourists fresh from cruise ships wander around, mingle with roosters and pigeons, then hunt for souvenirs at an outdoor mini-mall.

Come sundown, Mallory Square puts on its party face for the nightly sunset celebration. Cats jump through fire hoops. Jugglers do impossible feats. Be there a good half hour in advance of sunset. Hundreds of your closest friends will show up to help you celebrate the end of another day in paradise, or is the party just beginning?

Leaving Mallory Square in the daytime, continue on Front Street to the Museum of Art & History at the Custom House, built in 1891. The Custom House stands grand and gorgeous, three stories of resounding red brick graced with rounded archways,

Cruise ship docked at Mallory Square, Key West.

Past the Custom House, Front Street runs out of steam and ends. Turn left for a short half block on Curry Street, then right onto White-head Street one block to the entrance for Truman Annex, a U.S. naval station from 1823 to 1974. Old barracks are gone. In their place are single-family homes, townhouses, and condominiums.

The Truman Annex entrance has a small plaza with a tiered fountain and benches inviting you to sit and take a break. Pedestrians and bicyclists are welcomed inside the Truman Annex from 8 a.m. to 6 p.m.

Inside the annex you will find the Harry S. Truman Little White House in Key West. Built in 1890 as officers' quarters, it was converted to a single-family home in the early twentieth century. Truman liked to visit Key West. While here he enacted bills, prepared budgets, and even made a piece of civil rights history. On December 5, 1951, Truman signed an executive order requiring contractors to hire minorities.

Outside the Truman Annex, at Caroline and Whitehead Streets, there is more history. A small, white wooden building was once the Pan American Airways office. On October 28, 1927, Pan American flight number 1 taxied down a runway in Key West bound for Havana, took off, and made history as the first United States international air service operation.

Standing outside the Truman Annex on Whitehead Street, if you turn right and walk to the end of the street, you reach the southernmost point in the continental United States. Mileage wise, you will have walked a little over 1 mile from the parking garage to the southernmost point.

Mileage is a matter of perspective. At the southernmost point, you are standing 90 miles from Cuba and 150 miles from Miami.

Or turn right outside the Truman Annex and walk one block on Whitehead to Fleming Street. Take a photograph where U.S. 1 ends at Mile Marker 0, a sign so popular with visitors that souvenir shops in Key West sell copies.

From here, head one block up Fleming to Duval Street, famous for pubs, restaurants, people watching, and shopping. Some come to Key West, wander down Duval Street and that is all they do, which means they miss a lot. Wander off Duval onto the side streets. No two houses are alike. Some are falling down. Others have ongoing restoration.

Old Town Key West covers over 2 miles of prime real estate, and it is flat as a pancake. Locals sit on their porches smiling at visitors who scurry by in a hurry, their eyes fixed on some distant quarry.

Focus on the journey, not the destination. Look at details. Get sun-drenched. Feel the sky touch the water. Inhale island history. Breathe in the bougainvillea. Lounge with a strut.

Bonus Points

Old Town Parking Garage, phone (305) 293-6426, is located at the intersection of Caroline and Grinnell Streets. Bring cash. They don't take credit cards. Parking costs $2 per hour. You can park for an hour or all day. Garage hours are 7 a.m. to midnight.

Visit the Key West Chamber of Commerce, 402 Wall Street (Mallory Square), Key West, FL 33040, phone (305) 294-2587. Hours are 8:30 a.m. to 6:30 p.m. Monday through Friday; 9 a.m. to 6 p.m. Saturday and Sunday. Pick up free brochures, including those describing a number of free or paid walking tours.

Also on Wall Street (Mallory Square) is the Hospitality House/Mallory Museum, the office for the Old Island Restoration Foundation

SOUTHEAST FLORIDA

Inc. (OIRF). At both the chamber and the OIRF you can pick up a free brochure put together by the OIRF, "A Guide to Historic Key West on the Pelican Path."

Fifty buildings are listed by number, described, and marked on the map. The ones highlighted in pink are buildings where you pay a fee and can go inside, like the Harry S. Truman Little White House.

The Harry S. Truman Little White House in Key West is at 111 Front Street, Key West, FL 33040, phone (305) 294-9911. Web site: www.trumanlittlewhitehouse.com.

Admission is $11 for adults; $5 for children 5–12; children under 5 admitted free. Open 9 a.m. to 4:30 p.m. daily. Tours start about every 15–20 minutes and take 45–55 minutes to complete.

Wreckers and salvers have their history collected at Key West Shipwreck Historeum Museum, 1 Whitehead Street, Key West, FL 33040, phone (305) 292-8990. Web site: www.shipwreckhistoreum.com. Open 9–5 p.m. daily. Shows every 30 minutes. Admission is $10 adults; $5 children 12 and under.

Descendents of Ernest Hemingway's six-toed cats are used to visitors coming to see the house and them. You can visit the cats at Hemingway's Home and Museum, 907 Whitehead Street, Key West, FL 33040, phone (305) 294-1136. Hours are 9 a.m. to 5 p.m. every day. Admission is $11 adults; $6 children 6–12; children under 5 admitted free. Web site: www.hemingwayhome.com.

Free Key West pamphlets put out by www. SEE-KeyWest.com contain discount coupons for a number of these attractions.

To see the mother lode of sunken treasures recovered from seventeenth-century wrecks, visit Mel Fisher Maritime Heritage Society Museum, 200 Greene Street, Key West, FL 33040, phone (305) 294-2633. Web site: www.melfisher.org. Open 9:30 a.m.; last tickets sold at 5 p.m. daily. Admission is $10 adults; $5 children.

The address for the Museum of Art & History at the Custom House is 281 Front Street, Key West, FL 33040, phone (305) 295-6616. Over a nine-year period, the Key West Art & Historical Society spent $9 million to restore the Custom House to its original glory.

Admission is $10 adults; $9 seniors over 62; $5 children; those under 6 admitted free. Hours are 10 a.m. to 3 p.m. Monday through Friday; and 9 a.m. to 5 p.m. Saturday and Sunday.

Fort Zachary Taylor Historic State Park does, in fact, have a fort, built in 1866. Daily tours offered at noon and 2 p.m. Mailing address is: Fort Zachary Taylor Historic State Park, P.O. Box 6560, Key West FL 33041, phone (305) 292-6713. Hours are 8 a.m. to sundown. Web site: www.floridastateparks.org.

Admission is $3.50 for 1 person in a vehicle; $6.50 for 2 people or more in a vehicle. Call the park for more fee information. Located at the end of Southard Street in the Truman Annex, the park entrance is sandwiched between several commercial sites and is a bit hard to find.

Fort Zachary Taylor also has a great beach for swimming and snorkeling. Some say it is the best beach in Key West. Fishing is a good bet here. The west side of the park faces the main ship channel, about 33 feet deep. Saltwater fishing licenses are required.

Once a year, from January to March, Sculpture Key West mounts an outdoor show of contemporary sculpture at Fort Zachary Taylor Historic State Park. Many of the sculptures reside on the beach for three months. Other sculptures are placed around Key West. A free map, available at the chamber or the park, shows the location of every sculpture. The phone is (305) 295-3800, and the Web site is: www.sculpturekeywest.com.

Remember all those day-trip boats you saw along the Harbor Walk? One of their destinations is the Dry Tortugas National Park, a cluster of seven islands some 70 miles west of Key West. People often ask if they can drive their motor home or travel trailer there. The answer is no.

Ways to get there include seaplane, catamaran, private boat, or a ferry service. This is a full-day trip. Services providing charters to the Dry Tortugas are listed in free Key West brochures or check links on the National Park Service Web site.

The National Park Service oversees Dry Tortugas National Park. Admission is $5 for adults 17 and older, and your fee is good for seven days. Golden Eagle, Golden Age, Golden Access Passports are honored, along with the America the Beautiful annual pass. Mailing address is: Dry Tortugas National Park, P.O. Box 6208, Key West, FL 33041, phone (305) 242-7700. Their Web site is: www.nps.gov/drto.

Construction of Fort Jefferson on Garden Key, one of the seven islands, started in 1846 but was never finished. A visitor center is inside the fort. You can take a self-guided tour of the fort. Birders will find much to admire in the Dry Tortugas.

Swimming, snorkeling, scuba diving, and fishing are all popular. A 10-site primitive campground is on Garden Key just a short distance from the public dock. Camping fees are $3 a night per person. You have to bring everything—food, water, ice, and fuel, and pack out your trash.

Fort Jefferson is open during daylight hours, closed at night. Loggerhead, East, and Middle Keys are also open during daylight hours. From February through September, Bush Key is closed to allow nesting privacy for sooty and noddy terns.

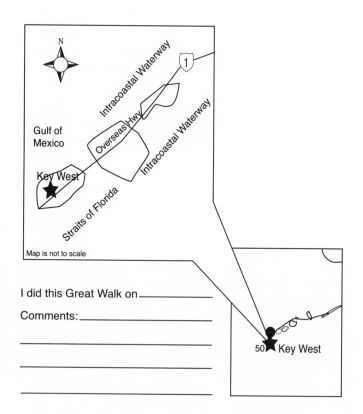

I did this Great Walk on _____

Comments: _____

_____

_____

_____

Trip Essentials

Name: Inhale Island History: Old Town Key West

Type of walk: Historic and scenic

Length of walk: 1-mile round trip on Historic Seaport Harbor Walk. Add 2–3 miles if walking Old Town Key West end to end.

Time to finish: 3 to 4 hours, more if you stay for sunset ritual at Mallory Square

Difficulty: Easy. Pavement. Wheelchair accessible.

Appeals to: People watchers, history buffs, souvenir hunters, and families

Guides: Self-guided or fee-based guided tours; walking & bike tours by Island City Strolls, phone (305) 294-0566; ghost tours by Haunted Tours, phone (305) 294-9255 and Ghosts & Legends of Key West, phone (305) 294-1713

Address: Historic Seaport Harbor walk goes from foot of Grinnell Street to foot of Front Street next to Mallory Square.

Phone: Key West Chamber of Commerce, phone (305) 294-2587

Web site: www.keywestchamber.org and www.keywesttravelguide.com

Cost: None for self-guided walks

Getting there: Old Town Key West is located at the southern end of U.S. 1.

GPS coordinates: (Fort Zachary Taylor) N 24° 54.722 W 081° 77.639

Hours: Key West never sleeps.

Restrooms: At Key West Chamber of Commerce, Bright Island Ferry Terminal

Water/food: Few fountains; many restaurants

Dogs: Allowed on sidewalks, none in buildings

Lunch and dinner ideas: Inventive menu, at Turtle Kraals, Historic Seaport at Lands End Village, Key West, FL 33040, phone (305) 294-2640; American, at Pepe's Café & Steak House, 806 Caroline Street, Key West, FL 33040, phone (305) 294-7192

SOUTHEAST FLORIDA

Index

Lucy Beebe Tobias is an award-winning columnist, photographer, and graphic designer who reported for the New York Times Regional Newspaper Group in Florida for twenty-three years.

She interviewed numerous Florida legends, historians, and environmentalists including Marjory Stoneman Douglas, Marjorie Harris Carr, and former governors Bob Graham and Lawton Chiles.

Artist Web site: www.Lucyworks.com

Writer Web site: www.Saturdaymorningswithlucy.com

Related-interest titles from University Press of Florida

30 Eco-Trips in Florida: The Best Nature Excursions (and How to Leave Only Your Footprints)
Holly Ambrose

Adventures on the Florida Trail: An 1100-Mile Walk through the Sunshine State
Johnny Molloy

Beach and Coastal Camping in Florida
Johnny Molloy

Exploring Florida's Emerald Coast: A Rich History and a Rare Ecology
Jean Lufkin Bouler

Fishing Florida's Flats: A Guide to Bonefish, Tarpon, Permit, and Much More
Jan Stephen Maizler

Florida on Horseback: A Trail Rider's Guide to the North and Panhandle Regions
Cornelia Bernard Henderson

Florida on Horseback: A Trail Rider's Guide to the South and Central Regions
Cornelia Bernard Henderson

Florida's Fairways: 60 Alluring and Affordable Golf Courses from the Panhandle to the Keys
Alan K. Moore

Highway A1A: Florida at the Edge
Herbert L. Hiller

Hiker's Guide to the Sunshine State
Sandra Friend

The Hiking Trails of Florida's National Forests, Parks, and Preserves, Second Edition
Johnny Molloy and Sandra Friend

Kayaking the Keys: 50 Great Paddling Adventures in Florida's Southernmost Archipelago
Kathleen Patton

Paddler's Guide to the Sunshine State
Sandy Huff

Waters Less Traveled: Exploring Florida's Big Bend Coast
Doug Alderson

For more information on these and other books, visit our Web site at www.upf.com.